The Nature of Art

The Problems of Philosophy: Their Past and Present

General Editor: Ted Honderich
Grote Professor of the Philosophy of Mind and Logic
University College, London

Each book in this series is written to bring into view and to deal with a great or significant problem of philosophy. The books are intended to be accessible to undergraduates in philosophy, and to other readers, and to advance the subject, making a contribution to it.

The first part of each book presents the history of the problem in question, in some cases its recent past. The second part, of a contemporary and analytic kind, defends and elaborates the author's preferred solution.

Private Ownership *James O. Grunebaum*
Religious Belief and the Will *Louis P. Pojman*
Rationality *Harold I. Brown*
The Rational Foundations of Ethics *T.L.S. Sprigge*
Moral Knowledge *Alan H. Goldman*
Mind–body Identity Theories *Cynthia Macdonald*
Practical Reasoning *Robert Audi*
Personal Identity *Harold W. Noonan*
If P then Q: the Foundations of Logic and Argument *David H. Sanford*
The Infinite *A.W. Moore*
Thought and Language *Julius Moravcsik*
Human Consciousness *Alastair Hannay*
Explaining Explanation *David Hillel-Ruben*
The Weakness of the Will *Justin Gosling*

The Nature of Art

A. L. Cothey

ROUTLEDGE
London and New York

First published 1990
by Routledge
11 New Fetter Lane, London EC4P 4EE

Simultaneously published in the USA and Canada
by Routledge
a division of Routledge, Chapman and Hall, Inc.
29 West 35th Street, New York, NY 10001

Typeset by LaserScript Limited, Mitcham, Surrey
Printed in Great Britain by Biddles Ltd, Guildford

British Library Cataloguing in Publication Data

Cothey, A. L. (Antony L.)
The nature of art.
1. Arts. Aesthetics. Theories
I. Title
700.1

Library of Congress Cataloging in Publication Data

applied for
Cothey, A.L. (Antony L.),
The nature of art / A.L. Cothey.
p. cm.— (The Problems of philosophy)
Includes bibliographical references.
ISBN 0-415-03357-8
1. Aesthetics. 2. Art–Philosophy. I. Title. II. Series:
Problems of philosophy (Routhledge (Firm))
BH39.C67 1990
701'.17—dc20
90–32935
CIP
ISBN 0 415 03357 8

To my parents

Contents

Preface

Keats warns that philosophy will clip an angel's wings (*Lamia*, II, 234). What some philosophers have written about the arts lends credibility to this accusation. When I began work on this book, and for some time afterwards, I was not at all sure how I could escape it myself; though I did not think it would be worthwhile to try to write about the arts and aesthetics unless in the end I had something more positive to say than that they are not matters that can be intelligibly discussed and explained.

That negative view has, I know, been widely held; but it now strikes me as fundamentally evasive. In so far as it expresses discontent at the superficiality of much that passes for theorizing about or verbal appreciation of the arts it is worthy of respect. But it can serve, I fear, as a smokescreen for an overnarrow and ultimately hollow conception of what is intelligible. It is possible, I believe, to explain art philosophically without belittling it or posing as a rival; but doing so has far-reaching implications. Often the true motive for the negative view is not, I regret, to pay homage to the arts but as an excuse to ignore difficult intellectual questions. This book has been written in the conviction that neglect of these issues is not justified.

I am grateful to Professor Ted Honderich for giving me the opportunity to write this book. I should also like to thank my parents for helping me in many ways while I have been doing so, and in particular to thank my mother for many hours of patient and efficient typing.

A.L.C.
St Ives, 1989

Introduction

1. Art is anomalous

Artists are supposed to have the capacity to create beauty; and beauty, Plato says, inspires love. Yet no one seriously believes in love potions. Apparently an alchemy is possible in the realm of artistic imagination which is impossible in reality. How can this be?

Some thinkers have believed that artistic creativity is so remarkable that nothing less than divine inspiration can account for it. Others have been sceptical, regarding artists as impostors whose products have a seductive charm that obscures rather than reveals true beauty. (Both these lines of thought appear in Plato's writings.) Still others, for example Tolstoy and Collingwood, have denied that art has anything essentially to do with beauty. Thus it has been held that artists are primarily concerned with expressing feelings or emotions, and that the true aim of art is not beauty or pleasure but to give knowledge of our inner experiences.

It remains that we enjoy works of art as we do things of beauty for their own sake. Art is not, except incidentally, a means to any further end. This creates an obvious and serious difficulty prior even to that posed by the existence of artistic creativity. In general, we explain our behaviour teleologically, that is, by describing how it helps us to satisfy our wants and needs. And our wants and needs are systematically interrelated. Indeed, many biologists would assert that all human behaviour, like that of any other species, can ultimately be understood in terms of its survival value. But if art is an end in itself it apparently makes no contribution, unless by accident, to any other aims. So from the standpoint of the usual teleological pattern of explaining behaviour, the existence of art is anomalous. Does this teleological pattern of explanation still apply to art? If so then how? If not then what are the implications of this?

2. *Forms of aesthetic scepticism: philistines and iconoclasts*

Many thinkers have responded to the above question by maintaining that art does in fact have a purpose, though this may be hidden or unobvious; and in so doing have taken a sceptical view of the idea that artists have the ability to create things the experience of which is an end in itself. Here the position is not like that with the usual varieties of epistemological scepticism. Much philosophical enquiry since Descartes has sprung from questions like 'How do I know that I am not at this moment dreaming?' and 'How do I know that other people have an interior mental life like my own?' Many philosophers have tried to refute the sceptical allegation that such questions are unanswerable. But here scepticism is only a device by which to pose philosophical difficulties. Only a madman would seriously doubt that there exist minds other than his own. In connection with the arts, however, genuine scepticism has been widespread.

There are two main types of sceptic about the arts. There are *philistines*, who deny the existence of beauty; and there are *iconoclasts*, who accept that beauty exists but have reservations about the capacity of human beings to create it. Philistines deny that anything is intrinsically valuable in the sense the experience of beauty and of the arts are commonly supposed to be. Iconoclasts, on the other hand, do not doubt that some experiences are intrinsically valuable; and they may allow that an inferior form of beauty can be created by human beings; but they regard art as at best a stepping-stone to the appreciation of true beauty. Several of the greatest philosophers of art – Plato and Plotinus, Kant and Hegel – have been iconoclastic. Of those empiricists who have written on aesthetics, many show philistine tendencies; and many other empiricists have propounded doctrines that are philistine by implication. *Prima facie* the existence of aesthetically enjoyable experiences shows that we have an inner life in a sense which behaviourists deny.

Philistinism and iconoclasm can both take hedonistic or puritanical forms. By a *hedonist* I mean someone who holds that pleasure or enjoyment is desirable in itself, though hedonists may vary in how discriminating they are, i.e. in whether or to what extent they distinguish higher from lower pleasures. A philistine whose attitude to the arts is hedonistic will accept that the arts can give pleasure and that this suffices to make them desirable, but will see no reason to assign to the arts a special position in human life. On the other hand, were a hedonist to be iconoclastic, in the sense of regarding the pleasure from art as inferior to certain other pleasures, then he might hold that the pleasure to be derived from *true* beauty is the chief good of all.

By a *puritan* I mean someone who believes that pleasure should be evaluated according to its effects, whether or not these be held to be specifically *moral* effects. Puritans are hedonists' most obvious opponents, though there are intermediate positions opposed to both. (For example, a *eudaemonist*, who believes that happiness is the goal of life, may go along with hedonists in holding that desirability is connected with pleasure while agreeing with puritans that pleasure alone does not make something truly desirable.)

A *philistine* puritan may accept that the arts give pleasure, but will evaluate individual works not on this basis but according to their wider impact. Moral puritans typically fear that the effects of enjoying art can be corrupting, and are accordingly disposed to advocate censorship. In one respect an *iconoclastic* puritan will be even more sweeping in his condemnation, rejecting whole categories of things that purport to be beautiful. But an iconoclastic in contrast to a philistine puritan might hold that *true* beauty is something that cannot be apprehended without having good effects. Broadly speaking, moral puritans tend to be iconoclastic while puritans who do not see the value of art in specifically moral terms tend to be philistines.

3. Historical note

Most philosophers of art have been sceptics in one or other of the senses just described. A consideration that can lend some credibility to such scepticism is that our present concept of fine art is relatively recent. The ancients and medievals distinguished the liberal arts, such as geometry, architecture and logic, from the mechanical or servile arts. The distinction between fine and applied arts only gained currency in the eighteenth century. It is not wildly implausible to suggest that this distinction is something of an historical aberration. And if the concept of fine art lacks secure foundation there is presumably no genuine problem of explaining how we can have autonomous artistic aims separate from other practical ones. The problem, on the contrary, is to explain what practical aims art serves; and the forms of scepticism just distinguished suggest some lines on which a solution might be attempted.

Our modern term 'aesthetic' dates from the same period. Baumgarten, who is credited with introducing the term, in fact gave it a much broader meaning than it now usually conveys. He wrote that: 'Aesthetics (the theory of the fine arts, the theory of the lower kind of knowledge, the art of thinking beautifully, the art of analogical reasoning) is the science of sensuous knowledge' (*Aesthetics*, 1750, section 1; in Carritt(ed.), p.84).

Here in the same breath Baumgarten speaks of aesthetics as the study of beauty and the arts while still using the term in more or less the original sense of the Greek *aisthetikos*, i.e. as having to do with sensory and perceptual knowledge. Baumgarten's use of the term thus expresses the thesis that our enjoyment of beauty and the arts – what has come to be known as 'aesthetic enjoyment' – can be explained in terms of the character of a certain kind of experiential knowledge: in terms of features of experience that are 'aesthetic' in the original Greek sense. Bearing this ambiguity in mind, it ought to be clear that it need not be a truism to assert that aesthetic enjoyment is the enjoyment of aesthetic experience. That this can so easily appear to be truistic illustrates how we tend to neglect what we are presupposing in believing that our enjoyment of beauty and the arts is set apart from other enjoyments. If there is a distinctive aesthetic form of enjoyment only if there is a separate activity which is here being enjoyed, then difficulties in specifying this activity will naturally tend to rebound on the supposition that there is any distinctively aesthetic enjoyment. Difficulties in specifying this activity will thus make it hard to resist philistine conclusions.

(As a rule I shall be using the terms 'aesthetic enjoyment' and 'aesthetic experience' in the sense that makes the above proposition a truism, i.e. I shall be taking 'aesthetic experience' to mean activity of that kind – whatever it is exactly – in the enjoyment of which we experience beauty or 'aesthetic enjoyment'. It has to be shown, of course, that this usage is valid.)

4. The central issues

The most basic problem, as I see it, in aesthetics and the philosophy of art is to answer the question about the applicability here of teleological explanation, without falling into either philistinism or iconoclasm. This means we have:

(a) to show that there is such a thing, distinct from other forms of enjoyment, as aesthetic enjoyment or the experience of beauty (non-philistinism); and

(b) to show how it makes sense to suppose that we can successfully make things intending that others will have such experiences in apprehending them (non-iconoclasm); while

(c) explaining how our aesthetic and artistic aims relate to our other practical concerns (the teleological question).

Problem (a) poses questions about what it is for an experience to be intrinsically satisfying in the way the experience of beauty is supposed to be. This raises general issues about the nature of pleasure and satisfaction. These, like those raised by (c), are in a broad sense *ethical* issues – in the sense, that is, in which Aristotle's *Nicomachean Ethics* is an ethical work. Indirectly (a) also poses difficult questions about the nature of *cognition*. For the experience of beauty entails a cognitive act – one of apprehending something by looking at it, listening to it, etc.; but it is hard to explain how in themselves such cognitive acts, as opposed to the opportunities that knowledge may open up for us, can be a source of pleasure or satisfaction.

Philistinism will have been refuted once it has been shown that we are capable of experiences that are intrinsically satisfying in the required sense. But to refute iconoclasm it has further to be shown that we have capacities to make things with aesthetic aims in mind (problem (b)). This again raises issues in the theory of cognition: ones to do with the different forms – experiential, verbal, and practical – that knowledge can take, and the relationships between them. The underlying problem here can be briefly stated. It would seem that before actually making it, the only kind of knowledge I can have of a thing I intend to make is *verbal* knowledge. But aesthetic enjoyment has to do with *experiential* knowledge. So how is it possible to have an ability to achieve any specific aesthetic aims?

These ethical and cognitive questions are exceedingly general. To anticipate, the key to resolving them lies, I believe, in certain points about the nature of *metaphor* and its role in cognition. The importance of metaphor ought in any case to be common ground in philosophical discussion of art and aesthetics since metaphor is such a prominent feature of what we say in describing works of art and reporting aesthetic experiences. Were we debarred from speaking metaphorically nothing in what we say would reveal that we took any interest in aesthetic or artistic matters.

It has also often been suggested, especially by recent writers, that the activity of making a work of art has a close affinity with speaking metaphorically. (If 'analogical reasoning' in the earlier quotation means thinking metaphorically then Baumgarten might have agreed.) I think there is important truth in this; but it is far from self-explanatory. Metaphor is only a metaphor for art. The primary importance of a correct understanding of metaphor is, I believe, that it enables us to comprehend aesthetic enjoyment. Many philosophers in attempting to explain aesthetic experience have relied on the notion that knowledge can take experiential as opposed to verbal or conceptual forms; but they have had little success in explaining why it should sometimes be satisfying to have such knowledge. It is necessary to explain this if we are to defend a non-philistine position. One of my central theses will be that certain claims about metaphor and its role in cognition are essential in doing this; and that having enabled us to connect aesthetic enjoyment with *experiential* knowledge the same claims will enable us to understand the connection between this enjoyment and the *practical* knowledge that artists possess.

5. *Aestheticism*

The nature of metaphor is, of course, a *semantic* issue. I have just been saying, therefore, that the central issues of aesthetics and the philosophy of art comprise ones drawn from ethics, the theory of cognition, and semantics. The philosophy of art lies at the intersection of these other areas of philosophical enquiry. One reason why it is hard to bring these issues into focus is that the boundaries of these other areas of enquiry have often been drawn too narrowly. Another reason is that the presumed adequacy or even unavoidability of a philistine or iconoclastic approach has sometimes made it appear superfluous to confront these other questions.

A line of thought which encourages this outlook is that we would otherwise be forced to agree with the *aesthete* who holds that the primary goal of life is none other than the enjoyment of beauty and works of art. This would be an objectionable conclusion not only because there can be something morally repellent about regarding the enjoyment of art and beauty as the paramount goals in life, but because it introduces a dualism into the practical sphere. It cannot be denied that we have aims besides aesthetic ones, e.g. food and shelter; and it can hardly be accepted without further ado that these other aims are really only means by which we attain the opportunity to contemplate works of art. This would leave unanswered the question how our biological goals could have acquired this further purpose.

If this sort of aestheticism is unacceptable, as I agree it is, then a satisfactory solution to problem (c) must, of course, give a different account of the relationship of our aesthetic to our other practical aims. Sometimes this has been attempted by appeal to a metaphysical purpose behind the experience of natural beauty – the purpose of preparing us to appreciate higher forms of beauty. This *metaphysical* aestheticism may succeed, as its 'mundane' counterpart apparently cannot, in integrating our ordinary practical concerns with our aesthetic aims. But evidently it does so only at the cost of taking an iconoclastic view of art and of natural beauty: appreciation of these is to be superseded by the appreciation of metaphysical beauty.

Philistine and iconoclastic theories are fuelled, then, by the suspicion that the alternative is a form of aestheticism that postulates a dualism among our practical goals; and this aestheticism does not solve satisfactorily the teleological problem (problem (c)). I shall be maintaining, however, that a satisfactory solution to (c) is possible consistently with solutions to (a) and (b). I shall be steering a middle course between the various forms of aesthetic scepticism, on the one hand, and dualistic aestheticism, on the other. Briefly, the destination will be a view that harmonizes aesthetic with other practical goals by regarding aesthetic satisfaction as quite generally the *source of meaning* – as what gives meaning to our actions, including literal meaning to linguistic utterances.

CHAPTER I

Hedonism and the Theory of Taste

1. General objections

The simplest theory of the arts is the hedonistic one that their purpose is to give pleasure. That the arts can give pleasure is beyond dispute; what is questionable is that this point is in any way explanatory.

The principal objection to hedonism is that the notion of pleasure cannot simply be taken for granted but requires explanation in terms of the features of pleasant activities that go to make them pleasant. One good reason for holding this is that feelings of pleasure do not differ just on their own but, in a stronger than merely causal sense, because of differences in the activities that are found pleasant. In fact it is plausible to hold that pleasure needs itself to be understood teleologically in that pleasure is in general connected with success in achieving the goals of an activity. In that case the hedonistic doctrine that pleasure is the goal of action reverses the true order of explanation.

The general shortcomings of hedonism are particularly evident when it comes to aesthetic pleasure. For this form of pleasure has peculiarities that cannot be accounted for merely in terms of qualitative differences between pleasures or differences in their causal origin. This is a deeper objection than the puritanical one that pleasure alone does not justify an activity: we shall see that puritanical theories are equally incapable of explaining the peculiarities of aesthetic enjoyment.

The crudest hedonistic theory asserts that the aim of art is to produce pleasurable sensations. In that case an artist would be like a manufacturer of perfumes or a purveyor of fine wines. The metaphorical use of the word 'taste' to denote the faculty of aesthetic discernment is evidence of the appeal of this theory. Were the theory true the metaphorical element in this usage would be slight.

The crudity of this theory becomes evident when we ask how many different aesthetic sensations there are. If there is some finite limitation on the variety of such sensations, then we should be able to classify everything according to the things to which it is aesthetically equivalent. We would then be indifferent between the members of each such class in the same way as we might between the taste of two apples; and there could come a time when there is no longer scope for aesthetic novelty. If, on the other hand, we allow indefinitely many kinds of aesthetic sensation to match the variety in the things we find aesthetically enjoyable, then a capacity to discriminate between aesthetic sensations will not be comparable to a capacity to discriminate between sensations proper.

Some sensations are indeed pleasant; but I can derive aesthetic enjoyment from many things that are not sensations, such as the qualities of proportion or expressiveness in a painting, or the elegance of a mathematical proof. Any type of thing – a tree or a poem, a musical composition or a piece of abstract reasoning – can be the object of aesthetic enjoyment. As Francis Jeffrey maintained, it is a decisive objection 'against the notion of beauty being a simple sensation, or the object of a separate and peculiar faculty' that there cannot be a property 'common to a flower and a demonstration, a valley and an elegant discourse' ('Essay on Beauty'; in Aschenbrenner and Isenberg (eds), pp.278–9). If there is an aesthetic faculty it can involve the understanding and the imagination as well as a sensibility to sensations. The fact is that aesthetic enjoyment is interwoven with cognition (perception, thought, and understanding) in ways that a simple capacity to detect sensations does not take account of.

But perhaps the idea is that aesthetic enjoyment always consists in experiencing a special type of pleasurable inner sensation, even though this enjoyment need not have a sensation in the ordinary sense as its object. This, however, makes the question 'What are you enjoying?' needlessly ambiguous in aesthetic contexts. I can correctly reply that I am enjoying, say, looking at a picture or following a proof. But on this theory I ought to acknowledge that the immediate object of my enjoyment is the pleasant inner sensation I gain from these activities. This is one reason why Hutcheson described the power of perceiving beauty as an 'internal sense' (*An Inquiry into the Original of our Ideas of Beauty and Virtue*, p.8). When, however, I enjoy a sensation in the ordinary sense, for example the taste of an apple, there does not appear to be the same duality: I simply enjoy the taste. If this case is uniform with aesthetic enjoyment, then there should be a distinction between enjoying the taste considered as a property of the apple, and enjoying the pleasurable sensation which the experience of this taste causes.

The advantage of this theory is that there is presumably no need to explain why some sensations are pleasant and others are not. For present purposes we can simply take this as an evident fact; and so, by analysing aesthetic experience in terms of the presence of sensations, there is no further need to explain why there should be such a phenomenon as aesthetic enjoyment. But as I indicated, the central objection to the theory is that it treats factors that are actually integral to aesthetic enjoyment as if they merely caused it. When I enjoy looking at a picture, I cannot separate from this activity any special aesthetic sensations which this activity itself merely serves to cause.

2. *Beauty as a secondary quality: Hutcheson, Reid, Burke*

The eighteenth-century empiricist writers who tried to develop a theory of aesthetic taste were strongly influenced by Locke's understanding of the mind; and it must be said that this was a prime factor in setting them on the wrong track. Locke held that mental processes of every kind – perceptions and sensations, thoughts and emotions – all consist in the presence of 'ideas' before the mind; and this assimilation obscures important differences. We experience aesthetic pleasure in performing various cognitive acts, e.g. in looking at certain things. The right question to ask is 'What is it about cognition that makes these particular cognitive acts pleasant?' But the empiricists, under Locke's influence, leapt to the conclusion that experiencing aesthetic pleasure is like another mode of perception. Instead of questioning the analogy with literal taste these writers were deflected into considering what kind of explanation there might be of how aesthetic taste operates, and whether, like literal taste, the aesthetic faculty gives knowledge of a type of 'secondary quality'.

Writers who upheld Locke's distinction between primary and secondary qualities were usually inclined, in view of the mind-dependence Locke believed distinctive of the latter, to classify aesthetic qualities along with secondary ones. This is implicit in Hutcheson's *Inquiry*, where he aimed to discover 'what real quality in the objects ordinarily excites' our idea of beauty (ibid., p.8). Thomas Reid asserted explicitly that 'The sense of beauty may be analysed in a manner very similar to the sense of sweetness' (*Essays on the Intellectual Powers of Man*, VIII, Ch.4).

But for the reasons already given, the capacity for aesthetic pleasure is not really like a sensory faculty. Hutcheson himself emphasized that we can find beauty in mathematical theorems and scientific theories (op. cit., p.9, pp.33–4); and in fact he makes no attempt to analyse it as if it really were a secondary quality. Locke had written that secondary qualities 'in truth are nothing in the objects themselves but powers to produce various sensations in us by their primary qualities' (*Essay*, II, viii, 10). But Hutcheson's thesis that the idea of beauty is caused by the perception of 'uniformity amidst variety' does not even pretend to be an account in terms of primary qualities: 'uniformity' and 'variety' are as problematic *vis-à-vis* primary qualities as is beauty itself. Reid's account also proceeds on different lines from those he initially appeared to be embarked upon. Instead of analysing beauty as a causal property which things have in virtue of their primary qualities, he concludes that 'all the beauty of the objects of sense is borrowed, and derived from the beauties of mind which it expresses or suggests to the imagination'. According to Reid, 'it is in the moral and intellectual perfections of mind, and in its active powers, that beauty originally dwells' (op. cit.).

Nevertheless, a comparison between beauty and secondary qualities can be apposite even if the causal mechanism is quite different in the two cases. An account modelled on Locke's treatment of secondary qualities might hold that only ideas can be strictly or literally beautiful, just as only certain taste sensations are literally sweet; but that we tend in both cases alike mistakenly to suppose that things which only cause these ideas and sensations are themselves beautiful and sweet. Thus many writers have claimed that beauty is fundamentally a matter of things prompting pleasant associations. For example, Jeffrey wrote that 'beauty is not an inherent property or quality of objects at all, but the result of the accidental relations in which they may stand to our experience of pleasures or emotions'. He says that beautiful things have 'nothing in common but this accidental power of reminding us of other emotions' (op. cit., pp.281–2).

But Reid's contrast between 'original' and 'derived' beauty introduces a complication. We now have not only a distinction between a thing and its pleasant associations, but also a distinction between things that are beautiful on their own account and ones that are beautiful only because of what they suggest to us. This creates an ambiguity in saying that the 'objects of sense' we describe as beautiful in fact only cause us to have ideas of beauty not present in the claim that things we describe as sweet in fact only cause us to have ideas of sweetness. For an 'idea of sweetness' is here taken to mean an idea that is literally sweet; but if an 'idea of beauty' may only be a thought of something beautiful it is not obvious that such thoughts must themselves possess 'original' beauty. Theorists who take it to be obvious that we will experience pleasure in associating something with pleasant things may not consider this a point worth dwelling on. But if Reid's 'original' beauty were equated with real beauty, the 'derived' sort being considered merely apparent, then clearly his distinction could be given an iconoclastic or puritanical twist.

In any event it is important to distinguish theories of aesthetic pleasure which adapt the original secondary quality model by introducing psychological intermediaries from ones which hold that certain sets of associations actually constitute aesthetic pleasure. Edmund Burke ventured an account of the latter type when he attempted to classify kinds of aesthetic enjoyment according to the different sorts of association that can feature in it.

Burke rejects the notion of a distinct faculty of aesthetic taste maintaining that it is made up only of 'primary pleasures of sense', the 'secondary pleasures of the imagination', and various 'conclusions of the reasoning faculty' (*A Philosophical Enquiry into the Origin of our Ideas of the Sublime and Beautiful*, p.23). Famously, he goes on to draw a basic distinction between the beautiful and the sublime. He identifies beauty with 'all such qualities in things as induce in us a sense of affection and tenderness, or some other passion the most nearly resembling these'. By contrast, 'The passions which belong to self-preservation . . . are delightful when we have an idea of pain and danger, without actually being in such circumstances . . . . Whatever excites this delight, I call sublime' (ibid., p.51).

Notice that with this distinction Burke loses a uniform explanation of aesthetic enjoyment. Since, as he himself stresses, the constituent emotions and sensations in experience of the sublime are not themselves pleasant, he obviously cannot explain delight in the sublime by reference to the pleasantness of the emotions and sensations that enter into our experience of it. Instead he attributes this delight to a 'conclusion of the reasoning faculty', namely to the knowledge that the sublime poses no real threat. On the other hand, he asserts that 'beauty demands no assistance from our reasoning . . . the appearance of beauty as effectively causes some degree of love in us, as the application of ice or fire produces the ideas of heat or cold' (ibid., p.92). He does, it is true, sketch crudely a physiological account of the sublime (dimly influenced by Aristotle's theory of catharsis) which might bring it and the beautiful closer together. Thus he suggests that when pain and terror 'clear the parts [of the system] of a dangerous and troublesome incumbrance, they are capable of producing delight' (ibid., p.136). But if delight in the sublime and in the beautiful are two species of aesthetic enjoyment the conclusion would seem to be that this enjoyment cannot after all be explained just by reference to a thing's psychological associations, and is independent of whether what it is associated with is itself pleasant or unpleasant.

Nonetheless a feature of aesthetic enjoyment which an account that stresses the role of psychological associations might seem well suited to explain is our tendency, even in a single instance of this enjoyment, to cite different sorts of thing as its object. For example, we may say variously that the object of aesthetic enjoyment is a picture that we are looking at; or the activity of looking at it; or the thoughts, feelings, and emotions that we experience in so doing. This is over and above the point that we take all manner of things to be capable of beauty. And at first sight this may appear to support the type of secondary quality account now under consideration. For there is some initial plausibility in the suggestion that this tendency displays a confusion on our part like that Locke believed makes us think that objects themselves are red or sweet.

This impression does not, however, withstand scrutiny. When I enjoy the taste of an apple I do not confuse my enjoyment with the taste I am enjoying: I find no contradiction in the thought that others might dislike the taste. But when I enjoy the beauty of a flower I do not allow that someone could experience this beauty and yet find it unpleasant. Unlike experience of a genuine secondary quality, experience of the beauty of something entails a specific manner – which is necessarily pleasant – of experiencing it. Hutcheson realized this very well – he spoke of the idea of beauty as '*necessarily* pleasant to us as well as immediately so' (op. cit., p.11). But the situation cannot be rectified by adjusting the secondary quality account either, as Hutcheson proposed, by thinking of taste as an internal faculty, or, like Burke, by stressing the role of associations. If we identify aesthetic pleasure with certain sets of association prompted by other experiences or with inner sensations that they cause, then the confusion to which we are liable, if a point corresponding to Locke's about secondary qualities applies, ought to consist in supposing that these original *experiences*, rather than their associations or the inner sensations they cause, genuinely possess the aesthetic qualities. (Perhaps within his own theory Burke actually does commit this sort of confusion.) However, we cannot simply say that having confused these we then make another confusion, again analogous to the one Locke thought characterized our beliefs about secondary qualities, which explains why we think of things as well as some of our experiences connected with them as beautiful. It is possible to confuse my enjoyment with the experiences I have in enjoying something; but it is not plausible to suggest that we have a general tendency to objectify enjoyment in the way, according to Locke, we do our ideas of secondary qualities. If we did we would always have a tendency – whatever this might mean – to project the state of enjoyment on to whatever we are enjoying.

Those who believe that it is only through experience that we come to realize that people have different likes and dislikes might dispute this last point. But unless philistinism is presupposed these grounds for disputing it do not support a secondary quality account of beauty. If we did commit the confusion spoken of, the qualities that correspond to secondary ones would not include beauty, but rather qualities like the pleasantness of a smell which depend, we learn, on the state of the perceiver. For if there is a genuine quality of beauty, it is something the apprehension of which is necessarily pleasant. In other words, a secondary quality account entails the philistine position that there is no such thing as beauty in the sense just understood. If, on the contrary, there is a quality of beauty in a non-philistine sense, then its existence vindicates in this case our alleged tendency to objectify enjoyment. Thus beauty turns out to have the status of a *primary* quality rather than a secondary one. Such indeed is the account proposed by Santayana.

3. *Beauty as a primary quality: Santayana, Bell*

Santayana writes that 'Every sensation we get from a thing is originally treated as one of its qualities'. And he claims that 'emotions are essentially capable of objectification, as well as impressions of sense'. Following Hume, he maintains that the distinction between primary and secondary qualities is due only to the fact that we 'reduce the qualities of an object to a minimum, and . . . regard most perceptions as an effect of these few qualities upon us.' But beauty, he claims, survives this process. It is 'an emotional element, a pleasure of ours, which nevertheless we regard as a quality of things'. Beauty is 'pleasure objectified' (*The Sense of Beauty*, pp.29–30).

This account cannot be correct as it stands because it treats the distinction between primary and secondary qualities as only a matter of 'convenience and economy of thought'. But the impossibility of discovering that beauty is a secondary quality is absolute (assuming philistinism is to be rejected). Unless we put the objectivity of all primary qualities on an absolute basis, we cannot classify beauty along with primary qualities. Moreover, even if the status of all primary qualities is absolute, the case of beauty remains exceptional if its only explanatory role is to correspond to our experience of beauty.

Belief in a primary quality of beauty restores the propriety in thinking that aesthetic enjoyment can be focused on the things we perceive rather than only on ideas and sensations; but it still does so at the cost of divorcing this enjoyment from the qualities we would actually cite as the ones that make an experience aesthetically enjoyable. For we do not merely say that a picture is pleasant to look at 'because it is beautiful'. We refer to qualities of expression and design, colour and texture. If, however, beauty were a primary quality, this alone would be the true source of aesthetic pleasure; and a capacity to detect it would have no obvious connection with any other capacities, except perhaps ones for recognizing other primary qualities. Clive Bell shows some tendency to accept this with respect to his much-derided notion of 'significant form', this being, he explains, 'the common quality which provokes' the 'peculiar emotion' which works of art cause in us (*Art*, pp.6–8). Bell asserts that 'to appreciate a work of art we need bring with us nothing from life, no knowledge of its ideas and affairs, no familiarity with its emotions' (ibid., p.25). This can be made to sound less antiseptic by allowing that beauty (or 'significant form') does nonetheless acquire emotional associations. Reversing the order of explanation in Burke's account, we could then say not that I regard things as beautiful because I associate them with tenderness and affection, but rather that I associate beautiful things with tender emotions because I associate beauty with these emotions. It remains true, however, that factors that are integral to aesthetic experience are not here being assigned their full weight. If a fault in a secondary quality model is to treat such factors as only causes of aesthetic enjoyment, a fault in regarding beauty as a primary quality is to reduce them to inessential associations.

Might this criticism be evaded by identifying specific manifestations of beauty with complexes of other qualities, while denying that any general analysis of beauty is possible? The idea that beauty is, in this sense, a Gestalt property has some credibility; but there is an obvious objection to the hope that it can be used to reconcile belief that beauty has the status of a primary quality with the diverse sorts of explanation we give of why we find things beautiful. If the beauty of a thing consists in a complex of qualities, then beauty has the status of a primary quality only if all these constituent qualities do. But we frequently cite secondary qualities among the features of things that contribute to their beauty. To be effective the reply will have to maintain not that beauty is a primary quality but that it has an objectivity comparable to that of a primary quality with respect to whatever qualities on specific occasions may constitute it regardless of the status of these qualities themselves. Beauty is not simply a further quality, either primary or secondary, alongside others. Bell tacitly concedes this when he gives a rather heterogeneous list in trying positively to specify the capacities needed to appreciate art: to do this 'we need bring with us nothing but a sense of form and colour and a knowledge of three dimensional space' (ibid., p.27).

Another objection to regarding beauty as a primary quality is that this creates difficulties about the relationship of aesthetic to other values. If we experience aesthetic pleasure in perceiving the quality of beauty, this being something it is necessarily pleasant to perceive, then the desirability of this perception is apparently independent of its effects, i.e. it requires no extraneous justification. The stage is thus set for conflict between the aesthete and the puritan. It now appears that a puritan who is not a philistine must simply make an exception of aesthetic values. Santayana's solution is to embrace aestheticism. He declares that 'All values are in one sense aesthetic', and that 'morality is a means and not an end' (op. cit., pp.19–20). In a similar vein, Bell asserts that art is 'beyond the reach of the moralist' (op. cit., p.20).

An aestheticism prompted by regarding beauty as having an objectivity like that of primary qualities rather than secondary ones tends, however, to confer a more than merely hedonistic value upon aesthetic experience. For if properties of every kind can figure in perceptions that are aesthetically enjoyable, and yet beauty is a property of the things we perceive not only of our perceptions themselves, then the implication is that there can be an affinity between things and how we experience them of a *deeper* kind than that between primary qualities and our perceptions. If this is so there is scope to maintain that aesthetic experience, in making us aware of this affinity, has a metaphysical or quasi-religious significance. Indeed Bell makes it clear that this is the nature of the significance which he believes 'significant form' possesses. He advances the 'metaphysical hypothesis' that significant form is 'form behind which we catch a sense of ultimate reality' (ibid., p.54).

It is a moot point how far this kind of view, which invites comparison with Neoplatonism and in a different way with Kant, can consistently avoid iconoclasm. But it evidently takes us a long way from hedonism. It no longer relies on the notion of aesthetic pleasure to explain art, but calls for a theory of the relation between mind and nature whereby aesthetic enjoyment can be taken to echo something beyond itself.

4. *Hume's theory*

A hedonist will have cause radically to modify his position if he thinks of beauty as a primary quality; but there remains the option of adhering to the adapted secondary quality account. A disadvantage with this sort of account is that its philistinism seems to commit it to regarding the beautiful as no more than a species of the agreeable; and we like to think that aesthetic evaluations have a more solid basis. However, in his essay 'Of the Standard of Taste' Hume attempted to show, in opposition to Lockean notions of objectivity, how there can still be a non-arbitrary basis for aesthetic evaluations even if beauty exists only in the mind that contemplates it.

According to Hume, 'Strong sense, united to delicate sentiment, improved by practice, perfected by comparison, and cleared of all prejudice, can alone entitle critics to this valuable character [of true judge]; and the joint verdict of such, wherever they are to be found, is the true standard of taste and beauty' (*Essays and Treatises*, p.238). This account, if it is not to be circular, must mean that greater authority ought to be given to the considered judgements of those who display superior powers of discrimination. We can test such powers, for example in connection with classifying wines or attributing paintings, independently of the subjects' likes and dislikes.

At one point Hume incautiously suggests that it may be possible to decide questions of beauty in the same sense as we can ones regarding 'true and real colour, even while colour is allowed to be merely a phantasm of the senses' (ibid., p.229). But even if the best judges do, as a matter of fact, deliver a 'joint verdict', the objectivity of their evaluations is not like that of judgements on colour. People possess compatible colour concepts if they make the same colour discriminations. If people agree in what they are prepared to describe as 'red' and as 'green' then there is some measure of agreement in what they mean by their classifications. But the possession of identical powers of discrimination entails no identity of preferences. 'Pleasant' and 'unpleasant' cannot be put on the same footing as 'red' and 'green' merely by restricting consideration to the judgements of those who display greatest discernment. Two qualified judges could agree perfectly in, for example, classifying wines as 'pleasant' or 'unpleasant' and yet give these words opposed meanings. The objectivity of taste as postulated by Hume is contingent upon a tendency for preferences to converge as powers of discrimination increase; but the objectivity of judgements about colours only requires consistency in discrimination. On Hume's theory there is an element of relativity in beauty absent from 'true and real colour'.

A question Hume's account raises is 'Why should I give greater weight to the judgements of those who can make finer and more reliable discriminations than myself?' It is not enough to reply that the opinions of superior judges give a foretaste of how my own preferences will evolve. For I may know that my limitations are such that my preferences will never develop to that point. Why, then, should the opinions of superior judges be of any interest to me? Why, anyway, should I regard any agreement reached by these judges as more than coincidence?

I do not think Hume has any real answer to these questions if his theory is regarded as a purely hedonistic one. If it is then the respect we have for superior judges can only be like that which a man with a poor sense of smell might have for the preferences of those who can smell better. This man may have to concede that those with keener senses have a truer perception than he does of how things smell. But it need not detract from his own enjoyment of a smell that others who can smell better do not share his preferences; and as regards the way he experiences a smell, his judgements of pleasantness may be as valid as the judgements which those with keener senses make with respect to how they experience it. If Hume's theory is a purely hedonistic one, the grounds for giving authority to qualified judges are just that their judgements are based on a truer perception of the objects. His account lapses if we are only interested in the evaluation of the way these objects appear to different individuals.

But Hume was not a pure hedonist. In his essay 'The Sceptic' he describes 'the chief triumph of art and philosophy' as being that 'It insensibly refines the temper, and points out to us those dispositions which we should endeavour to attain' (ibid., p.168). Hume hints, then, that the abilities exercised in appreciating art have an ethical significance which makes it desirable to develop them. It is important to Hume that the true judge is not just someone with superior powers of discrimination; his judgements have to be considered ones if they are to carry weight: the true judge displays a certain maturity. Consequently the evaluations of the best judges have authority not just because they are based on a truer perception of the object, but because they are a truer or deeper reflection of human nature.

This background, together with the assumption of a shared human nature, explains Hume's confidence that the best judges will tend to agree. Not that total agreement can be expected: perhaps there will always be 'a difference in degree of our approbation and blame'; but such differences will at any rate be explicable in terms of the factors that to a limited extent can modify human nature, such as the 'different humours of particular men' and the 'manners and opinions' of an age or country (ibid., p.240).

Thus Hume's belief that aesthetic enjoyment has ethical significance is integral to his attempt to explain how aesthetic evaluations can have an objective basis. And by this same means he makes his philistinism more palatable that it otherwise would be. If, as Hume maintains, there is no real quality of beauty, then the question arises why we should regard our aesthetically enjoyable experiences as having any importance. Belief in a genuine quality of beauty leads to the view that beauty must be a deeper feature of reality than primary qualities; and such a view has no difficulty in holding that aesthetic enjoyment is something of significance. But a secondary quality treatment apparently leads to the conclusion that beauty is an even more superficial feature of reality than colours and smells, or tastes and sounds, being only a matter of how we experience our own ideas and sensations. On the face of it this implies a very shallow estimate of the importance of aesthetic pleasure. But Hume avoids this conclusion by tempering his hedonism with claims as to the ethical value of this pleasure. In other words beneath his hedonistic surface Hume is a puritan, if only a mild one – he is not concerned to stress that art can be positively harmful.

The general point which Hume's theory illustrates is that a philistine has to become puritanical if he is not to trivialize art. The upshot is that there is very little territory for a consistent hedonist to occupy. If aesthetic pleasure is taken to reflect a genuine facet of reality, then we have to come to grips with the difficult notion of a metaphysical affinity between ourselves and nature. If aesthetic pleasure is not so regarded then hedonism either trivializes aesthetic experience or develops into a puritanical view that does not consider aesthetic pleasure to be an end in itself.

CHAPTER II

Theories that Assign a Direct Practical Purpose to Art

1. Nutritional and medicinal analogies

There are two main senses in which we can ask for an *explanation* of art and of aesthetic enjoyment. We can ask for an account of their *purpose*; or we can ask for an account of the *activities themselves* that are here being enjoyed. These two questions are interwoven, of course. In general it is impossible to say what the purpose of an activity might be without first being able to describe the activity itself; and a full and accurate account of an activity ought to lead to an account of its purpose, if it has one.

Of these questions the one about the point or purpose of aesthetic enjoyment is apt to seem the more pressing. Hedonism fails to explain why we should have a capacity for aesthetic enjoyment. Consistently adhered to it makes the existence of aesthetic pleasure appear quite pointless. One direction in which we might move in attempting a better answer is towards a metaphysical aestheticism which identifies the purpose of life with none other than the capacity to appreciate true beauty. But a more down to earth response is to try to identify some specific practical benefits beyond the pleasure itself which aesthetic enjoyment can bring.

An analogy often used in this connection is that of 'aesthetic nutrition' or art as 'food for the mind'. Indeed this metaphor is a natural complement to that of 'aesthetic taste'. Tolstoy, for instance, uses nutritional analogies repeatedly in his provocative *What is Art?* He says that 'Everybody understands that the satisfaction of our taste cannot serve as a basis for our definition of the merits of food .... In the same way beauty, or that which pleases us, can in no sense serve as a basis for the definition of art' (ibid., pp.116–17). In Tolstoy's view, the purpose of art is to provide 'real, important, necessary, spiritual food' (ibid., p.250).

Thinkers who believe the practical benefits art brings are chiefly remedial may prefer medicinal to nutritional analogies; but these are clearly variations on the same theme. A famous such use of a medicinal analogy is Aristotle's theory that tragedy can effect a catharsis or 'purging' of the emotions. Another well-known therapeutic theory is the Freudian one that art serves as a compensatory outlet for impulses that cannot be satisfied more immediately. Plato mixes such medicinal analogies with nutritional ones; for example, when he likens what he regards as the harmful effects of art to the consequences of unhealthy eating while comparing the influence of beneficial art to that of a healthy climate (*Republic*, 401).

These theories attempt to explain the enjoyment of art, in the sense of answering questions about its purpose, by relating it directly to practical benefits beyond the enjoyment itself. In this sense these are all puritanical theories even if their puritanism is not always of a specifically moral kind. They all evaluate aesthetically enjoyable experiences not by reference to how pleasurable they are but by reference to their outcome.

Those who have proposed such theories have not always, however, been concerned to explain art and aesthetic enjoyment in the other sense distinguished, i.e. in the sense of explaining the more immediate character of the activity here being enjoyed. But, as I said, these two explanatory issues – the purpose of art and aesthetic enjoyment, and the character of the enjoyed activity – cannot be divorced. Any attempt seriously to use nutritional or medicinal comparisons to explain art's purpose will face questions about how the experience of art brings about its supposed practical benefits.

2. *General difficulties*

It is often hard to follow closely the thought of those who use the nutritional analogy or its medicinal variant – not surprisingly, I think, since the analogy is flawed. Their theories anyway differ widely, the chief respect being over the question whether the purpose of art is something external to the experience of art which this experience causes, as the analogy would first suggest, or whether it is somehow internal to this experience. Freud's theory is along the former lines. But a factor that encourages the latter view is that art directly engages our emotions and feelings, and these have traditionally been regarded as belonging to the practical side of our nature. This point deeply impressed Plato, and it is central to Tolstoy's theory. Another possible ground for adopting this second interpretation is the belief that while the experience of art is primarily cognitive the attainment of certain kinds of knowledge is itself central to our practical goals. This is a guiding thought in the philosophy of Plotinus who took it over from Plato, in whose own writings it sits uncomfortably alongside the point about the immediate impact of art upon the emotions.

At first sight comparing art to food implies the philistine view that art is only a means to some other end; but because on some interpretations of the analogy the practical purpose of art is internal to our experience of it, this does not always follow. Non-philistine interpretations of the analogy do, however, tend to be iconoclastic. They would otherwise have difficulty in giving an integrated account of our aesthetic and other practical goals, i.e. works of art would be a distraction unless they lost their beauty once they had served their purpose.

The basic objection to all these theories is that however the nutritional analogy is used, no such account of the relationship between the experience of art and its supposed practical benefits can be explanatory in both the senses mentioned. The teleological question about the contribution art makes to our aims is not, then, to be answered by directly relating it to any specific benefits. The difficulty displays itself differently depending on how the analogy is used. Briefly, theories that maintain – embracing philistinism – that the practical benefits of enjoying art are a separate causal outcome find it impossible to explain the character of the enjoyed activity: specifically they are unable to explain the relation between the evaluation of art according to aesthetic criteria and its evaluation according to functional ones. These theories, lured by the prospect of a direct answer to questions about the purpose of art, are unable to explain how it can actually serve any such purpose. On the other hand, theories that locate the purpose of art within artistic experience, while they may have the merit of not being philistine, forsake the strategy of explaining art's purpose by reference to any independently recognizable aims. Consequently they face the difficulty of explaining how something internal to our experience of art can itself constitute a practical goal. Theories of this kind find themselves propelled towards iconoclasm and metaphysical aestheticism.

3. Art as substitute satisfaction: Freud

If art has a purpose it is not as evident as that of food: people who lack contact with art do not suffer effects as obvious as starvation and malnutrition. But perhaps in the sense art is like food it is only one element in the relevant 'diet'. A deeper difficulty than that of isolating art's practical purpose is that if it had one beyond the experience of art itself, this would raise questions about the relationship between aesthetic and functional criteria for evaluating the enjoyment of art, i.e. between evaluating the appropriateness of this enjoyment by reference to the sorts of factors we attend to in apprehending works of art, and evaluating it by reference to whether or not the experience served art's purpose.

If art has an external purpose the question of this relationship is bound to arise, assuming that the 'consumption' of a work of art is in some sense a matter of attending to the work and noticing relevant features of it. In that case enjoyment of the work will be misplaced if it involves mistakes or omissions regarding its relevant features. So questions about the appropriateness of enjoying a work of art can now be meant in two ways depending on whether the questioner has these matters or functional criteria in mind. In the food case, however, the only question is whether food that is enjoyed is nutritionally beneficial.

If the theory is to make good its claim to identify a purpose behind aesthetic enjoyment, it must explain how internal aesthetic criteria reflect or derive from the external practical ones, i.e. how the sorts of adjustments and revisions we make in our aesthetic responses as we get to know works better contribute to securing art's purpose. But if aesthetic and practical criteria are co-ordinated then there is not the same sort of contrast here as in the food case between enjoyment and its effects. Provided the enjoyment of art is appropriate as properly judged by *aesthetic* criteria this itself is an indication that it will fulfil its *practical* purpose. The relationship between food being appetizing and it being nutritious is different. Creatures who developed a taste for harmful foods would be at a serious survival disadvantage: it is not surprising, therefore, that there is a correspondence between things that we *like* to eat and things that are *good* to eat. But the position is not that we have developed a liking for art that is good for us. If it were it would make sense to say that something is good art although no one will ever like it. If there are both aesthetic and practical criteria for art these must correlate in the sense that these are criteria for the very same thing. Otherwise the theory would not be explaining aesthetic enjoyment by reference to its purpose, but would only be a theory of the possible uses to which this enjoyment can be put.

But if aesthetic and practical criteria are criteria for the very same thing, then does not art's practical purpose have to be *identified* with experiencing enjoyment that is appropriate by aesthetic criteria? And does not that mean that art's practical purpose, if it has one, cannot after all be something external to the enjoyment of art in the sense that the purpose of food is something external to the enjoyment of eating?

Freud's theory provides a possible response to this difficulty, namely that the internal enjoyment of art can simultaneously be regarded as an external effect because it can be equated with other satisfactions for which it stands as a substitute. Although Freud concedes that psychoanalysis has 'scarcely anything to say about beauty' (*Civilization and its Discontents*, p.20), he is ready to equate the enjoyment of art with 'satisfaction through phantasy' (ibid., p.17). He explains that 'at the time when the development of the sense of reality took place, [the life of the imagination] was expressly exempted from the demands of reality- testing and was set apart for the purpose of fulfilling wishes which were difficult to carry out' (ibid., p.17).

The principle behind this explanation is obscure. It is possible to enjoy fantasizing, of course; but it cannot merely be assumed that, for example, a man who has violent impulses will satisfy them to some degree if he indulges them in fantasy. The opposite is equally conceivable. Freud's sympathizers tend to take it for granted that fantasy can be a harmless arena for harmful emotions; Plato took a contrary view. But without belief in the therapeutic potential of art, Freud's theory would become a version of iconoclastic hedonism rather than of philistine puritanism, i.e. it would maintain that art offers no more than an inferior form of satisfaction.

It is not clear, anyway, that enjoying a fantasy need have anything to do with satisfying what is fantasized. Obviously a hungry man cannot satisfy his hunger by imagining a meal. And it does not help to suppose that he is unaware that he is only imagining it, e.g. that he is dreaming, or that he imagines a meal unconsciously. No doubt the satisfaction that art can bring may compensate for some disappointments or frustrations. But this is possible because art is satisfying: its being a compensation or a substitute does not explain why it is satisfying but rather the other way around.

Despite this Freud believes that he can explain the compensatory or substitute character of our enjoyment of art by appeal to the workings of the unconscious. He believes that art has a symbolic content, and that we can satisfy instinctual impulses in unconsciously discerning this content. But there ought in that case to be two ways of enjoying works of art. Besides or instead of enjoying a work because of the unconscious fantasy it provokes, it ought also to be possible to admire it because it is a well-constructed symbol. This, of course, is the point artists are likely to stress against Freud. Art can be used as a vehicle for fantasy; but artists want their work itself to engage our interest. The philosophical objection is that if there were an explanation of how art fulfils the function Freud assigns to it, this would create a gap between internal and external criteria for evaluating art. There would then be ways of enjoying art that are independent of fantasy satisfaction; so the theory cannot explain what it is to enjoy art as such, but only certain of its enjoyable uses.

Very likely Freud would not have been bothered by this conclusion: his aim was probably only to explain what he took to be, as a matter of fact, the chief causes of enjoyment of the arts. If he meant to give a deeper explanation of this enjoyment he would have had to maintain, as more than an empirical generalization or a stipulation, that the only criterion in judging works of art is how well they serve the purposes of fantasy. There is, however, an element of paradox in this claim.

Compare the situation with evaluating an artefact such as a hammer or a saw. The only relevant criterion in judging a saw is how good it is at cutting. But it is possible to judge the quality of a saw on indirect grounds: saw manufacturers rely on this fact. Consequently it is possible to admire the quality of a saw without actually using it or having any wish to do so. But the present Freudian claim is that fantasy purposes are the sole criterion in art in a sense that excludes any grounds for judging works that could analogously serve as a separate basis for admiring them. This means that the Freudian theory's own symbolic analyses can only prompt admiration of works of art if these explanations are themselves enjoyable because of a fantasy content. The corollary is that the theory cannot give an independent explanation of how art achieves its purpose analogous to one of a saw's effectiveness. So the mystery of art is finally impenetrable. It is impossible to explain it on a purely rational basis. Perhaps this is a point upon which Plato and Freud could have agreed.

4. Tolstoy's theory

Tolstoy develops a theory of art which, like Freud's, conceives it as having a direct practical purpose, but which, unlike Freud's, regards art as strictly indispensable to attaining this purpose. For Tolstoy, art is no mere substitute: its purpose is internal to it in a stronger sense than Freud acknowledges. So, unlike Freud, Tolstoy is no philistine. He is, however, astonishingly iconoclastic.

Tolstoy's leading idea is that 'whereas by words a man transmits his thoughts to another, by art he transmits his feelings' (*What is Art?*, p.121). He says that:

> *Art is a human activity consisting in this, that one man consciously by means of certain external signs, hands on to others feelings he has lived through, and that others are infected by these feelings and also experience them.*
>
> (ibid., p.123; italics in original)

Tolstoy concludes that the best art is that which best transmits feelings; and he recognizes two criteria for this. Good art should transmit feelings vividly and readily; and should also do so to the widest possible audience. 'Great works of art are only great because they are accessible and comprehensible to everyone' (ibid., p.177).

Tolstoy resolves the problem of how art's purpose can simultaneously be something internal to our experience of it and something that has broader significance by maintaining that the sharing of feelings art makes possible is necessary to the goal of human well-being. Art 'is a means of union among men joining them together in the same feelings, and indispensable for the life and progress towards well-being of individuals and of humanity' (ibid., p.123). Tolstoy clearly holds that the union of feeling that art creates is a constituent of human well-being, not just a means to its attainment. Art, he says, achieves a 'freeing of our personality from its separation and isolation' (ibid., p.228). And he regards this in a moral and religious light: he believes that when art performs its true function, it achieves something morally good in itself.

This explains Tolstoy's insistence on accessibility. If the experience that art affords is a necessary constituent of human well-being, then unless everyone can share this experience, some will be denied the opportunity to attain this well-being: 'if art is an important matter, a spiritual blessing essential for all men . . . then it should be accessible to everyone' (ibid., p.148). Tolstoy unflinchingly concludes that almost everything regarded as great art is only a counterfeit. (He extends this condemnation to include, with two small exceptions, all his own earlier work.)

Tolstoy's emphasis on accessibility is not matched, however, by a corresponding claim as to the universality of the ability to create works of art. He believes that this ability is relatively rare, because 'only that is a true work of art which transmits fresh feelings not previously experienced by man' (ibid., p.149), and only a few individuals are capable of spontaneously experiencing such fresh feelings. Here Tolstoy gives a religious explanation. It is with 'the movement forward of humanity which expresses itself in religious consciousness' that 'men experience new and fresh feelings' (ibid., p.150). But few have this necessary religious consciousness. ('Religions are the exponents of the highest comprehension of life accessible to the best and foremost men at a given time in a given society – a comprehension towards which all the rest of that society must inevitably and irresistibly advance' (ibid., p.127)). The result is that Tolstoy conceives of art's function, in promoting unity of feeling, as an evolutionary process. He says that 'the evolution of feeling proceeds by art – feelings less kind and less necessary for the well-being of mankind being replaced by others kinder and more needful for that end. That is the purpose of art' (ibid., p.231).

Tolstoy also introduces religious considerations in evading what would otherwise appear to be a decisive objection to his theory, namely that many people admire art which by his criterion of accessibility they ought not to. He asserts that 'good art pleases everyone' (ibid., p.176). But what he really means is that everyone *ought* to find good art pleasing – since what art achieves is morally good in itself, and one ought to delight in what is morally good. So when people fail to enjoy accessible works, or enjoy ones that are not accessible, this reflects, Tolstoy believes, their state of moral corruption. He puts this down to their want of religion: good art pleases everyone except 'erudite, perverted people destitute of religion' (ibid., p.179). Apparently the capacity spontaneously to experience fresh feelings is something confined to a religiously aware creative elite whereas the capacity to receive such feelings through works of art is open to all provided they acknowledge religion.

One reason, perhaps, why Tolstoy imposes a requirement of novelty upon true art is the thought that there can be no point in trying to transmit feelings which the audience has already experienced. This would imply that art becomes obsolete once it becomes familiar. More seriously this raises the question whether the pleasure that true art causes is pleasure merely in (a) the experience of a feeling; or in (b) its transmission; or in (c) the knowledge that the feeling so transmitted is one that potentially unites mankind. If (c) is the important consideration as regards the purpose of art, then the content or novelty of the feeling hardly seems to be relevant as such; so it would be a confusion to think that (a) is the object of this pleasure. But clearly my own experience of a work of art is only of the transmission of a feeling to me. It would seem therefore that the pleasure I derive from true art is, in the first instance at least, pleasure in (b), not (c). What is the relationship between enjoying a work of art because it transmits a feeling to me and enjoying it because it can transmit this feeling to everyone?

This corresponds to the question for the Freudian theory about the two ways of enjoying a work of art – as a well-constructed symbol or as a vehicle for fantasy. And although Tolstoy suggests religious and moral grounds for holding that a work can transmit a feeling universally if it can transmit it to any one person, this does not go far enough. A religious guarantee that the transmission of feelings through art to a given individual contributes to securing the purpose of art, namely to unite men in the highest comprehension of life, does not explain the enjoyment of art as something that brings about this direct practical benefit, but merely ensures that it always does. Save for the religious hypothesis, the two need not coincide. Circumstances are certainly possible where the most 'infectious' feelings are detrimental to human well-being, or where different susceptibilities to 'infection' among different groups are a source of social discord.

The interest of Tolstoy's theory is that it represents an attempt to explain art as having a practical purpose but without regarding it as a means to some other end. His theory has set a pattern for non-philistine Marxist theories of art. For example, Ernst Fischer writes that man 'feels that he can attain wholeness only if he takes possession of the experiences of others that might potentially be his own .... Art is the indispensable means for this merging of the individual with the whole' (*The Necessity of Art*, p.8). The sentiment is Tolstoy's – though, of course, in a Marxist context Tolstoy's appeal to religious consciousness has to be replaced by one to knowledge of the forces shaping social reality.

Tolstoy's basic point is that if art is desirable as an end in itself then it must itself be something good or a constituent of goodness; and it must in that case be open to direct moral evaluation. Good art is morally good. The cogency of this reasoning is hard to question. But Tolstoy fails to establish a sufficiently close link between the experience of art and its supposed practical value. A symptom of this, though his evolutionary view of feeling tends to obscure it, is his tendency to vacillate between saying that good art merely fosters a community of shared feeling and saying that it promotes certain specific feelings. The same problem also exercised Plato, some of whose conclusions about art resemble Tolstoy's. (Tolstoy refers favourably to Plato (op. cit., pp.261–2).) But Plato's approach is founded upon a different and philosophically much deeper analysis of the nature of goodness.

5. *Art as a pseudo-capacity: Plato*

Tolstoy startles us by condemning almost everything that is generally acknowledged as great art: but Plato's indictment of art is even more severe. Tolstoy believes iconoclastically that artistic capacities can easily be and have often been corrupted; but his reservations do not undermine his conviction that true art is possible and that it is something desirable in itself. Plato, however, argues that art is inherently corrupt: he does not believe that art by itself can produce anything of value. He does not deny that art has its uses; but this is not due to any merit in art but only to the wisdom of those who know how to use it. Bluntly, Plato's view is that art has a potential for good only as a useful lie.

But Plato is not philistine. Far from it – the importance of the experience of beauty is one of his recurring themes. Modern readers may find it puzzling that Plato praises beauty while condemning art; for we have come to assume that these go together. We tend consequently to suspect that Plato lacks a properly developed concept of art. But Plato is not at all guilty of overlooking the point that art aspires to be beautiful. His thesis is that it cannot attain this aim though it may appear to do so. It is because of this deficiency, and because he believes that the experience of true beauty is of such paramount importance, that Plato is so severe on artists.

Plato holds, as a defining characteristic, that we love and desire the things we take to be beautiful; but that the good is the only proper object of desire. He infers that something is truly beautiful only when it is truly desirable, i.e. when it is something good. The problem, as Plato sees it, is that we can easily be led astray because many things that appear to be beautiful or pleasant are not truly desirable. He goes as far as to say that 'the object of education is to teach us to love beauty' (*Republic* 403, trans. H.D.P. Lee), i.e. to love *true* beauty; for delight in true beauty is delight in what is truly good.

Plato denies that the enjoyment of works of art is something truly desirable because he thinks it can manifestly be a bad influence. (He has drama particularly in mind.) He believes that art 'has a terrible power to corrupt even the best characters, with very few exceptions', because here 'our better nature . . . relaxes its control'; and if, for example, 'we let ourselves feel excessively for the misfortunes of others [as depicted in a work of art] it will be difficult to restrain our feelings in our own' (ibid., 605–6).

Plato concludes by advocating censorship. He writes that in his ideal republic 'we must issue . . . orders to all artists and prevent them portraying bad character, ill discipline, meanness or ugliness in painting, sculpture, architecture, or any work of art' (ibid., 401). He believes that if artists are required to 'represent good character', then art can make a valuable contribution to moral education (ibid.).

It may be agreed that sometimes works of art have a bad influence; but it does not follow that the purpose of art is to be a good influence any more than it follows that because there are dangers in driving motor vehicles the purpose of driving is to promote road safety. If art had a valid purpose of its own the most that would follow from the possibility of its being a bad influence is that access to it should be limited to those responsible enough to use it properly. Plato must believe, then, that art has no such purpose. He has several reasons for holding this, some relatively superficial, others more profound.

In Book X of the *Republic* Plato labours the point that an artistic representation of something, e.g. a bed, stands at 'third remove from reality' (ibid., 597), i.e. from the ideal Form of the bed. Whereas a craftsman who can make a bed knows what a bed is, i.e. the Form of a bed, a painter, Plato insists, only knows what a bed looks like. Works of art are in his view only a very inferior means of bringing us into contact with the true objects of knowledge, viz. the Forms.

But it nowadays hardly enters our heads to imagine that artists are interested in conveying *this* kind of knowledge. Plato has a deeper point, however. Whatever else artists may be trying to do, they are certainly concerned to give pleasure. And whatever pleases appears to be good. But we can only regard something as good if we can say what kind of good thing it is – a good knife, a good soldier, a good day for sailing, etc. And the kind of thing it is supplies the criteria for judging its goodness. As applied to art this means that there can only be good works of art as such if there is some standard, other than the pleasure it gives, for judging whether or not a work of art is good. But since the primary concern of artists is precisely to produce pleasure, there cannot, Plato reasons, be any such independent standard. Artists do not aim to please by doing something else well, as a craftsman might in trying to make a good bed.

This point does not depend on Plato's metaphysics. In a different way it arises again in Kant's notion of 'purposefulness without purpose'. And Aristotle, like Plato, holds that there is no 'art' of producing pleasure, distinguishing this from the case of the perfumer or chef (*Nicomachean Ethics*, Bk.VII, Ch.xii). Pleasure or beauty are not things that can be aimed at as such. Kant believes that despite this he can explain artistic abilities; but Plato draws the plausible conclusion that artists have no genuine ability to produce things of beauty.

Plato infers that artists deal in appearances not merely in the sense that a painting of a bed is remote from the Form of the bed, but in the sense that artists, in so far as they are only concerned to please, are necessarily concerned only with apparent goodness. Plato regards artists as a species of sophist. Reciprocally he accuses lovers of music and the theatre of being like dreamers who confuse image with reality because they delight in sounds, colours and forms which appear to be beautiful without being capable of delighting in beauty itself (op. cit., 476).

Seen in this light, Plato's theory makes no attempt to explain art by revealing its underlying purpose – rather he rejects it as an activity beneath explanation. It must be said that even if the idea of a pseudo-capacity that cannot be rationally explained is a coherent one, the matter cannot be left here. It still needs to be explained how we come to have such pseudo-capacities. (From an evolutionary standpoint their very existence would be baffling.) But while he is in this frame of mind Plato's only concession is that some art can be put to good use. When it portrays virtue in an attractive light it can, by sugaring the pill so to speak, serve an educational purpose. But, significantly, art is not mentioned when, in the *Symposium*, we hear Diotima's account of the ascent, beginning with the love of physical beauty, through the love of knowledge, to the love of beauty itself (*Symposium*, 209–12).

6. Beauty and inspiration: Plato

Yet Plato sometimes falters in the severity of his condemnation of art. Although he says at one point, while deploring certain passages in Homer, that 'the better they are as poetry the more unsuitable they are for the ears of children or grown-ups' (*Republic*, 387), he says later that 'Good literature . . . good music and beauty of form generally all depend on beauty of character' (ibid., 400). He goes on to say that this can also be seen:

> in painting and similar arts, in weaving and embroidery, in architecture and furniture, and in living things, animals and plants. For in all of these we find beauty and ugliness. And ugliness of form and disharmony are akin to bad art and bad character, and their opposites are akin to and represent good character and discipline.
>
> (ibid., 401)

Plato continues shortly with the observation that:

> Our artists and craftsmen must be capable of perceiving the real nature of what is beautiful, and then our young men, living as it were in a good climate, will benefit because all the works of art they see and hear influence them for good.
>
> (ibid., 401)

The implication is that if artists only knew what beauty really is, then no censorship would be needed; for they would then of their own accord produce works that comply with Plato's moral aims. It is also noteworthy that Plato is apparently willing to credit beautiful things with a beneficial influence even if they lack any representational content in the ordinary sense. This willingness would exculpate him from the charge that he attributes art with a moral purpose only because he confuses a tendency to enjoy works in which morally bad actions are depicted with a tendency to enjoy the bad actions themselves.

The implication of these passages appears, however, to conflict with Plato's argument that art is a pseudo-capacity. He was saying that there is no knowledge of beauty as such which could equip artists to produce beautiful things in the way a craftsman's knowledge of what a bed is equips him to make one. But he now appears to be saying that there is knowledge of beauty that would have this effect. There are, perhaps, two ways, neither very satisfactory, of trying to reconcile these statements. These reflect an ambiguity, characteristic of Plato, in speaking of 'knowing beauty'. This can mean being able to tell what things are beautiful, or it can mean knowing what it is that makes all these things beautiful.

One way of trying to reconcile Plato's statements is to take it that when, in the last quotation, he speaks of being 'capable of perceiving the real nature of what is beautiful' he is only referring to the capacity to distinguish particular beautiful things from ugly ones, e.g. to recognize particular beautiful tables. His point would then be that provided an artist or craftsman knows properly what he is doing, he will know whether or not what he is making is good of its kind: he will thus be incapable of producing something bad of that kind out of mere ignorance. Of course this point only applies where the agent can have explanatory knowledge of what he is making. If Plato is now applying it to what we call the 'fine arts' then he is forgetting his claim that it is impossible to credit artists with any true knowledge of what they are doing.

The other way of trying to reconcile the statements is to imagine that Plato is alluding to the possibility of artists somehow having access to that knowledge of beauty itself which, he believes, crowns the pursuit of knowledge. If this is possible then artists may be in a position to recognize that what they produce is really beautiful, and not merely something that pleases an audience, despite the fact that its beauty is not explicable in terms of its being a good example of any specific type of thing. This interpretation demands that the apparent beauty which artists produce is not always bound to be illusory but can sometimes be genuine.

This raises difficult questions about knowledge of beauty itself. As I said, Plato's basic problem is how we can distinguish what is truly desirable from what is only apparently so. Owing to the connections between desirability, goodness and beauty this is equivalent to asking how we can distinguish real from apparent goodness, or true from false beauty. Plato sets out by trying to subsume this question, which concerns moral goodness in particular, under a more general one about what it is for things, of whatever kind, to be good. He maintains that to tell, for example, whether something is a good knife, we need to know what a knife is, i.e. know what it is to be a knife (having the purpose of cutting things and so on). This sets the standard for goodness in knives; and this is the sort of knowledge Plato has in mind when he speaks of knowing the *Form* of the knife. But he detects a problem about real and apparent goodness over and above that which may arise from not knowing what standards are relevant in evaluating particular things. There is a problem about what it is for these various standards all to be standards of *goodness*. To put it another way, he in effect envisages the possibility that someone may in one sense know very well what things are – he may know what Forms the things exemplify – and yet misapply this knowledge. To know in the full sense how to evaluate things and how to use them it is further necessary to know goodness itself. Plato says that the Form of the good is 'what gives the objects of knowledge their truth and the mind the power of knowing'. Again, the Form of the good is the 'cause of knowledge and truth', and is itself 'higher than knowledge and truth' (*Symposium*, 508–9). (Plato's problem about goodness itself has affinities with the one Michael Dummett claims to uncover about the notion of truth; see 'Truth', reprinted in *Truth and Other Enigmas*.)

Over and above knowledge of particular Forms, Plato acknowledges, then, a need for there to be such a thing as knowledge of the good or of beauty itself, these two being inseparable because we experience beauty in apprehending the good. This is a further reason why the first attempt at reconciling Plato's statements is unsatisfactory. Even if standards of goodness and badness applied to art in the way they do to crafts, knowing these standards would not itself guarantee that the things made are truly good and beautiful: the knowledge could be misapplied.

But how could knowledge of beauty itself – the Form of beauty – help in trying to produce genuinely beautiful works of art? The craftsman's knowledge of the Form of the bed enables him to make beds; but knowledge of the Form of beauty does not correspondingly enable its possessor to do anything in particular – to make beautiful things. What it enables him to do is quite different, namely to recognize for what it is goodness and beauty wherever it is found. Knowledge of true beauty and goodness is not expressed in any specific activities but in knowing how to live a good life generally. So the possibility of attaining such knowledge does not overturn the point that there is no knowledge of beauty that could enable an artist to produce beautiful things.

Indeed, the availability of knowledge of beauty itself not only fails to overturn this point but strengthens it. The relationship of particular things to the Form of beauty is not like that of particular beds to the Form of the bed. Beauty and goodness themselves lie beyond the other Forms. So the distinction between particular beautiful and ugly things, as judged by the standards of true beauty, is not on the same footing as that between well-made and badly-made beds. The things that well exemplify the Form of beauty, as opposed to well exemplifying the other Forms, are not the particular beautiful things we experience through our senses but the Forms of these things. As judged by the standards of beauty itself, the whole world of sense experience stands condemned as capable at most of an inferior or illusory beauty.

These considerations apparently confirm and reinforce Plato's contention that art cannot produce anything of positive value. They ought to mean that anyone who knew beauty itself would have no inclination to be an artist. Although Plato's system demands that there be such a thing as knowledge of beauty itself this is not only irrelevant to the problem of artistic creativity but seems to be inimical to its possibility. Nevertheless Plato's attitude to art is ambivalent. Despite all these negative considerations, there is a side to Plato that still wants to allow that some artists can produce things of real beauty. His efforts at explaining how this is possible rest finally on his theory of inspiration sketched briefly in the *Phaedrus* (245) and *Ion* (533). Drawing upon this Plato believes artists can have the contact with true beauty necessary to produce genuinely beautiful works, but without this undermining, as full knowledge of true beauty would, their inclination to do so. This is possible because artists do not themselves have this knowledge but are only the mouthpiece of the gods or the muses who do: Plato describes the true artist when he creates beautiful things as divinely possessed or inspired.

Whatever exactly this idea is taken to mean – and in less fanciful language it persists in the notion that artists have 'gifts' of a different order from learned skills – it evidently implies an opposite assessment of art from Plato's earlier, negative one. Instead of the artist being a mere sophist who has less than the knowledge of an honest craftsman, he now appears to have something infinitely more precious: an unbidden contact with the divine or with creative forces deeper than reason. What remains, however, whether because it is inferior to reason or superior to it, is that the ability to produce works of art is by ordinary standards inexplicable.

Doubtless there is an important element of truth in this. But we should notice how deep and indeed paradoxical this inexplicability is for Plato. It is not just that we cannot explain the ability to produce works of art; from Plato's viewpoint it is also beyond reason to understand what it is that artists succeed in producing. While art was regarded as beneath reason this hardly mattered. But the point cannot be brushed aside when art is allowed to have positive value. Whatever the merits of the inspiration theory, it does not remove the paradox for Plato in the idea that some things in the world of sense exemplify the Form of beauty itself as opposed to exemplifying beautifully one of the other Forms. We are entering the area where a claim that something is incomprehensible is being taken as an excuse for accepting an incomprehensible theory.

7. Metaphysical aestheticism: Plotinus

Plato believed that if the experience of beauty (or of art) is desirable in itself, then there must be an internal link between beauty (or art) and moral goodness. He sought to understand this by identifying the experience of true beauty with knowledge of true goodness. This explains the intrinsic desirability of the experience of beauty; but it apparently does so at the cost of making art impossible; for nothing in the world of sense experience can display true beauty.

By the same token, however, it ought to follow that nothing we do can exemplify true *goodness* – except, perhaps, contemplating the Forms. Anyone who finds this or Plato's rejection of art unacceptable, but who sympathizes with his outlook, will naturally wonder what adjustments in his system would be needed to allow ordinary things and actions to have positive value of their own. If I understand it, the overhaul of Platonic thought that Plotinus conducted was intended among other things to achieve this.

From the present point of view, the root of Plato's difficulty is his assumption that apparent desirability (beauty) is always unreliable until it has been ratified by reference to some ultimate standard of unmistakable goodness. Plato's attitude is that things can only be reliably evaluated as good when they are seen in the light of an ultimate standard. This is what lies behind the ambiguity characteristic of his thought noted earlier about the objects of knowledge: he believes that we only truly know what things exemplify a given Form if we first know the Form itself. Despite the *Symposium*, Plato does not believe that the perception of lower beauty is alone an effective means by which to develop progressively capacities to appreciate higher beauty. On the contrary. Knowledge of the good, as he conceives it, is not something we can have any *ability* to attain: that would presuppose the knowledge being sought. This point corresponds to the argument against artistic abilities. Plato conceives of the ascent to knowledge of the good as a journey whose final destination will reveal that we have taken the correct route, but which we cannot plan for ourselves. In advance we can only accept the advice of those who have already reached the destination as to the route to take. This is the source of Plato's authoritarian politics. Since there is no technique for acquiring it, knowledge of the good is a precious and precarious possession which has to be safeguarded; and those who lack this knowledge must defer to the judgement of those who do. Plato's authoritarianism is a political counterpart to his theory of artistic inspiration.

Although Plotinus is often highly obscure there is no doubt that his attitude to art is very different from Plato's. He would seem to believe that our capacity to apprehend lower beauty has its own power to develop and lead us to higher beauty. He speaks of a process of 'purification' and 'training' whereby the soul develops the capacity to see true beauty (Ennead I, Tractate vi, sections 6 and 9; Ennead V, viii, 2; trans. A.H. Armstrong). And he maintains, crucially, that the soul itself becomes beautiful and good in apprehending beauty (I, vi, 9). There are two principles behind this: an Aristotelian one, namely that in perception a perceptual faculty takes on the form perceived; and a quasi-Platonic one, namely that 'things in this world are beautified by participating in form' (I, vi, 2). In Plotinus's system Plato's Forms become, roughly, what things would be were they fully developed. As such the Forms are 'more real' than things in this world.

It follows from the quasi-Platonic principle that a thing has 'more reality in so far as it is beautiful' (V, viii, 9). This, in conjunction with the Aristotelian principle, entails that on perceiving beauty the soul itself acquires beauty and thereby both develops itself more fully and knows itself better. Plotinus's idea that in experiencing beauty we gain *self*-knowledge is a notable departure from Plato. Similiar ideas proved potent again in many nineteenth-century theories of art. Another important respect in which Plotinus diverges from Plato is in conceiving the apprehension of beauty as something intrinsically creative or developmental. He does not, like Plato, require an ad hoc theory of inspiration. Plotinus speaks of the assimilation of form that occurs in perceiving beauty as itself like being possessed by a god (V, viii, 10).

Plotinus finally identifies the knowledge of true beauty in which this developmental process culminates with the attainment of the good. As one would expect he is iconoclastic about this. His account of the ascent to knowledge of true beauty echoes with modifications Plato's account in the *Symposium.* This involves turning away from physical beauty. 'Shut your eyes', says Plotinus, 'and change to and wake another way of seeing, which everyone has but few use' (I, vi, 8). In the course of its training the soul passes through a stage when it ceases to look at the beauty 'which the arts produce, but [looks instead at] the work of men who have a name for goodness' (I, vi, 9). Finally 'the man who has seen [the good] glories in its beauty . . . he laughs at other loves and despises what he thought beautiful before' (I, vi, 7).

But Plotinus's iconoclasm is not like Plato's. Plotinus allows art a definite role in the soul's training; and he is even prepared to speak of the 'beauty of art' as 'greater and more beautiful than anything in the external object' (V, viii, 1). This is because he does not share Plato's view that lower forms of beauty are potentially dangerous illusions. His attitude is rather that as I gain more experience of beauty I cease to notice beauty where I previously found it because I become capable of appreciating greater beauty elsewhere.

It is a moot point whether for Plotinus enlarging one's capacity to appreciate beauty necessarily means rejecting as worthless all those things previously found beautiful or can still leave room for some in a subsidiary role. The above quotation from Ennead I, vi, 7 suggests he took the former view; but there is nothing, I think, in his system that definitely prevents him taking the latter, even if this is not very likely to apply to art. It is anyway striking that Plotinus's aestheticism, in identifying the good with the experience of true beauty, seems better able than Plato's theory to assign positive value to lower forms of beauty, such as that found in morally good actions, despite the fact that Plato began with the aim of discovering how we can improve ourselves morally. Plato wanted – as seems reasonable on the face of it – to regard knowledge of beauty and goodness as necessary means to living a good life; but he found it hard not to conclude that true virtue consists just in contemplating the Forms. Plotinus, who seems to reverse here the ends and the means, can in fact assign a higher place to ordinary morality than Plato.

CHAPTER III

Perfection and the Play of Cognition

1. Aristotle's theory of pleasure

As we have seen, a request for an explanation of art and aesthetic enjoyment might focus either upon their *purpose* or upon descriptions of the *activities themselves* that we here find enjoyable. These two ways of taking the question correspond to two different sorts of explanation: to use Aristotelian terminology, they correspond respectively to explanations in terms of *final* and of *formal* causes.

If pleasure is thought of as a concomitant of actions, for example as a sensation that accompanies some of them, it would seem that any sort of explanation of it will relate to its causes and effects. This can hardly avoid introducing factors that make it appropriate to ask if the pleasure is desirable or not. From this viewpoint pleasure always belongs to the practical side of our nature, i.e. pleasurable activities can always be evaluated directly in terms of how beneficial and desirable they are. As applied to art this means that unless we accept the hedonistic belief that artistic pleasures on their own make art worthwhile, we ought to entertain puritanical reservations about the repercussions of these pleasures.

But there is another, quite different view of pleasure which does not oblige us to approach art from the practical point of view, and so which makes it unnecessary to suppose that this is the choice before us. This can briefly be formulated as the view that pleasure is a quality of our actions, or a matter of how they are experienced, rather than something separate from them with which they are associated. On this view there is scope to maintain that some cognitive activities – acts of perceiving or apprehending things – are pleasurable in their own right.

This looks a promising idea to apply to art and aesthetics since, as we have found, it is the cognitive element in aesthetic experience that makes it difficult to explain it by connecting it with any practical effects.

Instead, on the present approach, we should think of the pleasures of art as autonomous cognitive pleasures. This does not mean simply ignoring the question of how aesthetic experience relates to our practical goals; but this question now demands only an indirect answer, for example one that describes the practical benefits of having the cognitive skills exercised in aesthetic experience.

The best known theory of pleasure as a quality of our actions is Aristotle's. He maintains that pleasure is not a 'process'. He explains what he means by this by saying that pleasure is not the outcome or end result of an activity in the way that, for example, the construction of a temple is the outcome of the activity of building. Pleasure pervades a pleasurable activity: the quality of pleasure is 'complete at any given moment' (*Nicomachean Ethics*, Bk. X, Ch.iv; trans. J.A.K. Thomson, p.319).

Aristotle goes on to develop the theory that pleasure 'perfects' or 'completes' an activity. His thought would appear to be that since pleasure is not the end result of an activity, it must consist in factors internal to it – specifically on how well the activity is being conducted. Thus he says that the activity of a sense organ 'is most pleasurable when it is most perfect, and most perfect when the organ is in a healthy condition and directed toward the worthiest of its objects; and the pleasure perfects the activity' (ibid., p.320). In general Aristotle believes that when the exercise of a faculty is as 'complete' or 'perfect' as it can be, it will be experienced pleasurably. The pleasure then completes the activity in a sense over and above the completeness that explains the pleasure. Hence Aristotle speaks of pleasure as 'a sort of supervening perfection, like the bloom that graces the flower of youth' (ibid., p.321).

These ideas obviously need to be developed and supplemented before we can claim to have a comprehensive theory of pleasure. There is, notably, the question of harmful pleasures: so far Aristotle has only given a sufficient condition for pleasure. He introduces a range of considerations to explain other pleasures, including impairment of our faculties and failure to develop them properly. But we need not go into this to recognize that his general approach has much to commend it. By regarding pleasure as a quality of activity, differences between pleasures can be immediately put down to differences in the respective activities. Aristotle writes, for example, that 'the activities of the intellect differ in kind from those of the senses, and both differ among themselves; therefore so do the pleasures that perfect them' (ibid., X, v, p.322). But as Kenny points out, it would only be a contingent fact, were pleasure only a sensation, that pleasurable experiences vary according to the activities found pleasant (*Action, Emotion and Will*, p.133). Kenny also argues that it would be impossible to explain why pleasure is ever desirable were it merely 'an internal impression' (ibid., p.134). But Aristotle's theory allows us to hold that true pleasure is desirable because when we experience it we are fulfilling those aims and purposes that truly belong to us. Furthermore his theory can explain why there is no 'art' of pleasure as such. If pleasure is not properly regarded as the end result of any of our activities, but is an internal quality of some of them, then it makes no sense to postulate a skill whose aim is just to produce pleasure. There are merely diverse capacities that each yield pleasure when well exercised.

As I say, the idea that pleasure is a quality of activity gives a promising approach to problems about aesthetic enjoyment. But how exactly should it be applied in this case? Aquinas observes that 'beauty relates to the cognitive faculty; for beautiful things are those which please when seen' (*Summa Theologiae* I, q.5, art.4; in Beardsley, p.101). Again, 'the *beautiful* is something pleasant to apprehend' (*S.T.* I-II, q.27, art.1; in Beardsley, p.102). This is true enough so far as it goes. But it is exceedingly hard to spell out in any genuinely explanatory way what it is about these pleasurable cognitive acts that makes them pleasurable.

Not surprisingly many thinkers have seized upon Aristotle's notion of perfection and suggested that aesthetic pleasure occurs when cognitive faculties and the objects upon which they are directed are in such condition as to 'perfect' cognition. It should be stressed, however, that the general approach we are now considering does not necessarily entail that the correct explanation of which activities are pleasant must always use the notion of their being 'perfect'. The point that pleasure is not a 'process' but is due to factors internal to the activity does not necessarily commit us to the idea that the Aristotelian notion of 'perfection' applies, or applies relevantly, to all pleasurable activities. Nonetheless, the idea that we experience aesthetic enjoyment (beauty) when cognition is 'perfect' has, of course, been enormously influential. It lies behind the longstanding identification of beauty with perfection.

2. *Beauty and perfection: a dilemma*

It is, of course, entirely schematic to explain our experience of beauty as the 'perfection' of cognition. Two things would be needed to turn this into a real explanation: an account of what constitutes perfection in cognition; and an account that enables us to recognize that when we experience aesthetic pleasure (beauty) the activity being enjoyed is indeed perfect by the criteria given. The first account spells out the proposed general explanation of aesthetic pleasure; the second gives the justification for supposing that the explanation actually applies.

Cognition aims at knowledge; so its perfection should be reflected in a 'perfect' type of knowledge. What, then, is this 'perfect' knowledge that constitutes aesthetically pleasant cognition?

Unless we take the iconoclastic view that true beauty is only to be found in abstract thought, there would seem to be overwhelming reasons for denying that this is always knowledge of *truths*. If it were we ought, on the face of it, to be able to state what we learn from any experience of beauty; for it is generally assumed that knowledge of truths can always be formulated verbally. Moreover, if the enjoyment were due to the experience imparting this item of knowledge, someone who understood a verbal statement of it ought to be able on that basis to share the same experience of beauty. This may be true of abstract beauty, for example a beautiful theorem, but it is not true of beauty perceived through the senses. If it is said for some reason that the truths learned in the perceptual experience defy verbal formulation, so this situation can never arise, there is still the point that we can enjoy works of art and beautiful things repeatedly. This implies that it is not the learning of any truth as such that is responsible for the enjoyment but, if truths are relevant at all, the way the experience imparts them. It is this knowledge of the experience itself that counts, not knowledge of the truths as such.

We reach, then, the idea that the knowledge responsible for the pleasure – whose possession constitutes the experience of beauty – is knowledge of something that cannot be known verbally but only experientially, this knowledge not being detachable from whatever is being apprehended in the way knowledge of a truth is. But this conception of an essentially experiential form of knowledge is full of difficulties. It raises hard questions about the relationship between experiential and verbal knowledge. In the present context it poses the paradox that if the knowledge that is 'perfected' in aesthetic enjoyment is of the experiential kind, then it cannot be formulated verbally; so apparently we cannot develop a theory that explains why particular items of experiential knowledge count as 'perfect', since to do that we would have to be able, contrary to hypothesis, to formulate the knowledge in words.

Although this paradox has a sophistical air, we have here, I think, the makings of a genuine dilemma. To give an account of what constitutes cognitive perfection we have to describe the general features that go to make any cognition (knowledge) perfect. The perfection of an individual cognitive experience would then be explained in terms of its satisfying the general description. But we said that we cannot explain aesthetic enjoyment by reference to knowledge of any truths learned in having the experience. If, however, its perfection could be explained in the manner supposed then the knowledge that the experience satisfies the general description ought, after all, to explain the enjoyment. It seems, therefore, that we either have to abandon the sort of explanation of aesthetic enjoyment being attempted, or else develop a theory that enables us to explain in words how knowing a truth experientially differs from knowing it verbally.

3. *Rationalist aesthetics: Leibniz, Baumgarten*

Descartes, with his hostility to the imagination, had little interest in aesthetics. But his concern, in his theory of knowledge, for the reliability of individual 'ideas' suggested some new ways of understanding how there might be a standard of perfection in knowing individual perceived things. Previously the tendency, always implicitly iconoclastic, had been to value knowledge that is general or all-embracing to the exclusion of knowledge of the individual. The generality of the truth known was the accepted standard of cognitive perfection. Aristotle, it is true, saw no obstacle to evaluating literary works by this criterion. Famously, he maintains, aiming his remark at Plato no doubt, that 'poetry is something more philosophical and more worthy of serious attention than history; for while poetry is concerned with universal truths, history treats of particular facts' ('On the Art of Poetry', Ch.9, trans. T.S. Dorsch, pp.43–4). But it is obviously more difficult to apply this line of thought to many paintings or pieces of music. Literary works can, perhaps, be seen as illustrating universal truths; but it is not easy to see how instrumental music can be so regarded.

Descartes had used jointly his two criteria of *clarity* and *distinctness* in evaluating 'ideas'. In different ways Leibniz and Baumgarten both thought that by separating these two criteria they could explain a form of cognitive perfection that applies to knowledge of individual things.

According to Leibniz, to know something *clearly* is to know it with certainty; whereas to know it *distinctly* as opposed to *confusedly* is to be able to explain what one knows. Using these conceptions he thought he could circumvent the obvious difficulties in generalizing Aristotle's estimate of poetry to the other arts by maintaining that sometimes in knowing individual things we have clear but indistinct knowledge of general, explanatory truths. He writes that:

> we sometimes know *clearly*, without being in any kind of doubt, if a poem or a picture is good or bad, because there is a *je ne sais quoi* which satisfies us or displeases us. But when I can explain the marks which I have, my knowledge is called *distinct*.
>
> (*Discourse on Metaphysics*, section 24, trans. Mary Morris and G.H.R. Parkinson, p.33)

Leibniz explains our pleasure in works of art by holding that the clear but indistinct knowledge we have of them would, if known distinctly, give intellectual pleasure. He writes:

> sensuous pleasures are really confusedly known intellectual pleasures. Music charms us, although its beauty only consists in the harmonies of numbers and in the reckoning of the beats or vibrations of sounding bodies, which meet at certain intervals, reckonings of which we are not conscious and which the soul nevertheless does make. The pleasures which sight finds in proportions are of the same nature.
>
> ('Principles of Nature and of Grace', trans. G.M. Duncan; in Beardsley, p.154)

So although Leibniz agrees with Aristotle that knowledge that pleases does so because it concerns general, explanatory truths, this does not prevent him from holding that our enjoyment of works of art, which has no evident connection with such knowledge, is nonetheless due to it. Despite our inability to state explicitly any intellectually pleasing knowledge of works of art, Leibniz believes that our enjoyment of them is due to our having such knowledge – we possess it clearly but not distinctly. Leibniz thus opts for the second horn of the dilemma posed at the end of section 2.

Leibniz has his own not very compelling reasons for identifying perception with confused knowledge of causes. But even allowing that in perception one can have indistinct knowledge which if known distinctly would give intellectual pleasure, it hardly follows that there will be anything pleasing in knowing it confusedly. Aristotelian principles tend to imply that knowledge that is confused is *ipso facto* imperfect, and so ought never to be pleasurable. If, moreover, as is not unlikely, distinct knowledge of the causes of any perception would give intellectual pleasure, Leibniz's account ought to entail that *all* perception is pleasurable.

Baumgarten's approach is different. Instead of using the notions of clarity and distinctness to characterize different ways of possessing the *same* item of knowledge, Baumgarten allocates to each of these notions an autonomous sphere of cognition in which it is the dominant criterion of perfection. He distinguishes 'things perceived' from 'things known', maintaining that '*things known* are to be known by the superior faculty as the object of logic; *things perceived* [are to be known by the inferior faculty as the object] of the science of perception, or AESTHETIC' (*Reflections on Poetry*, section 116, trans. K. Aschenbrenner and W.B. Holther, p.78). Logic is to study the kind of perfection proper to thought, namely distinctness as opposed to confusion; while aesthetics studies the perfection proper to perception, namely clarity as opposed to obscurity.

This can be understood as an attempt to slip through the horns of the above dilemma. There is all the difference, it may be said, between knowing that something is clear, and perceiving its clarity. The latter demands no capacity on the part of the perceiver to describe what he perceives; but that need not hinder us in using words ourselves to describe his perception. So we can explain why he finds a perception pleasurable – because it is clear – without supposing that his pleasure depends on his knowing that it is clear. *We* need to know that it is clear to explain the pleasure; but to experience the pleasure *he* needs only to experience the perception's clarity.

This, of course, is the thought behind the suspicion that the paradox outlined in section 2 is sophistical. The problem this thought overlooks is how the clarity of a perception (or any other experiential feature) can explain why it is pleasurable, i.e. the justification for holding that clarity constitutes a perfection proper to perception. If we are genuinely to explain aesthetic enjoyment in terms of cognitive perfection we cannot simply declare that the experiential features of this enjoyment constitute a form of such perfection. A genuinely explanatory account has to bring together the two things mentioned at the beginning of section 2: an account of cognitive perfection; and a demonstration that aesthetically enjoyable experiences comply with it.

Baumgarten faces a general difficulty in doing this. He speaks of the intellect and the senses as respectively 'superior' and 'inferior' cognitive faculties. The role of the latter in cognition as a whole is to provide material for the intellect. But if sensory perception is merely a subordinate capacity in cognition, how can it be capable of perfection on its own? Of course some creatures have sensory capacities without intellectual ones; but it is not plausible to suggest that aesthetic pleasures are sensory ones in just this sense. Aesthetic pleasures are supposed to be perceptual pleasures experienced by creatures (ourselves) who use their perceptual capacities to further the aims of intellectual cognition. Does not it follow that such perceptual experiences can only themselves be described as pleasurable in a derived sense – in the sense that they contribute well to pleasurable intellectual cognition? If this does follow then we should abandon any separate criterion of perceptual perfection, and revert to the idea that enjoyment of these experiences is really enjoyment of them as a means to intellectual knowledge, or, following Leibniz, as an indistinct perception of something intellectually satisfying.

It might appear that we could evade this conclusion by relinquishing the idea that the intellect is superior to other cognitive capacities, and by putting other forms of knowledge on a more equal footing, each with its own separate potential for perfection. But the difficulty is not so easily shaken off. Even if we are not to explain what constitutes per- fection in perceptual knowledge by relating it to higher forms of know- ledge, the question remains how its perfection is to be understood, i.e. how we are to understand the aim or purpose in perceptual cognition so as to explain perceptual enjoyment as enjoyment in achieving this aim.

It is beginning to look as if no such explanation is to be had. For in the special case of aesthetic enjoyment we cannot separate the activity being enjoyed from the experience of the enjoyment. Pleasure, we have said, is a quality of activity. It is a matter of how we experience our activities. But we are now regarding aesthetic pleasure as pleasure in an activity that is itself experiential: the activity here enjoyed is itself one of having certain experiences. So there is not here the same contrast as there is generally between the type of activity in question and how it is experienced, including whether or not it is pleasant. Hence the usual pattern of explanation of pleasure in terms of perfection fails to apply in this particular case.

Notice that this mirrors the predicament that confronts attempts to explain aesthetic enjoyment as having a direct practical purpose. Just as it proved impossible to discover a practical purpose external to aesthetic experience by which to explain why it is enjoyable, it now proves to be impossible to identify any activity external to the enjoyment whose perfection can explain it. Accordingly we can trace parallels between theories as to art's practical purpose and ones as to the kind of knowledge it yields. For example, saying, as Leibniz does, that aesthetic experience constitutes valuable knowledge, albeit in a confused form, can be compared to the Freudian view that this experience is unconscious instinctual satisfaction. Saying that there is an experiential form of knowledge specific to aesthetic enjoyment is like the hedonistic view that this enjoyment has a purpose just in the pleasure it yields. And the idea that art is a means of imparting valuable knowledge of truths, as in Aristotle's view of poetry, can be compared to the belief that its purpose lies in moral education.

We shall see that the parallel goes further. We saw that, being unable satisfactorily to explain art as having an external purpose, theories that wish to relate it directly to a practical purpose have little option but to explain it by a reverse procedure of supposing that all our other practical aims contribute to the central aesthetic one. These theories culminate in metaphysical aestheticism. Something analogous is true of many cognitive theories of art. They find it necessary, in order to explain the connection between aesthetic and other forms of knowledge, to suppose that the true role of these other forms is to contribute to aesthetic knowledge. Many aspects of Absolute Idealism can be seen in this light. Not unnaturally Absolute Idealism invites comparison with Plotinus.

We should not, however, leap to the conclusion that an aesthetic theory of this type is the inevitable outcome of identifying aesthetic with cognitive enjoyment. For one thing there remains the first horn of the dilemma posed in section 2, namely that of seeking a different sort of explanation than one that speaks of their 'perfection' of what it is about cognitive activities that makes them pleasant. This means, in effect, locating an aim inherent to cognition other than that of acquiring knowledge. Kant's aesthetic theory is an attempt to do just this.

4. Kant's theory (1): the existence of a non-cognitive aim of cognition

In his *Critique of Judgement* Kant maintains that there can be a pleasurable mode of exercising our cognitive faculties which yields no knowledge of objects, but which consists merely in experience of a harmonious relationship of 'free play' between such faculties themselves, specifically between the faculty he here calls the 'imagination', which has to do with the reception and handling of sensory 'intuitions', and the 'understanding', which is the faculty of concepts. When these faculties yield cognition, intuitions are brought under concepts – Kant regards all cognition as conceptual. But when we experience aesthetic enjoyment he believes that they are exercised in a manner that produces no cognition.

In his earlier writings Kant had entertained views closer to his rationalist predecessors. For example, he wrote at one time that 'the perfection of the objects of experience is harmony with the law of the senses, and this, as appearance is called beauty' (Guyer, p.119); and again that 'the form of sensibility which facilitates the perfection of the understanding is the independently beautiful' (ibid., p.21). When he wrote the *Critique of Judgement*, however, Kant was clear that beauty is not 'reduceable to the concept of perfection' because the 'judgement of taste', i.e. the judgement that something is beautiful, is not a cognitive judgement at all (*Critique of Judgement*, Pt.I, pp.41–2, 69–71; trans. J.C. Meredith). But although Kant ceased talking of beauty as that which promotes the perfection of our cognitive faculties, he was unswerving in the view that the experience of beauty should be explained as a distinctive manner of exercising these faculties.

In the Introduction to the *Critique of Judgement* Kant enunciates what he apparently regards as a general truth about pleasure when he writes that 'the attainment of every aim is coupled with a feeling of pleasure' (ibid., p.27). Two things about this soon emerge. First, an 'aim' does not, for Kant, necessarily require an intention; for he speaks of our *faculties* including cognitive ones as having aims and of the attainment of these as pleasurable. To this extent Kant aligns himself with the Aristotelian–rationalist tradition which does not confine pleasure to the practical side of our nature. Second, Kant soon quali- fies his original remark by conceding that some of our faculties have aims whose attainment does not yield pleasure; for example, we take no pleasure in the routine exercise of our understanding, i.e. from 'the coincidence of perceptions with the laws in accordance with the universal concepts of nature (the Categories)' (ibid., p.27). Kant's explanation of this amounts to the claim that attaining an aim is pleasurable if and only if that aim is one whose attainment is only contingent.

In developing his theory of aesthetic pleasure Kant makes extensive use of a rather difficult technical notion of 'finality' (as Meredith translates it). I think this notion, which Kant does not explain clearly, is best understood as integral to his view of pleasure. The *finality* of something – be it an object, or a mental representation, or nature itself –

is the contingent condition of its being such as to contribute to attaining a specified aim. In general, the finality of things in a certain respect is that to which we have to appeal to explain the existence of any pleasure. So to explain aesthetic pleasure in particular we have to explain the 'finality which it evinces.

As mentioned, Kant rejects any attempt like Baumgarten's or Leibniz's to do this using the notion of perfection. His grounds for this lie deep in his mature philosophical system. He believes that if perfection explained aesthetic pleasure then in principle we could demonstrate by conceptual reasoning that something is beautiful. But we would then have demonstrated rationally that it should be apprehended with delight; and Kant holds that the only things of which this can be done are actions in accordance with the moral law.

Kant also firmly rejects the view held by many empiricists that aesthetic pleasure is fundamentally only a matter of finding certain things agreeable. He maintains that beauty pleases 'universally' in a sense incompatible with its being only a reflection of individual preferences. This may seem a curious claim in view of the actual diversity in what people consider to be beautiful. But this claim is really a consequence of his belief that aesthetic pleasure is independent of the moral law. For in that case it must, he takes it, be independent of our desires; and if it is independent of our desires then it is 'disinterested' ('interest', for Kant, entails delight in the satisfaction of a desire (ibid., p.42)). And if it is 'disinterested' then it is something that everyone is in a position to experience (ibid., p.51).

The problem, then, that Kant sets himself is to explain how there can be a universal pleasure – aesthetic pleasure – that has no rational or conceptual basis. Such pleasure is, he says, 'connected with the mere apprehension [*apprehensio*] of the form of an object of intuition, apart from any reference it may have to a concept for the purpose of a definite cognition' (ibid., p.30). Because of his general view of pleasure, this problem becomes one of identifying the aim whose attainment in this apprehension is responsible for aesthetic pleasure. This means explaining in what respect beauty is 'final' for our cognitive faculties despite the fact that our apprehension of it yields no 'definite cognition', i.e. despite the fact that its finality is not explicable in terms of any truths known.

Here Kant does, I think, identify perhaps the most fundamental philosophical problem posed by aesthetic pleasure, though his route to its formulation is questionable. The problems in explaining how there can be such a thing as aesthetic enjoyment are independent, I would maintain, of the considerations Kant imports from his moral philosophy. This is not an incidental point since his moral philosophy influences not only his understanding of how the problem arises but also his attempts to solve it.

It follows from his general view of pleasure that the finality Kant is seeking consists in the contingent attainment of an aim that is necessary to our cognitive faculties even though attaining it yields no 'definite cognition'. It is impossible, then, to state conceptually any end that this finality serves – judgements of taste would otherwise be cognitive (conceptual) judgements. Kant is thus driven to his celebrated notion of 'finality apart from an end' (ibid., p.69), or 'purposiveness without purpose' as it is sometimes rather loosely put. An 'end', for Kant, is always something conceptual (ibid., pp.19, 61), unlike, evidently, our 'aims'.

Kant speaks, then, of there being an aim behind judgements of taste while maintaining that it is impossible to state conceptually what this aim is. This sounds absurd. Kant thinks it is not because, for one thing, he thinks, despite the absence here of an end, that he can characterize more positively the circumstances that reveal that this aim has been achieved. He refers to the 'play of the cognitive faculties whose harmonious accord contains the ground of this [aesthetic] pleasure' (ibid., p.39). Again, he describes this as 'pleasure in the harmony of our cognitive faculties' (ibid., p.59). 'The cognitive powers . . . are here engaged in a free play, since no definite concept restricts them to a particular rule of cognition' (ibid., p.58).

Kant goes on to suggest that the *faculty* of the imagination is here subsumed under the *faculty* of concepts in a manner analogous to the subsuming, in ordinary cognitive judgements, of particular sensory intuitions under specific concepts (ibid., p.143). And he maintains that in experiencing this harmony we become aware in a special, general way of an accord between our cognitive faculties and nature. He says that 'as this accordance of the [beautiful] object with the faculties of the Subject is contingent, it gives rise to a representation of a finality on the part of the object in respect of the cognitive faculties of the Subject' (ibid., p.31). But since no 'definite cognition' is here involved the finality in question can only consist in a general compliance of natural objects with our cognitive aims. Kant refers to this as the 'finality of nature' for our cognitive faculties.

This notion of the 'finality of nature' for cognition is not very convincing. Why should there be any need to experience this finality as such? Are we not already sufficiently aware that nature accords with our cognitive faculties when we know what we are experiencing in the usual way, i.e. when experience *does* yield definite cognitions? One would have thought furthermore that the proper exercise of these faculties was in the service of cognition, and hence that the sort of exercise of them that Kant is envisaging ought properly to be regarded as one where the aims of cognition are *frustrated.* This point also tends to undermine Kant's attempt, by claiming that the aims of the understanding are necessarily achieved within experience, to explain why cognition as such is not pleasurable.

5. *Kant's theory (2): the sublime and the moral significance of beauty*

Kant sometimes tries to meet these objections by distinguishing the understanding's aim of bringing intuitions under concepts from the larger aim of the faculty of judgement to discover systems of empirical laws to which experience conforms. He maintains that the finality of nature responsible for aesthetic pleasure lies in nature's accord with the latter aim. But most of his efforts to meet these objections spring from another quarter. Having satisfied himself that no specific cognition is achieved in experiencing beauty, he is unable to resist the thought that cognitive experience here partakes of aims that originate outside cognition altogether, in particular of ones that relate to the validity of moral experience. He thereby strives to give greater substance to his notion that there is an aim which is not an end to which our experience of beauty attests.

Kant's theory of the sublime helps him greatly in this task. Kant was familiar with Burke's *Enquiry* which he praises highly in the *Critique of Judgement*; and it was probably this work that persuaded him that an account of beauty needs to be complemented by one of the sublime. In any event, Kant attempts a distinct account of the kind of aesthetic delight it is possible to take in things that are vast or terrifying. This account parallels that he gives of beauty with the important exception that in this case the cause of our delight is not a relationship of harmonious accord between imagination and understanding but a relationship of conflict between imagination and our powers of judgement which prompts in us a sense of our moral superiority over nature.

Natural beauty, according to Kant, appears to be 'preadapted to our power of judgement' (ibid., p.91), whereas things that excite the feeling of the sublime appear to 'contravene the ends of our power of judgement, to be ill-adapted to our faculty of presentation, and to be, as it were, an outrage on the imagination' (ibid., p.91). Since we nevertheless derive pleasure from the sublime, he concludes that it '*evidences a faculty of mind transcending every standard of sense*' (ibid., p.98). There would otherwise be no aim whose attainment would explain why we find it pleasurable.

Kant is ready with a suggestion as to the identity of this faculty. He believes that we have a faculty of reason whose concepts, or 'ideas' as he calls them to separate them from the concepts of the understanding, have the distinctive feature that they cannot be presented fully in sensory intuition. He thus maintains that the sublime 'cannot be contained in any sensuous form, but rather concerns ideas of reason, which although no adequate presentation of them is possible, may be excited and called into mind by that very inadequacy itself which does not admit of sensuous presentation' (ibid., p.92). Since, according to Kant, reason is responsible for the moral law, he infers that the capacity to appreciate the sublime has moral relevance.

Having connected ideas of reason with the sublime, Kant also tries, rather tortuously, to link them with beauty. One point where this comes out is in his discussion of 'genius', i.e. the capacity to produce beautiful works of art, taste being 'merely a critical, not a productive faculty' (ibid., p.174).

Kant begins by rehearsing in his own way the same problem about artistic creativity as had worried Plato. Something cannot be the product of a skill, Kant holds, 'unless there is a preceding rule' whereby it is 'represented as possible' (ibid., p.168). But since judgements of taste are not cognitive judgements, there is no *concept* of beauty from which a rule for the production of works of art could be derived. Kant concludes that genius 'derives its rules' from 'ideas' not concepts: genius is 'the faculty of *aesthetic ideas*' (ibid., p.212). These 'aesthetic ideas' share with ideas of reason the feature that they cannot be captured in concepts. (An 'aesthetic idea' is a 'representation of the imagination which induces much thought, yet without the possibility of any definite thought whatever, i.e. *concept*, being adequate to it' (ibid., pp.175–6).) Kant therefore feels entitled to assimilate them. He declares that 'both kinds of ideas, aesthetic ideas as well as rational, are bound to have their principles, and the seat of these principles must in both cases be reason – the latter depending upon the objective, the former upon the subjective, principles of its employment' (ibid., p.212). Thus Kant says that 'an aesthetic idea is the counterpart (pendant) of a *rational idea*' (ibid., p.176). He goes on to speak of aesthetic ideas as seeking to provide rational ideas with a 'substitute' or 'approximation' for the sort of presentation in sensory intuition possible in the case of concepts of the understanding: aesthetic ideas give to rational ideas the 'semblance of an objective reality' (ibid. p.176–7).

Kant appears to be unperturbed by the point that if genius sprang from reason's 'subjective principles' then it ought to be as universal as reason itself. Perhaps this is because he is eager to exploit the implications of these conceptions for the nature of beauty. Genius is supposed to be the capacity to produce *beautiful* works of art; but having understood it as the capacity to give sensory presentation to the ideas of reason its products ought, according to Kant's own definitions, to be *sublime* rather than beautiful. Sometimes he seems to think that this outcome needs to be rectified, for example when he suggests that genius has to work under the supervision of taste (ibid., p.183). On the positive side he finds the thought that there is a sublime element in beauty a welcome one in so far as it indicates that beauty has moral significance. If genius creates beauty and genius is the capacity to present aesthetic ideas, then, Kant infers, 'Beauty (whether it be of nature or of art) may in general be termed the *expression* of aesthetic ideas' (ibid., p.183). This enables him to give a fuller explanation of delight in beauty than the earlier rather meagre one which relies on the notion of pleasure in the 'free play' of our cognitive faculties. He remarks on the tendency for delight to wear off where 'the fine arts are not, either approximately or remotely, brought into combination with moral ideas, which alone are attended with a self-sufficing delight' (ibid., p.191); 'only when sensibility is brought into harmony with moral feeling can genuine taste assume a definite unchangeable form' (ibid., p.227).

In saying this Kant is not suggesting that beauty comes in two varieties – an inferior one that prompts only the free play of our faculties; and a superior one that expresses moral ideas. But what moral idea can natural beauty be taken to express – the sort of beauty with which the earlier account appears to be primarily concerned? The conclusion to which Kant is drawn is that natural beauty, because experiencing it consists in a *free* exercise of our cognitive faculties, expresses the rational idea of *freedom* itself, which idea he considers to be central to morality (ibid., pp.224–5). He thus speaks of aesthetic pleasure as betokening 'a finality on the part of the Subject, answering to the concept of freedom' (ibid., p.33). And he is apparently willing to accept that the beautiful therefore cannot be distinct from the sublime. The same aesthetic judgement, he says, 'refers not merely, as a judgement of taste, to the beautiful, but also, as springing from a higher intellectual feeling, to the *sublime*' (ibid., p.33). Both the beautiful and the sublime are 'final in reference to the moral feeling' (ibid., p.119).

Since our true inner nature, according to Kant, is our nature as moral beings, this means that beauty reflects not merely an accord between the world we experience and our faculties of knowledge (the finality of nature for cognition), but also more profoundly an affinity between that world and our own ultimate inner nature (a finality of nature for moral freedom). This, I take it, is the significance of Kant's obscure remarks relating beauty to the 'supersensible that lies at the basis of nature' (ibid., p.14). He holds as a general principle that 'Intuitions are always required to verify the reality of our concepts' (ibid., p.221); and that even concepts (ideas) of reason 'to which no sensible intuition can be adequate' must be capable of a 'symbolic presentation' in intuition (ibid., pp.221–2). In particular, then, a 'symbolic presentation' of the moral idea of freedom is needed to verify that our freedom is real. We find this symbolic presentation, he maintains, in things of beauty: the beautiful is 'the symbol of morality' (ibid., p.221). More precisely, this experience shows us, Kant believes, that our moral freedom is compatible with our actions all being bound by natural laws. The experience reveals 'a ground of the *unity*' of the supersensible underlying all nature, including our own, 'with what the concept of freedom contains in a practical way' (ibid., p.14). To put it differently, the faculty of judgement, 'with its concept of a *finality* of nature, provides us with the mediating concept between concepts of nature and the concept of freedom' (ibid., p.38).

In experiencing beauty we experience, then, the reality of our moral freedom. This, of course, is a point of great importance to Kant; and because it applies only to aesthetic judgements specifically about beauty, he dismisses the 'concept of the sublime in nature', notwithstanding the point that beauty is not independent of the sublime, as 'far less important and rich in consequences than that of its beauty' (ibid., pp.92–3).

Up to a point these conclusions enhance the coherence of Kant's system; but he is reluctant to embrace them wholeheartedly. And rightly so. For it is now becoming very hard to preserve the distinction which means so much to him between the beautiful and the morally good. Although delight in beauty is disinterested he cannot deny that it produces interest, i.e. that we form desires to experience beautiful things. But having regarded the beautiful as 'the symbol of the morally good' (ibid., p.223) how can Kant effectively distinguish such desires from the desire to act morally? He admits the affinity is close: interest in beauty is 'akin to the moral' (ibid., p.160); 'the feeling in the judgement of taste comes to be exacted from everyone as a sort of duty' (ibid., p.154); such an end as that served by the existence of beauty is only met with 'in that which constitutes the ultimate end of our existence – the moral side of our being' (ibid., pp.160–1).

Kant seeks escape in drawing an invidious distinction between natural beauty and the beauty of art. It is 'always a mark of a good soul', he says, 'to take an *immediate interest* in the beauty of *nature*' (ibid., p.157); for this presupposes deep interest 'in the foundation of the morally good' (ibid., 160). But all he is prepared to concede to the beauty of art is that it 'promotes the sensibility of the mind for moral feeling' (ibid., p.39).

Kant has no good grounds for such a distinction. The conclusion he cannot swallow is that the production of beautiful works of art is an end comparable in worth to performing actions in conformity with the moral law. He cannot hide his contempt for '*virtuosi* in matters of taste' who are 'one might say as a general rule, vain, capricious, and addicted to injurious passions' (ibid., p.157). Kant seems to imagine that if natural beauty alone bears comparison with the morally good then the pursuit of beauty can safely be put aside as no threat to the demands of morality. But his case against beauty in art amounts only to pointing out that works of art often 'minister to vanity, or, at least, social joys' (ibid., p.159). It would anyway be little help to him even to withdraw altogether his theory of genius and to maintain a more extreme iconoclasm. Even if true beauty can never be created by human beings the sort of conflict he fears with the morally good can still arise if we are able to recognize beauty in nature and form the desire to experience it.

Kant's position is crumbling. He begins, drawing upon his moral theory, by reasoning that in aesthetic pleasure a non-cognitive aim is realized within cognitive experience. He goes on to argue that this non-cognitive aim is a moral one in the sense that it relates to the validity of moral experience. But he then finds himself unable to counter the allegation that this is a moral aim in the direct sense that the experience of beauty is morally desirable. This undermines his initial premisses. Where has Kant gone wrong?

The short answer, I think, is that Kant grafts his investigation into the aim achieved in aesthetically pleasurable experiences on to a preconceived understanding of cognition which is already defective. He holds rightly that beauty is not in his sense a *concept* and is therefore inexplicable using the notion of perfection. But he neglects the possibility of there being other forms of knowledge. Having concluded, wrongly, that aesthetic delight indicates the existence of an altogether non-cognitive aim within cognitive experience, Kant eventually finds himself maintaining that this experience serves some ill-defined practical aim.

The generation of philosophers after Kant who took his work as their point of departure tended to respond to this by seeking a more thoroughgoing understanding of how conceptual cognition is bound up with and reflects processes beyond itself and so participates in their aims. I think they were wrong in this. The real problem in explaining aesthetic experience is to discover an aim that underlies cognition rather than one that extends beyond it. This demands examination of fundamental questions about the nature of cognition. But one way or the other, Kant's third *Critique* does not merely crown the edifice of his philosophical system but initiates the process of its reconstruction.

CHAPTER IV

Art as the Experience of Metaphysical Truth

1. The reception of Kant's theory; Schiller, Schelling

Kant himself wrote apologetically that the solution to the problem of taste involves 'a certain amount of hardly avoidable obscurity' (*Critique of Judgement*, Pt I, p.7). Few of his readers will have difficulty in agreeing that his own account merits the apology.

His theory, we saw, is founded on the Aristotelian view that pleasure is a quality of activity. This is a promising approach to problems in aesthetics since, assuming that the activities in question here are cognitive ones, it allows us to sidestep for the moment at least problems about the practical purpose of this pleasure and attempt instead a different sort of explanation – one in terms of its 'formal cause', i.e. of the features of the pleasurable activities that go to make them pleasant.

However, Kant had the insight that in the case of aesthetic pleasure this approach cannot be implemented in the usual Aristotelian manner by explaining it as something experienced when the pleasurable activity is 'perfect'. In this special case there is the problem that we cannot spell out conceptually what aim is being achieved when the activities concerned are pleasurable. So what kind of aim can this be? If we cannot explain conceptually the circumstances in which it is attained, is not any theory of it in danger of being self-defeating? For will not the explanation be trying to capture in words something which, it has been agreed, cannot be formulated verbally but can only be experienced? Ought not we in fact to conclude, as Wittgenstein did in his *Tractatus*, that art and aesthetics should be placed beyond the boundary of what can be intelligibly discussed as things whose significance can only be 'shown' and not 'said'?

Anyone who resists this conclusion while agreeing with the soundness of Kant's fundamental insight is now in a tight corner. If attainment of an aim entails having certain experiences that does not, it is true, in itself prevent us developing a theory to explain why we possess this aim. But in the case of aesthetic enjoyment, attainment of the aim is internal to the experience in a sense that excludes explaining the aim by relating it to any end the experience serves beyond the experience itself. Kant himself fell into the trap of attempting to explain it as if it had an external aim in maintaining that the experience of beauty verifies the moral idea of freedom. But if it is impossible to give this form of explanation of the aim, what kind of explanation is open to us?

Schiller, like many of Kant's early readers, felt that Kant's conception of freedom and of the role of art were both insufficiently positive. Freedom, for Kant, is not something we have to struggle to attain, but something we already possess in virtue of our rationality: we are free because we can act in accordance with the rational dictates of morality rather than out of inclination or appetite. Schiller, by contrast, conceived of freedom as a yet to be attained fulfilment of our nature. And he held that aesthetic pleasure does not merely verify our freedom but has an active role in realizing it: 'it is only through Beauty that man makes his way to Freedom' (*On the Aesthetic Education of Man*, trans. E.M. Wilkinson and L.A. Willoughby, p.9). By modifying Kant's claims about the moral significance of beauty Schiller escapes the incoherence in Kant's account of the aim of aesthetic pleasure. In Schiller's theory something positive – freedom itself – is realized within aesthetic experi- ence. This theory implies a reversed appraisal from Kant's of the im- portance of art and natural beauty.

The 'harmonious free play' of our faculties of which Kant spoke becomes for Schiller an experience that actively harmonizes previously conflicting impulses. Schiller credits us with two opposed drives: a '*sensuous drive*' (ibid., p.79), and a '*formal drive*' (ibid., p.81), 'the one pressing for change, the other for changelessness' (ibid., p.85). But he maintains, in a manner that set the pattern for Hegel's dialectic, that these are harmonized in the 'play-drive . . . as the one in which both the others act in concert' (ibid., p.79). Schiller writes that 'The object of the sense-drive . . . we call life' (ibid., p.101). Since the play-drive reconciles the sensuous and formal drives, Schiller concludes, in a telling phrase, that 'The object of the play-drive . . . may therefore be called *living form*' (ibid., p.101).

Because the play-drive reconciles the conflicting elements in our nature, Schiller asserts that 'man only plays when he is in the fullest sense of the word a human being, and *he is only fully a human being when he plays*' (ibid., p.107). Here alone, according to Schiller, can man:

> have a complete intuition of his human nature, and the object which afforded him this vision would become for him a symbol of his *accomplished destiny* and, in consequence (since that is only to be attained in the totality of time), serve him as a manifestation of the *Infinite*.
>
> (ibid., p.95)

Obviously, however, an account of the circumstances in which the elements in man's nature are all harmoniously reconciled will be incomplete until it acknowledges our dependence upon society and the rest of nature.

So far as the social dimension is concerned, the point Schiller emphasizes is that social harmony consists in individuals each attaining the aesthetic harmony of which he has already spoken. He introduces a conception of the '*aesthetic* State' where 'conduct is governed by beauty' (ibid., p.215). 'Taste', he says, 'alone brings harmony into society, because it fosters harmony in the individual' (ibid., p.215). The Aesthetic State 'exists in every finely attuned soul', though there are unlikely to be many societies where every soul is 'finely attuned': 'as a realized fact, we are likely to find it . . . only in some chosen circles' (ibid., p.219).

This still leaves the broader question of our dependence on nature. This seemed to Schelling a grave omission, as also did Schiller's failure to develop a theory of artistic creativity. Schiller offers no account of how the play-drive succeeds in reconciling the disparate objectives of the sensuous and formal drives. But Schelling believed himself to be equipped, through his own response to Kant, to rectify these two omissions simultaneously. In his exciting but highly obscure *System of Transcendental Idealism* he produces a theory which seeks to reconcile freedom with nature by regarding artistic creativity as a manifestation of a process whereby nature, acting through the individual, itself develops freely. This leads Schelling to stress 'the unconscious factor which enters into art' (ibid., trans. P. Heath, p.223).

Schelling's idea that the artist has a special rapport with nature had a profound impact on Romanticism. The point that concerns us, however, is that his theory appears to open up a way of regarding art as contributing to some larger aim without compromising the point that its aim is internal. It contributes to a larger aim not as a means of attaining it, but as an element that is both a constituent in its attainment and a reflection of it. One side of this idea had already been present in Schiller's notion that harmony in the Aesthetic State consists in harmony in the souls of its individual members. Schelling's thought was the bolder one that the artist's individual aims not only realize nature's aims but reciprocally can only be understood by reference back to them. The present question is whether or not using this difficult idea we can resolve the problem Kant uncovered about understanding the aim that is satisfied when we experience aesthetic pleasure.

2. Art and nature: Schelling

Schelling, like Hegel in his turn, agreed with Kant that aesthetic experience is cognitive and that it has no aim external to itself. Against Kant, however, they insisted as Schiller had that, in Hegel's phrase, art has a '*substantial* end' (*Introduction to Aesthetics*, trans. T.M. Knox, p.48), and that this end actively realizes human freedom.

Now the only candidate, it would seem, for a substantial end internal to cognition is self-knowledge, or thought gaining knowledge of itself. But to understand how the aim of freedom can be realized in aesthetic experience they took it that the aims achieved in this experience constitute and reflect nature's own ultimate aims. (Otherwise nature and freedom might be in conflict.) These points jointly yield the astonishing conclusion that art is the vehicle of nature's own self-knowledge, and that in art we participate in the highest thing reality contains. The attempt to understand this conclusion gave birth to Absolute Idealism.

In line with the above, Schelling writes that 'art is at once the only true and eternal organ and document of philosophy . . . . Art is paramount to the philosopher precisely because it opens to him, as it were, the holy and holies' (op. cit., p.231). In beauty and in beauty alone we find 'the infinite finitely displayed' (ibid., p.225). No philosopher has had a loftier conception of art. Schelling even ranks art above philosophy. 'Philosophy attains, indeed, to the highest, but it brings to this summit only, so to say, the fraction of the man. Art brings the *whole* man, as he is, to that point, namely to a knowledge of the highest' (ibid., p.223).

The intelligibility of this depends on being able to understand the relation between individuals' thoughts and aims, and the aim of nature for which they are supposed to be the vehicle. Even Hegel found Schelling obscure; but it is fair, I think, to interpret Schelling's understanding of this relation as springing from an attempt to overcome problems in Kant's system by amalgamating some of Kant's most difficult conceptions.

Recall that for Kant the finality we apprehend in experiencing beauty is both a finality for cognition and a finality for freedom. The experience of beauty somehow reveals both that nature accords with our cognitive aim of discovering empirical laws, and that there is a 'supersensible' basis to nature that 'unifies' its conformity to these laws with the possibility of moral freedom. Schelling was wholly dissatisfied with Kant's treatment of the latter point, but he thought he could better understand how art serves freedom by developing further Kant's ideas about the former kind of finality.

Schelling here drew heavily upon the second part of Kant's *Critique of Judgement*, namely the 'Critique of Teleological Judgement'. What chiefly impressed him was Kant's notion of an '*intuitive* understanding' (*Critique of Judgement*, Pt II, trans. J.C. Meredith, p.62). This, Kant explains, would not be an understanding which has no need of intuition, but rather 'a faculty of *complete spontaneity of intuition* . . . distinct from sensibility and wholly independent of it' (ibid., p.62). Kant's idea appears to be that a faculty of intuition that was spontaneously comprehensive would itself accomplish the synthesizing work of the understanding.

Kant's interest in this notion is connected with his longstanding concern, so central to the *Critique of Pure Reason*, to understand, as against Hume, the *necessity* of causation – a topic which obviously has a bearing upon the possibility of free action. In the first *Critique* his arguments had really only shown that it is necessary that experience as a whole should exhibit causality, not, as he wished, that all particular causal relations are necessary. The third *Critique* was intended to fill this lacuna (whose existence in his theory empiricist commentators have built up a tradition of ignoring). He says that empirical laws 'may be contingent as far as the light of our understanding goes, but still, if they are to be called laws, (as the concept of a nature requires), they must be regarded as necessary on a principle' (*Critique of Judgement*, Pt I, p.18). The relevant principle, he suggests, is that particular empirical laws should be regarded as having 'a unity such as they would have if an understanding (though it be not ours) had suggested them for the benefit of our cognitive faculties' (ibid., p.19). His notion of an intuitive understanding is intended to explain how from the point of view of this hypothetical understanding the laws would be necessary. He says that such an understanding 'not being discursive like ours, but intuitive, moves from the *synthetic universal*, or intuition of a whole as a whole, to the particular – that is to say, from the whole to the parts' (*Critique of Judgement*, Pt II, p.63). For such an understanding there would be no '*contingency* in the synthesis of the parts' (ibid., p.63).

Whatever else may be said about this conception, it would seem to be insufficient for Kant's purposes that it merely be hypothetical: the necessity of empirical laws is not guaranteed merely by the necessity that we judge as if there were an understanding from whose point of view they can be seen as necessary. Briefly, Schelling transformed Kant by postulating the actual existence of an intuitive understanding; using it to replace Kant's 'supersensible'; and by regarding it as an activity which resolves those conflicts we apprehend as limitations on our freedom. The result, for Schelling, is that nature is a process whose aims are realized in aesthetic experience, this being an experience both of self-knowledge and of freedom. Schelling writes that:

> the real world evolves entirely from the same original opposition as must also give rise to the world of art, which has equally to be viewed as one great whole, and which in all its individual products depicts only the one infinite . . . . it can be given to art alone to pacify our endless striving, and likewise to resolve the final and uttermost contradiction within us.
>
> (op. cit., p.231; 222)

Obscurity apart, there is an immediate cause for dissatisfaction with this account. Let us grant that cognition demands the existence of a form of understanding that intuits everything spontaneously and thus apprehends immediately the mutual relationship of whole to parts. It may well be true that experience of a work of art can be characterized as comprising an analogous apprehension of the relation of whole to parts. And it may further be true that the experience of freedom must also share this same feature. But even supposing that the demands of freedom can thus be compared with those of cognition, Schelling has produced no real argument to show that these demands are actually met in aesthetic experience. These experiences may present themselves as ones in which we act freely; and it may also be possible to picture them as ones in which we participate in nature's self-knowledge. But what grounds have we for believing that this way of looking at them is actually correct? Nothing very convincing has been said to establish that in having them we do in fact realize any broader aim of nature. Without an argument to this effect, we have no grounds to accept, as Schelling optimistically does, that nature and freedom must act in concert, nor for holding, more to the present point, that reference to the aims of nature provides a means, consistent with Kant's fundamental insights, of explaining the aim of aesthetic pleasure.

3. Art as 'the sensuous presentation of the Absolute' : Hegel

Hegel took up the challenge of remedying the deficiencies of Schelling's theory. Schelling has only offered us analogies, together with the unsubstantiated claim that the 'real world' and the 'world of art' are products of the same activity. Schelling's problem, in short, is how the resolution of conflicts between ourselves and the rest of nature can be equated with the resolution that gives rise to nature as a whole. In this connection he does, it is true, make extensive and influential use of the dichotomy between the conscious and the nonconscious: 'the concurrence of the two (the conscious and the nonconscious) *without* consciousness yields the real, and *with* consciousness the aesthetic world' (ibid., p.12). But such remarks only highlight the difficulty. If the real world and the world of art spring alike from the concurrence of the conscious and the nonconscious, ought not they to be present in both?

Hegel's response, recognizing that it is bound to be unsatisfactory to try to explain nature as a whole in terms of the reconciliation of any particular kind of conflict, was to generalize to its abstract limit the notion of conflict he used for his own explanatory purposes. He identified the force which generates nature and all the changes that occur within it with the demand that conflict in this abstract, general sense be resolved. His audacious thought was that conflict in this abstract sense is equivalent to contradiction; and therefore that the motive force, the basis of nature, is none other than reason itself moving 'dialectically' progressively to resolve contradictions in reality. His remarkable ambition was to explore and to defend in detail the thesis that reality as we experience it is in all its aspects the embodiment of the demands of rationality.

One of the chief attractions of this thesis is that it offers a not unconvincing answer to the question of how an individual's experience can reflect something about the whole of reality. This is possible because reason is the same wherever it is found. Hegel puts this by saying that 'the rational intelligence does not belong to the individual person as such in the way that desires do, but to him as at the same time inherently universal' (*Introduction to Aesthetics*, p.37). For Hegel, our rationality is our point of contact with the underlying basis of reality. Our purely rational ends are not only ones whereby we participate in the universe's own ends but ones in which the insight we gain can be identified with that of the universe into itself.

Hegel makes a determined effort to apply this line of thought to art. This looks a highly implausible venture. He wants to maintain, as he puts it, that 'the work of art . . . belongs to the sphere of conceptual thinking' (ibid., p.13), i.e. that we achieve purely rational ends in the pleasure we derive from art. Hegel rejects firmly Kant's contention that the experience of art, though cognitive, does not yield conceptual cognition. But are not purely rational ends ones achieved in the medium of thought alone? So does not the sensory element in art preclude this kind of treatment?

Hegel is undaunted by this consideration, probably because the notion of *embodied* rationality is already one his system demands. If reason explains absolutely everything then it must not only explain all the events occurring within the reality we experience but also why there should exist such a reality at all. One of the dictates of reason is that reason be embodied in reality. So Hegel's 'Absolute Idea' which explains everything is not detached from empirical reality like Plato's 'ideas', but is integrally bound up with it. As such it is explanatory in a sense that goes beyond and synthesizes several usually distinct notions of explanation – which of course it must do if it is to sustain its pretensions to be *totally* explanatory. (This had been anticipated in Kant's discussion of an intuitive understanding (see *Critique of Judgement*, Pt II, section 16).)

Thus the Absolute Idea, besides allowing no separate question of the *material* causes of things, can also, considered as a pattern which is embodied in particular things, be thought of as their *formal* cause. Regarded as something ontologically more fundamental than particular empirical events which in some sense brings these events about, the Absolute Idea has the character of an *efficient* cause. And considered as the object of the self-knowledge to which the universe is progressing, it is like a *final* cause, i.e. the explanations it yields of particular events have a teleological significance. An image that goes some way to combining all these elements is to think of the Absolute Idea as like the soul of a wholly self-sufficient creature.

Having developed this doctrine of the Absolute Idea as embodied rationality, Hegel sees no obstacle in principle to regarding the end of art as '*the sensuous presentation of the Absolute itself*' (op. cit., p.70). But what exactly is there in the experience of art to warrant this conclusion? If, for the reasons given, this experience is a vehicle for the universe's ultimate aim, and attainment of this aim consists in knowing the Absolute Idea, then it follows that the experience of art is one in which the Absolute presents itself. But this argument's first premiss requires confirmation. Hegel is fully aware of this. Having maintained that the 'ultimate end' points to 'a higher standpoint' in which all 'oppositions' are reconciled, he asserts that 'we will have to vindicate this higher standpoint for art too' (ibid., p.55).

Hegel's procedure in attempting to do this is to argue that our experience *vis-à-vis* a work of art possesses just that same internal integration as his analysis shows the Idea does *vis-à-vis* the reality which embodies it. Whereas Schelling left us wondering what justification there is for identifying our artistic aims with those of nature itself, Hegel claims that his own understanding of what the Idea's self-knowledge would consist in has an independent, purely rational basis. So by showing that the experience of art conforms to this understanding he believes he can vindicate his view that the end of art is a purely rational one which is simultaneously internal to our experience and a vehicle for the Idea's own ends.

Perhaps the central point Hegel wishes to make here – one that has been deeply influential on its own account – is that works of art have a quasi-organic relation to our apprehension of them by which we experience them as embodying ourselves. Hence we achieve through art both self-realization and self-knowledge. This is why, in Hegel's view, our relationship to art can be equated with the relationship of the Idea to the reality that embodies it when the Idea knows itself.

Art, Hegel says, has its 'basis and necessary origin' in 'the free rationality of man' (ibid., p.32); and this gives man:

> the impulse, in whatever is directly given to him, in what is present to him externally, to produce himself and therein equally to recognize himself. This aim he achieves by altering external things whereon he impresses the seal of his inner being and in which he now finds again his own characteristics. Man does this in order, as free subject, to strip the external world of its inflexible foreignness and to enjoy in the shape of things only an external realization of himself . . . . The universal need for art . . . is man's rational need

> to lift the inner and outer world into his spiritual consciousness as an object in which he recognizes again his own self.
>
> (ibid., p.31)

Later Hegel writes:

> in the beautiful . . . universal and particular, ends and means, concept and object, perfectly interpenetrate one another . . . thought is incarnate in the beauty of art, the material is not determined by thought externally, but exists freely on its own account.
>
> (ibid., p.60)

Hegel believes that such considerations entitle him to conclude that 'the content of art is the Idea, while its form is the configuration of sensuous material' (ibid., p.70).

4. Hegel's iconoclasm

Hegel himself qualifies this conclusion however. Art is only one of the human activities constituting the Idea's self-knowledge: philosophy is another. And Hegel is anxious to assert the superiority of the latter: 'the form of appearance acquired by a topic in the sphere of *thinking* is the truest reality' (ibid., p.9). Hence 'the Idea as the beauty of art is not the Idea as such, in the way that a metaphysical logic has to apprehend it as the Absolute, but the Idea as shaped forward into reality' (ibid., p.73). 'Only one sphere and stage of truth is capable of being represented in the element of art' (ibid., p.9). In art 'spirit is not in fact represented in its *true* nature' (ibid., p.79).

Hegel believes furthermore that only at one period of its development has art been capable of fully accomplishing even its limited aim of presenting the Idea sensuously. He claims that art has gone through in turn a 'Symbolic', a 'Classical', and a 'Romantic' phase; and that only Classical art, in which sculpture is central, affords 'the production and vision of the completed Ideal' (ibid., p.77). (The *Ideal* is the embodiment of the Idea as 'an individual configuration of reality'(ibid., p.73).) In Symbolic art, to which architecture is particularly appropriate, 'the incompatibility of Idea and shape still remains unconquered' (ibid., p.77); while in Romantic art, to which painting, music and especially poetry all lend themselves, 'the connection of spiritual meaning with sensuous material grows into a deeper intimacy than was possible in architecture and sculpture', but this 'can only come about at the expense of the objective universality of the content and its fusion with the immediately sensuous element' (ibid., p.86).

Hegel concludes that Romantic art is a transitional phase in the quest for true philosophical understanding: 'at this highest stage, art now transcends itself, in that it forsakes the element of reconciled embodiment of the spirit in sensuous form and passes over from the poetry of imagination to the prose of thought' (ibid., p.89). Hence 'art, considered in its highest vocation, is and remains for us a thing of the past' (ibid., p.11). Croce comments that 'The Aesthetic of Hegel is thus a funeral oration: he passes in review the successive forms of art, shows the progressive steps of internal consumption and lays the whole to its grave, leaving Philosophy to write its epitaph' (*Aesthetic*, trans. D. Ainslie, pp.302–3).

But all this would seem to contradict Hegel's original premiss, namely that in aesthetic experience we participate in the ultimate ends of the universe. If this premiss is true, then whatever else the realization of these ultimate ends might include, the experience of beauty ought to figure among them. If the need for art is something we transcend, then its ends cannot be truly ultimate. The only way to make this coherent is to regard sensuous beauty in an iconoclastic light as something whose purpose is to prepare us to experience a higher beauty, which experience consists in purely rational insight into the Idea.

This confirms the initial impression of implausibility about Hegel's approach to art. The notion that we attain in aesthetic experience internal ends that are purely rational cannot be saved from this implausibility even by Hegel's zig-zag strategy of developing independently an account of what it would be for such ends to be realized and then seeking confirmation that the experience of art bears this out. His ambition to show that art 'acquires its real ratification only in philosophy' (op. cit., p.13) is hollow. He regards aesthetic experience as a kind of impure knowledge of the Absolute; and in so doing runs into the same problem, writ large, as Leibniz did in trying to explain aesthetic enjoyment as confused knowledge of intellectually satisfying truths. For the fact remains that it is only in an analogical or metaphorical sense that the experience of art conforms to his account of knowledge of the Absolute. This account does not explain why we find art satisfying.

The obvious question is whether Hegel has misconceived the demands of the final rational synthesis. He believes that this can only be attained at the level of thought because only here can an all-embracing unity be established. More exactly:

> it is only the *whole* of philosophy which is knowledge of the universe as in itself that *one* organic totality which develops itself out of its own Concept and which, in its self-relating necessity, withdrawing into itself to form a whole, closes with itself to form *one* world of truth.
>
> (ibid., p.24)

This is likely to prompt the objection (among others) that it is hardly sufficient, so far as our practical aims are concerned, to attain intellectual understanding of the universe, however complete. This was Marx's response. But Hegel cannot really be accused of thinking otherwise. His view, officially at least, is that a reconciliation of all oppositions at the level of thought will subsume a reconciliation of them at all lower levels. The implication is that all practical experience aspires to the condition of concrete reconciliation which art exemplifies. This harks back to Schiller's notion that art is a 'symbol' of man's 'accomplished destiny'. And it ameliorates Hegel's iconoclasm to the extent of allowing us, in the final reconciliation, the experience of sensuous beauty, even if this beauty is inferior to the purely rational variety. What it does not do is enable us to assign a role to art when this destiny has been accomplished. If the ultimate end is one in which all experience has a positive aesthetic character, then art, considered as something that has a special role in giving us the opportunity for such experience, would become superfluous. This point has caused difficulty to some Marxist theorists. Hegel cannot evade it as Schiller can by holding that our destiny can never be finally accomplished since that would entail that reason is subject to limitations. So far, then, as the beauty of art is concerned, Hegel's theory emerges as irredeemably iconoclastic. Those who reject such iconoclasm will consequently be disposed, turning Croce's metaphor around, to regard art as the death warrant of Hegelian rationalism.

5. Art as respite: Schopenhauer

Of all those philosophers upon whom Hegel left his mark none rejected more bitterly his belief in the supremacy of reason than Schopenhauer. For Schopenhauer the basis of reality is not reason but the *will*: 'the will is the *thing-in-itself*. . . . It is that of which all representation, all object, is the phenomenon, the visibility, the *objectivity*' (*The World as Will and Representation*, trans. E.F.J. Payne, Vol.I, p.110). And the will is not rational at all but more like 'a blind impulse, an obscure, dull urge' (ibid., Vol.I, p.149); the will is 'an endless striving' (ibid., Vol.I, p.164).

For all that, Schopenhauer's thought retains many Hegelian features. In particular, Schopenhauer believes that the will is *universal* rather in the sense Hegel believed this of reason: 'all things in the world are the objectivity of one and the same will, and consequently identical according to their inner nature' (ibid., Vol.I, p.144). Again, 'in every individual the whole will-to-live, the being-in-itself, appears' (ibid., Vol.II, pp.590–1). Schopenhauer's philosophy can be seen as a bold variant of Hegel's system: it works out the consequences of modifying it in the fundamental respect of substituting for reason a wholly irrational force. One of the interesting things to emerge from this is a philosophy of art which is free from the iconoclastic implications of Hegel's theory.

Schopenhauer shares with Kant and Hegel the belief that aesthetic experience is cognitive; but he differs from both in how he understands this. Kant had held that although aesthetic enjoyment is enjoyment in a mode of exercising our cognitive faculties we do not obtain here any definite knowledge. There is merely the 'free play' of our faculties. Schopenhauer agrees with Hegel that aesthetic experience has a more definite cognitive outcome; but he firmly rejects Hegel's contention that this is *conceptual*. According to Schopenhauer the knowledge we gain through art is directly *perceptual*.

Of course, Schopenhauer loses Hegel's explanation of the significance of the ends we achieve when we acquire knowledge through art. Hegel had been able to identify this knowledge with attaining freedom because his metaphysical theory relates the internal ends of aesthetic cognition to the universe's own rational ends. Schopenhauer has no such optimistic belief in a metaphysical force that harmonizes our individual aims with the rest of the universe. The keynote of his philosophy is the opposed thought that there is no escape from the ceaseless, unlimited striving of the will. For Schopenhauer, freedom in Hegel's sense is simply unattainable.

Unable to avail himself of Hegel's positive account of the significance of artistic cognition, Schopenhauer offers a negative account. We may not achieve positive freedom in experiencing art; but at least we are here temporarily 'delivered from the miserable pressure of the will' (ibid., Vol.I, p.196). Art is a respite from the frustrations that inevitably accompany all our other activities. This gives a new twist to the idea that through its participation in a broader process art's aim is both internal and external. The enjoyment of art now has external significance not by contributing to a broader process but in virtue of not sharing the negative characteristics of other things we do.

In developing this idea Schopenhauer relies on a distinction between two kinds of knowledge: a kind that serves the will, and a kind that is free from it. The former 'really knows nothing more about objects than their relations' (ibid., Vol.I, p.177). This is characteristic of intellectual knowledge; and the intellect 'does not penetrate into the very essence of things' (ibid., Vol.II, p.176). This is in contrast to *perceptual* knowledge. '*Perception*', writes Schopenhauer, 'alone is the unconditionally true genuine knowledge, fully worthy of the name' (ibid., Vol.II, p.77). He takes the object of perceptual knowledge to be an *Idea*; but he uses this term in a quite different sense from Hegel. Schopenhauer's Ideas are not to be confused with the intellectual concepts which form 'the object of rational thought and of science . . . . The *concept* is abstract, discursive . . . . The *Idea* . . . is absolutely perceptive' (ibid., Vol.I, pp.233–4). Partly to avoid confusing these two, Schopenhauer refers to his Ideas, rather idiosyncratically, as *Platonic* Ideas.

We gain perceptual knowledge, according to Schopenhauer, by a process that liberates us from the will: 'the transition . . . from the common knowledge of particular things to knowledge of the Idea takes place suddenly, since knowledge tears itself free from the service of the will precisely by the subject's ceasing to be merely individual, and being now a pure will-less subject of knowledge' (ibid., Vol.I, p.178). In a remark that brings out how his theory of art is connected with his views on perceptual knowledge, Schopenhauer asserts that 'knowing is the purer and more perfect the more it has freed and severed itself from willing, whereby the purely objective, the aesthetic apprehension appears' (ibid., Vol.II, p.244).

One might well think that perceptual knowledge ought to be more rudimentary than the intellectual kind, providing it with material. But Schopenhauer holds that 'all perception is intellectual' (ibid., Vol.II, p.378). Knowledge of Ideas is attained, he maintains, when the intellect goes beyond its normal task of serving the will and, so to speak, acts on its own behalf. Thus he says that while genius lies 'in the completeness and energy of the knowledge of *perception*', possession of this faculty 'consists in an abnormal excess of intellect' (ibid., Vol.II, pp.376–7). The intellect can detach itself from its root, the will (ibid., Vol.II, p.383).

But why, when the intellect acts in this way, is this not experienced as a mere distraction? If the will is the inescapable driving force behind everything we do, then obtaining perceptual knowledge which is of no use to it ought only to be an irritant. Schopenhauer is presupposing that the pursuit of knowledge has a capacity to satisfy us which can counterbalance the usual demands of the will. Perhaps this is what he means when he says that a 'sharp distinction between will and knowledge . . . constitutes the fundamental characteristic of my philosophy' (ibid., Vol.II, p.495).

Another difficulty is that Schopenhauer sometimes characterizes aesthetic experience in ways apparently inconsistent with what he says about knowledge of Ideas. He writes that in aesthetic contemplation 'We lose ourselves entirely' in the object and 'we are no longer able to separate the perceiver from the perception' (ibid., Vol.I, p.178). But he also says that the will is 'the one thing really known to us immediately and completely', since only here do 'knower and known coincide' (ibid., Vol.I, p.112). An Idea, however, is 'not as yet the essence of the thing-in-itself [i.e. the will], for the very reason that it has sprung from knowledge of mere relations' (ibid., Vol.II, p.364).

6. Schopenhauer on music

This last difficulty does not arise with Schopenhauer's theory of music. Although he asserts that art's 'only source is knowledge of the Ideas; its sole aim is communication of this knowledge' (ibid., Vol.I, pp.184–5), he treats music as an exception. Music does not present Ideas but 'a *copy of the will itself*' (ibid., Vol.I, p.257). Music expresses 'the inner being, the in-itself of the world' (ibid., Vol.I, p.264). In knowing Ideas our knowledge is free from the demands of the will in the sense that it becomes detached from the standpoint of individual desires; but in knowing music our knowledge is free from these demands in the deeper sense that we know here the activity of the will before it has acquired an individual standpoint.

This apparently introduces a new kind of knowledge over and above the intellectual and perceptual sorts already described – direct knowledge of the will, the thing-in-itself. But in ordinary experience we only encounter the 'objectivity' of the will. So how is this direct knowledge possible? Because of the will's universality, Schopenhauer is able to understand this as a kind of inner knowledge: '*we ourselves are the thing-in-itself*. Consequently, a way *from within* stands open to us to that real inner nature of things to which we cannot penetrate *from without*' (ibid., Vol.II, p.195). But how does this help us to understand the special capacity of music to express the 'in-itself' of the world? A musical performance is as much an event in the 'world as representation' as, say, the recitation of a poem.

To understand Schopenhauer here we have to recognize that he detects a significant analogy between the qualities of musical experience and characteristics of the will itself, rather as Hegel had done between aesthetic experience in general and features of the Absolute Idea. Because of its striving the will is purposeful; but in so far as its striving is ceaseless it lacks any definite purpose. Precisely this quality of purposeless striving is distinctive, Schopenhauer believes, of our experience of music. When we 'lose ourselves' in a piece of music the inner knowledge we have of our own experiences is at the same time knowledge of the will as it is in itself. Music has a positive capacity to reveal the will's own nature.

This suggests a possible answer in the case of music to the question why knowledge gained in aesthetic experience is a genuine respite and not merely distracting. Because of the will's universality, when in music we know the will as it is in itself, the will knows itself. So Schopenhauer can explain why this knowledge is positively satisfying by crediting the will with the desire to attain self-knowledge. The Hegelian parallels here are evident. Although Schopenhauer rejects utterly Hegel's conception of freedom, in the case of music he has room to maintain that we participate in the aims of the universe as a whole.

Since his account of music has this advantage over his account of the other arts the question arises whether Schopenhauer was right to treat the other arts differently. I cannot see that he was. What impresses him about music is the quality of purposeless purposefulness in our experiences when we lose ourselves in it. But he believes that in all aesthetic experience we lose ourselves in the object; and he offers no grounds for denying that in their own fashion all these experiences display purposefulness without purpose. He singles out music only because he finds here the peculiar quality of restlessness he associates with the will. The correct conclusion may be that the will is not as restless as he supposes. There is also the point, if music is a direct copy of the will, that 'we could just as well call the world embodied music as embodied will' (ibid., Vol.I, pp.262–3). But music is itself embodied in sounds. A capacity to hear the music in these sounds ought to be a special case of a more general capacity to 'hear the music' in all things.

Perhaps this reveals that Schopenhauer's accounts of music and of the other arts are not really separate after all. The last point suggests a possible synthesis of his claims about Platonic Ideas and about inner knowledge of the will. 'Hearing the music' in things and perceiving an Idea are, it may be said, two aspects of the same activity: we know the will directly through our inner experiences; but these experiences are necessarily *of* something (real or imaginary sounds, sights, etc.); and the process of detachment required to perceive Ideas is one and the same as that required to recognize in our experiences that purposefulness without purpose which directly reflects the will's inner nature.

This account would make it unnecessary to suppose that Schopenhauer is introducing another form of knowledge distinct from the intellectual and perceptual when he talks of our having inner knowledge of the will. It might also help to remove some difficulties in Schopenhauer's claim that each individual person can be regarded 'to a certain extent as a special Idea' (ibid., Vol.I, p.132). This claim prompts the question 'How can each of us know his "special Idea"?' – a question that seems unanswerable on his previous account. But if perceiving one's own 'special Idea' is an aspect of perceiving one's inner nature, this nature being the will itself, then the capacity to perceive one's own Idea can now be regarded as a further side to the general capacity to perceive Ideas.

This synthesized account also enables us to see how Schopenhauer's theory of genius as an enhanced capacity for perception might be extended to the case of music; for a composer's concern to articulate the immediate activity of the will no longer appears to be separable from his perceiving Ideas – in particular not separable from perceiving his own 'special Idea'. This point suggests, moreover, a possible account of the special value of artistic as opposed to natural beauty. Schopenhauer sometimes appears to be suggesting that art is only a useful tool in gaining knowledge of Ideas, for example when he speaks of works of art as 'facilitating' the apprehension of Ideas (ibid., Vol.II, p.370). But if one of the Ideas whose apprehension a work of art makes possible is the artist's own special Idea, then this knowledge might only be obtainable through art.

It has, of course, often been held since Schopenhauer's day that works of art express the artist's individuality. But I think the possibility of interpreting Schopenhauer's theory as entailing this has a more backward-looking significance. His attitude is that in acquiring self-knowledge we align ourselves with the metaphysical basis of reality, this alignment being a process that entails deeper insight into the things of ordinary experience and which culminates in a form of direct non-conceptual contact with reality. The philosophy of Plotinus is often compared with Absolute Idealism; but the parallels with Schopenhauer are, I think, closer. A notable point is that for Plotinus knowledge of true beauty, like knowledge of the will itself for Schopenhauer but unlike Hegel's knowledge of the Absolute, is entirely non-conceptual: it is not 'discursive' knowledge expressible 'by reasonings' (Enneads V, viii, 4–6) but consists in a direct participation in what is known. Seen in this perspective Schopenhauer's use of the term 'Platonic Ideas' ceases to appear eccentric; and his notion of 'objectification' of the will can be compared to Plotinus's notion of *emanation.* (J.M. Rist verges on identifying the One of Plotinus with the will (Rist, pp.78–82).)

7. Conclusion: the need for a theory of forms of knowledge

This affinity between Schopenhauer and Plotinus illustrates again the parallels I spoke of (Chapter 3, section 3) between theories that try to explain aesthetic enjoyment as having a direct practical purpose and ones that defend a notion of autonomous cognitive enjoyment. Pleasure appears to demand explanation in terms of an aim satisfied, whether this be a *final* cause, i.e. a practical purpose to the pleasant activity, as viewing pleasure as a sensation would seem to demand, or a *formal* cause, i.e. a feature of the pleasant activity itself, as implied by Aristotle's theory that pleasure perfects an activity. But aesthetic experience is valued for its own sake. It serves no aims beyond itself, practical or cognitive. It can therefore only be assigned a direct practical purpose by adopting a metaphysical aestheticism such as Plotinus's which identifies our practical and aesthetic goals. The notion, as against this, that we attain autonomous cognitive aims in aesthetic experience does not really escape the difficulty. Now we find ourselves having to regard ordinary knowledge as the means by which we attain knowledge of the aesthetically satisfying variety.

There is also still the problem, assuming it is always satisfying to have this aesthetic knowledge, that any correct explanation of it ought itself, in using words to convey what this knowledge is, to be aesthetically satisfying, and so should be able to replace the original experience. Hegel was willing to conclude iconoclastically that the truest cognitive enjoyment does indeed take an abstract, conceptual form. Schopenhauer disagrees; but only by compromising the sense in which his theory is explanatory. In the end he interprets his theory of distinct conceptual and perceptual forms of knowledge as entailing that it is impossible to say what aesthetic experience teaches us. We can only experience it. The corollary is that the intellectual understanding of reality with which science and philosophy are concerned is inferior to that which art offers.

Thus Schopenhauer asserts that 'the ultimate and most important information about the inner nature of things can only be drawn from self-consciousness' (op. cit., II, p.178), and that as such 'the actual, positive solution to the riddle of the world must be something that the human intellect is wholly incapable of grasping and conceiving' (ibid., II, p.185). It is not, however, beyond the power of the arts, particularly music, to grasp this. Schopenhauer tells us that 'The composer reveals the innermost nature of the world, and expresses the profoundest wisdom in a language that his reasoning faculty does not understand' (ibid., I, p.260). These ideas were probably the source of a number of Wittgenstein's themes in his *Tractatus*, including his distinction between what can be 'said' and what can only be 'shown' and his belief that 'the value of this work [the *Tractatus* itself] shows how little is achieved' when the problems of philosophy are solved (Preface, trans. D.F. Pears and B.F. McGuinness).

From this point of view there cannot be a theory that genuinely explains why we find aesthetic experience satisfying: there can only be a theory that explains why such explanation is impossible. Broadly, the possibility of a genuinely explanatory theory depends on being able to distinguish verbal knowledge from the experiential knowledge we have in aesthetic experience in a way that still permits us to discuss and theorize about this experiential knowledge verbally. What is needed is a more developed theory of forms of knowledge than Schopenhauer or his predecessors attempted – a theory which not only allows the same knowledge to take experiential or verbal forms but which explains how possessing it experientially can differ positively from possessing it verbally.

CHAPTER V

Art as Language

1. Knowledge by acquaintance

Unless we are philistines or iconoclasts, a genuinely explanatory aesthetic theory calls for a theory of forms of knowledge that enables us to discuss experiential knowledge in words. In this connection Russell's notion of 'knowledge by acquaintance' has found favour among many writers on aesthetics. But Russell's account of this notion is far from straightforward.

Russell says 'there are two sorts of knowledge: knowledge of things, and knowledge of truths' (*The Problems of Philosophy*, p.25). He first explains 'acquaintance' by identifying it with knowledge of the former sort. But since some truths are about things he soon qualifies this by maintaining that knowledge of things can itself be of two kinds. Besides knowledge of things by acquaintance, which is 'logically independent of knowledge of truths', there is also 'knowledge of things by *description*', which 'always involves. . . some knowledge of truths as its source and ground' (ibid., p.25). Russell goes on to speak of acquaintance as 'direct' or 'immediate' knowledge of things. Thus what began as an attempt to distinguish different types of knowledge according to differences in their *objects* (truths or things) becomes also a distinction between two kinds of cognitive relation in which it may be possible to stand to the *same* thing.

Not that on Russell's reckoning there are many types of things with which one can be acquainted. I cannot, for example, be acquainted with any physical objects or other people's minds, but only with such *recherché* objects as sense-data and universals. Russell bases this highly restrictive thesis on the point that 'knowledge of truths, unlike knowledge of things, has an opposite, namely *error*' (ibid., p.69). From this he concludes that if there is scope for error about the existence of a thing then that thing cannot be of a kind with which I could be acquainted. The inference is invalid. Russell holds, contrary to what he said about acquaintance being logically independent of knowledge of truths, that if I am acquainted with a thing then I know that thing's identity. ('If I am acquainted with a thing which exists, my acquaintance gives me the knowledge that it exists' (ibid., p.23).) However, the significant point just now is that Russell's thought here reflects a third understanding of the distinction between acquaintance and description, namely as a distinction between different ways knowledge can be *acquired*. Influenced by the idea that acquaintance and description are both *sources* of knowledge, Russell holds that acquaintance yields the knowledge that the thing with which one is acquainted exists. Since acquaintance 'has no opposite', he concludes that knowledge of this truth enjoys an infallibility lacking in knowledge gained through description. (Even so, Russell's restrictive thesis does not follow: he ought to have distinguished knowing that the thing, whatever it is, with which one is acquainted exists from knowing the identity of that thing.)

The immediate moral of all this is that there are three strands to 'knowledge by acquaintance'. First, there is the idea that this knowledge has its own special *objects*. Second, there is the idea that knowledge by acquaintance is a *mode* in which objects of knowledge are known – we may have knowledge by acquaintance and knowledge by description of the same thing. Third, there is the idea that acquaintance and description are two different *sources* of knowledge.

In the last sense knowledge by acquaintance of a truth is knowledge that has been gained through acquaintance. Naturally there would be little point in continuing to add here the qualification 'by acquaintance' unless the source of the knowledge made a difference to it even after it had been acquired. There is the possibility, then, which Russell does not bring out, that acquaintance and description may not only be distinct modes in which the same thing can be known, but may be distinct modes in which the same truth is known. This could well be relevant to the problems we have been discussing in aesthetics. But, as we shall see, it will be necessary to examine some difficult general questions about the nature of cognition in order to develop a theory of experiential knowledge that unravels sufficiently the issues just adumbrated.

In view of these points it does not get us very far simply to say that in aesthetic experience we have knowledge by acquaintance. The amplification this claim needs must indicate whether this knowledge has its own special objects; in what sense it is a mode of knowledge; what its relation is to verbalizable knowledge; and the means by which it is acquired.

These are large questions. How can we tackle them? One possible way that has been influential springs from the conception of art which seems to be implied by the present view of aesthetic experience. If aesthetic experience consists in having knowledge by acquaintance the natural view of art is that its role is precisely to articulate and to communicate knowledge of this kind. And instead of thinking that we first need a theory of this type of knowledge and then a theory of how it can be communicated, we may adopt a reverse procedure. We may seek to explain the nature of the experiential knowledge with which art is concerned by investigating the means artists use to articulate it. It is natural to think of these means by analogy with language: just as ordinary verbal languages serve to communicate conceptual knowledge, the 'languages' or symbolic means used by artists serve to communicate experiential knowledge. Perhaps this is the clue we need to break through the impasse to which the previous discussions appear to have brought us. We cannot directly formulate experiential knowledge in words; but we can still theorize about art and aesthetic experience because we can discuss the special symbolic means used to express it.

2. *The phenomenological approach: Dufrenne*

We find, however, a related though somewhat different approach in the writings on aesthetics by thinkers belonging to the current of thought known as phenomenology.

Phenomenologists take to heart Schopenhauer's claims that the experiential knowledge we gain in aesthetic experience is uniquely objective, and that its source is adoption of an attitude of detachment. The phenomenological approach is to practise the adoption of this attitude more widely. Thus Merleau-Ponty writes that phenomenology is 'as painstaking as the works of Balzac, Proust, Valéry, or Cézanne – by reason of the same kind of attentiveness and wonder, the same demand for awareness' (*Phenomenology of Perception*, trans. C. Smith, p.xxi). Mikel Dufrenne asserts that 'metaphysical truths, in the widest sense of the term, proceed from an attitude which is not without affinity with the aesthetic attitude' (*The Phenomenology of Aesthetic Experience*, trans. E.S. Casey *et al.*, p.430). (Schopenhauer himself had said that the capacity for philosophy and for fine art are the same (*The World as Will and Representation*, Vol.II, p.407).)

The implication of this approach is that what we ought to be seeking in raising questions about the knowledge we gain in art is further knowledge of this same experiential sort. In other words, we ought not, at least primarily, to be concerned with developing an explicit theory of this form of knowledge: our concern ought rather to be to enrich our experiential knowledge itself. Phenomenologists tend themselves to be uncertain about the possibility of an explicit theory of the knowledge they seek and the extent to which, if one is possible, it can be explanatory or is only one of the channels through which facets of experience can be expressed. This uncertainty makes it hard to say definitely whether phenomenologists are pursuing a rival to the outlined approach or differ only in their emphasis. Certainly we find efforts in, for example, Dufrenne's work to organize an interest in the nuances of aesthetic experience within a theoretical framework; though he still feels that systematic philosophy 'exists in tension with art' (op. cit., p.323).

As one would expect, Dufrenne devotes much energy to conveying vividly the special qualities of aesthetic experiences. For example, he emphasizes the quality of fusion between a work of art and its audience. He describes this as 'reciprocal possession', saying, for example, that I 'exist in the symphony' and 'the symphony exists in me' (ibid., p.56). He also stresses the capacity of an aesthetic object to 'retain its thinglike characteristics while still being more than a thing' (ibid., p.lxvi). This prompts him to say that a work of art is a 'quasi subject' (ibid., p.146).

Although such descriptions can be strikingly evocative they do not, I think, make any really novel points bearing in mind the extensive discussions of aesthetic topics that followed in the wake of Hegel. (This, of course, is not a relevant criticism if the chief aim of the descriptions is to evoke the experiences.) The idea that man finds an embodiment of himself in art was, after all, prominent in Hegel's writings. And it had for long been a familiar thought that *empathy* (*Einfühlung*) – the feeling of subjectively entering into an object – is central to aesthetic experience. Isaiah Berlin credits Herder with inventing this notion (*Vico and Herder*, p.173). But it is chiefly associated with Theodor Lipps. Explaining the notion of empathy, Lipps says that I can find a storm, for example, expressive of things that 'can only be felt within me', as when 'in the storm I seem to find rage and threat'; and that in such a case 'I experience or feel myself in it [the storm]' ('Empathy and Aesthetic Pleasure', trans. K. Aschenbrenner; in Aschenbrenner and Isenberg (eds), p.405). On their own Dufrenne's remarks about my 'existing in the symphony' only highlight the empathic element in aesthetic experience.

But Dufrenne goes on to make broader claims which jointly add up to a more general if fragmentary theory. He is prepared to say that in aesthetic experience we gain a form of knowledge which is distinguished by its source, namely 'feeling' (or 'affectivity'), and by its object, which he refers to variously as an 'affective quality' (op. cit., p.143); a 'world atmosphere' (ibid., p.178); 'an interiority' (ibid., p.376); and 'the unconditioned' (ibid., p.194). Feeling, for Dufrenne, is like a mode of perception. 'Feeling is simply another direction which perception can take... feeling, in which perception is realized, is not emotion. It is knowledge.... Feeling is... a capacity of receptivity, a sensibility to a certain world, and an aptitude for perceiving that world' (ibid., pp.377–9). A key point about the knowledge feeling yields is that it is not verbalizable: 'the aesthetic object manifests a certain quality which words cannot translate but which communicates itself in arousing a feeling (ibid., p.178).

According to Dufrenne a thing's affective quality is something it *expresses*. ('Expression is the mode of revelation for what ever lacks a concept': ibid., p.131.) And receptivity to expressiveness gives us access, he believes, to a level of reality more fundamental than the conceptual. Thus he says that 'The unconditioned is revealed only through affectivity. This is why aesthetic experience may lie at the heart of being in the world' (ibid., p.230); 'knowledge by acquaintance is... complete in the aesthetic experience' (ibid., p.432). In this respect affectivity has a similar place in Dufrenne's thought to our inner knowledge of the will in Schopenhauer's.

But expression for Dufrenne is not only the means by which affective quality reveals itself. It is also 'the foundation of language' (ibid., p.134). In a general sense Dufrenne holds that anything that is expressive possesses 'meaning', the meaningfulness of ordinary verbal languages being only a special, developed case. Consequently, since affectivity is such a pervasive phenomenon, he is prepared to apply the notion of language in the general sense very widely. 'The aesthetic object is always a language' (ibid., p.79). Indeed, 'every object constitutes a language' (ibid., p.125). These 'languages' express something non-conceptual – a world atmosphere. Quite how the conceptual meaning of verbal languages is supposed to develop out of this Dufrenne does not make clear.

Dufrenne is more preoccupied with the question of how it is possible for there to be such a spontaneous accord between things and the feelings they arouse in us. Our knowledge of what a thing expresses cannot, he declares, be 'the result of an empirical generalization' because it is 'immediately immanent in feeling' (ibid., p.470). He responds by proposing a curious theory of the 'affective *a priori*': 'one's sense of the affective. . . [is] a sort of prior comprehension which is responsible for the fact that feeling is a knowing by acquaintance' (ibid., p.471). But since, as Dufrenne himself acknowledges, aesthetic objects are 'essentially singular' (ibid., p.476), a prior comprehension that could explain our receptivity to affective quality would have to encompass every case individually. The notion of an affective *a priori* is unworkable. It would, anyway, be superfluous were Dufrenne prepared to pursue further the parallels between his own theory and Schopenhauer's. The latter had no difficulty in explaining the felt affinity between ourselves and other things as a reflection of the inner identity all things share as manifestations of one and the same will. It is not so easy, certainly, to find a name in Dufrenne's case for the shared inner identity. But he himself goes as far at one point as to assert obscurely that 'Being is the very becoming of meaning' (ibid., p.554). He also says that 'it is by means of the artist that nature seeks to express itself' (ibid., p.550). This suggests a metaphysical picture akin to Schopenhauer's, but purged of both his pessimism and the Platonic ingredients, where the will's desire for self-knowledge is replaced by a process revealed through affectivity in which 'being' seeks to become 'meaningful'.

Whatever the merits of this, if it does accurately encapsulate Dufrenne's position, the considerations behind it certainly raise points pertinent to hopes of explaining experiential knowledge by investigating the means used to articulate it. If the experiential knowledge we are concerned with is as pervasive as Dufrenne believes affectivity to be then it is impossible to characterize this knowledge by isolating any symbolic means specific to it. We can thus discern in the phenomenological approach pursued by Dufrenne grounds for scepticism about hopes for an explicit theory of the experiential knowledge we have in aesthetic experience that go beyond its general reservations about the value of verbal knowledge. There are positive grounds for scepticism in the thesis that any symbol, indeed anything at all, is expressive of this knowledge. In that case there is apparently nothing more fundamental by reference to which this expressiveness and this form of knowledge can be explained: it is simply a basic fact of experience. We shall have to see if those who advocate a 'symbolic' view of art have a good reply to this.

3. Croce's theory of intuition and expression

In criticizing Schopenhauer, Croce writes, as Dufrenne could well have done, that 'To free oneself from common perception. . . does not mean rising to a Platonic contemplation of the ideas, but descending once again into the region of immediate intuition' (*Aesthetic*, trans. D. Ainslie, p.370). Many of Croce's remarks about 'intuition' resemble what phenomenologists have to say about the immediate content of experience. For example, Croce differentiates intuition from perception because 'the distinction between reality and non-reality is extraneous, secondary to the true nature of intuition' whereas perception is 'the apprehension of something as real' (ibid., p.3). Moreover Croce's most prominent thesis about intuition is that 'Every true intuition or representation is also expression' (ibid., p.8). He consequently believes, since he regards intuition as the fundamental level of knowledge, that expressiveness is pervasive. Those things we select for special attention as works of art differ from other things only in being 'very complicated and difficult expressions'(ibid., p.12). It would seem, then, that the points Dufrenne was making were anticipated by Croce. This does not, however, prevent Croce from developing a theory of intuitive knowledge. For Croce:

> Knowledge has two forms: it is either *intuitive* knowledge or *logical* knowledge; knowledge obtained through the *imagination* or knowledge obtained through the *intellect*; knowledge of the *individual* or knowledge of the *universal*; of *individual things* or of the *relations* between them.
>
> (ibid., p.1)

This makes it clear that intuitive and logical knowledge are supposed to differ both in their objects and in their sources. It would appear that over and above this they are meant to be different modes of knowledge only in the sense that the same thing when known individually is known intuitively but when known in relation to other things is known logically. It later emerges, however, that the distinction is less clear than this initial account suggests.

Croce stresses that 'intuitive knowledge has no need for a master' (ibid., p.2). Intuitive knowledge is autonomous. In maintaining this he departs from Kant's view that the role of intuition is merely to supply material for the understanding. A further Kantian thesis Croce firmly rejects is that the faculty of intuition is only passive and receptive. Kant described the understanding as an active faculty which 'synthesizes' intuitions. But Croce speaks of intuition itself as a synthesizing activity: its synthesis is an 'aesthetic', i.e. experiential, one; it synthesizes the 'matter of impressions' (ibid., p.22) so as to give them an intuitive 'form'. ('The aesthetic fact . . . is form.' (ibid., p.16).) Obviously this only coheres with what he said earlier if impressions are not 'individual things' in the previous sense whose relations we know in synthesizing them aesthetically. Croce takes account of this when he says that aesthetic synthesis is 'a fusion of the impressions in an organic whole' (ibid., p.20). The impressions are not known separately but through their place in the organic whole formed in the aesthetic synthesis.

Now, 'The spirit only intuits in making, forming, expressing. . . . Intuitive activity *possesses intuitions to the extent that it expresses them*' (ibid., p.8). It would appear, though Croce does not spell this out, that by 'expression' he means the process by which we know intuitions. In identifying the two his point is that the activity of having an intuition is one and the same as the process by which we know it. There are persuasive grounds for holding this. Logical (conceptual) knowledge can come about through applying concepts to things previously known; but by hypothesis things cannot be known prior to intuition, so this form of knowledge cannot derive from any corresponding two-stage process. Intuitions (the things we know) must *make themselves known*.

Since Plato, a recurring question in discussions of art has been 'What kind of knowledge explains the artist's ability to produce his works?' Croce believes that having identified intuition with expression he has an elegant and simple answer. The problem, as he sees it, is that the knowledge a work of art communicates cannot be abstracted from it; hence in producing the work the artist cannot be understood as employing means to communicate something he previously knows. Croce's response is to claim that it is a fundamental error to suppose the artist has need of any such means. The knowledge the work communicates is intuitive knowledge of the work itself. But since intuition and expression are identical, the artist's intuition of the work he produces is the very same process as the one by which he produces an expression of this intuition. Croce pours scorn on those who 'believe that anyone could have imagined a Madonna of Raphael; but that Raphael was Raphael owing to his technical ability in putting the

Madonna upon canvas' (ibid., p.9). For 'He who separates intuition from expression never succeeds in reuniting them' (ibid., p.8). And such expressive abilities do not, in Croce's view, require further explanation. The 'aesthetic activity' of the imagination, i.e. intuition, is the 'firstborn of the spiritual activities, mainstay of the others' (ibid., p.xxviii). It follows that all men have aesthetic expressive abilities, though 'some men are born great poets, some small' (ibid., pp.14–15).

The plausibility of this depends, however, on using 'expression' ambiguously. Croce is reasoning as if the production of a painting were the expression of an intuition in the sense in which these two can be identified. But were that so, the intuition of the painting by spectators, or for that matter by the artist himself after he has painted it, could not be the same as the one the painting originally expressed; for knowledge of *that* intuition is inseparable from the process of painting it. This point is the source of Croce's notorious doctrine that strictly speaking 'the work of art (the aesthetic work) is always *internal*' (ibid., p.51). He tries to evade the difficulty by regarding 'external' works of art as only '*physical stimulants of reproduction*' (ibid., p.97) of the intuitions that are the true works of art. When artists produce their 'external' works they achieve, according to Croce, a 'translation of the aesthetic fact into physical phenomena (sounds, tones, movements, combinations of tones and colours, etc.)' (ibid., p.96). Of course this only reintroduces the problem he earlier claimed to solve: there is now the question of how the artist is able to 'translate' his intuitions.

In fact Croce faces an even deeper difficulty. Intuitive knowledge is knowledge of individual things; and he identifies the individual things known (intuitions) with the expressive activities by which he knows them. It would seem to follow that each intuition is an individual event and as such is unrepeatable. In that case the very notion of communicating intuitions is self-contradictory. As E.F. Carritt, who is sympathetic to Croce, puts it 'we seem forced to conclude that [Croce] must abandon his identification of intuition with expression or his belief in the communicability of aesthetic experience' (*The Theory of Beauty*, p.137). If Croce's reply is that he is only interested in qualitative identity between intuitions, the question arises how it can be known that two intuitions are qualitatively identical.

Evidently things are going badly for Croce's theory of intuitive knowledge. What is more he is unable to prevent these difficulties from engulfing the other form of knowledge he distinguishes, logical knowledge. For logical distinctions, he admits, cannot be known 'otherwise than in expressions and words, that is to say, in imaginative form' (*Aesthetic*, p.123). Thought, he says, 'cannot but assume an intuitive form, in becoming objective to the spirit' (ibid., pp.22–3). How, then, can logical knowledge be more than a subclass of the intuitive kind? Croce has no very clear answer to this. He refers sometimes to 'aesthetico-logical expressions' (ibid., p.35) apparently conceding the point. He even says that 'the principle of contradiction itself is at bottom nothing but the aesthetic principle of coherence' (ibid., p.44). But he also speaks as if there were only a difficulty about having 'pure' logical knowledge. He says that 'the logical fact, *the only logical fact*, is *the concept*, the universal, the spirit that forms', and 'The concept, the universal considered abstractly in itself, is *inexpressible*' (ibid., p.42). If this means that his original distinction between intuitive and logical knowledge is really one between intuition and knowledge that blends intuitive and logical elements, it should follow, if logical knowledge has its own object, that we can possess logical knowledge in two different forms – in a pure, inexpressible form, and an impure, intuitive one. The seeming clarity of Croce's initial distinction is lost. (Elsewhere he concludes that 'there is no other mode of conceiving simultaneously of the independence and dependence of the various spiritual activities' than to conceive them as a process of *circular development* (*Guide to Aesthetics*, trans. P. Romanell, p.50).)

The true implication of Croce's doctrines would appear to be that there is only a single, intuitive form of knowledge, his distinction between intuitive and logical knowledge being an infelicitous way of distinguishing knowledge itself from the formative capacity which creates it. Certainly Croce cannot divide individual items of knowledge into intuitive and logical. And since he allows no distinction between the means used in expressing intuitive knowledge and the knowledge expressed, he denies that there can be any sub-classification of intuitive knowledge according to its means of expression. Indeed he makes 'the non-existence of classes of expression' (*Aesthetic*, p.143) one of his central doctrines: 'a classification of intuition-expressions is certainly permissible', he admits, 'but is not philosophical: individual expressive facts are so many individuals, not one of which is interchangeable with another, save in its common quality of expression' (ibid., pp.67–8). Notice that in putting the point like this Croce assumes, as is questionable, that were there a distinction between knowledge and its means of expression then the same knowledge could be expressed using different means. Be that as it may, Croce infers in particular the 'identity of Linguistic and Aesthetic' (ibid., pp.142–3), i.e. that there is no valid distinction between linguistic and aesthetic expressions of knowledge. He emphasizes that '*Philosophy of language and philosophy of art are the same thing*' (ibid., p.142).

All this is a consequence of Croce's identification of intuition with expression. But, as we have seen, there are already compelling grounds for thinking he goes too far in making this identification. While it is plausible to hold that knowledge is connected with the capacity to express it, to make the activity of expressing it identical with what is known prevents the knowledge from being accessible once it has been expressed. The sense of 'expression' we want here is, on the contrary, one where the expression of an item of knowledge can serve to communicate it.

Croce's identification of intuition and expression was not, however, a mere whim. It was motivated by the requirement, if there is knowledge of things in their individuality, that the individuals themselves actually be present in such knowledge. If we agree with Croce that aesthetic experience has to do with knowledge of things as individuals we need to examine how else this requirement might be met.

4. Presentational symbols: Langer

All knowledge, let us agree, can be communicated; but if knowledge has to be communicable by means separable from its object then knowledge of things in their individuality is not genuine knowledge at all.

Perhaps the solution to this is that knowledge of things as individuals differs from other knowledge just in this very respect, namely that the presence of the individual known is indispensable to communication of this form of knowledge. This need not mean identifying the individuals known with the act of expressing or communicating the knowledge if we recognize modes of symbolism in which individuals can stand in a symbolizing relation to themselves or their own properties. This is Goodman's approach. Another possibility is that the object of this knowledge, though distinct from the symbols used to communicate it, is not distinct from the sorts of experiences we have in apprehending these symbols. This is what Susanne Langer has in mind when she says that Croce's theory of intuitive knowledge awaited 'a recognition of non-discursive symbolization' (*Feeling and Form* (*F and F*), p.377). By means of a theory of this type of symbolism Langer believes she can answer questions about qualitative identity among experiences and thereby overcome the problems, to which Croce had no good solution, about how it is possible to communicate knowledge of our experiences in themselves. Neither Goodman nor Langer accepts Croce's identification of the individuals we know with the expression of this knowledge.

Langer writes that 'there is a great deal of experience that is knowable. . . yet defies discursive formulation, and therefore verbal expression: this is what we sometimes call the *subjective element* of experience, the direct feeling of it' (*Problems of Art* (*P of A*), p.22). According to Langer, although this knowledge defies discursive formulation, it can be formulated using non-discursive or 'presentational' symbols; and works of art are such symbols. Works of art 'objectify the life of feeling' (*F and F*, p.374). In so doing art gives '"knowledge by acquaintance" of affective experience, below the level of belief, on the deeper level of insight and attitude' (*Philosophy in a New Key* (*PNK*), p.263); 'it is the radical difference in their symbolic forms that makes art and discourse (logic, science, matter of fact) fundamentally different realms' (*F and F*, p.385).

What, then, are 'presentational symbols'? And how do such symbols 'objectify feeling'? In answering the first question Langer relies on the contrast with discursive symbols. She characterizes a 'true language or discourse' as possessing a vocabulary and syntax, and as comprising terms that can be defined and translated (*PNK*, p.94). Presentational symbols are symbols that lack these features. Her answer to the second question is based, she indicates, on Wittgenstein's picture theory of meaning (*PNK*, p.79). She maintains, for example, that 'musical structures logically resemble certain dynamic patterns of human experience' (*PNK*, p.226). In virtue of this resemblance music can objectify these patterns of experience.

The obvious complaint is that this is no explanation at all since we only speak of musical structures as resembling patterns of experience because we first hear the music as objectifying the experience. Langer gives no independent account of what constitutes a presentational symbol, nor any true explanation of the means by which they perform their symbolic role. But she is not, in fact, seriously concerned to attempt either of these things. Despite some remarks suggesting that symbolism can take autonomously discursive or presentational forms, her belief is that the presentational variety is fundamental, discursive symbolism being a later development. She believes that our capacity to apprehend things as presentational symbols is basic and spontaneous.

As such it is not analysable into anything simpler. We cannot expect a positive account of presentational symbols except in terms of what is achieved when they are functioning symbolically.

Because our capacity for presentational symbolism is basic and spontaneous, Langer is ready to detect it, as Dufrenne is prepared to detect expressiveness, anywhere that things can be experienced as fused with feeling. She even speaks of sense-data and images as (presentational) symbols (e.g. *PNK*, pp.21, 145; *P of A*, p.131); and of 'the stream of symbols which constitutes a human mind' (*PNK*, p.42). She does not appear to regard it as an objection that in such cases there is no clear distinction between the symbol and what, considered presentationally, it symbolizes. But if this distinction disappears then the presentational symbols become after all like Croce's 'expressions': they only symbolize themselves.

Occasionally indeed Langer makes remarks implying that for her presentational symbolism has the same basic function in cognition as Croce assigns to expression. Croce holds that intuitions – the things we know as individuals – must be 'expressions' because our capacity to know intuitions depends upon them making themselves known. In a similar way Langer maintains that our capacity to have any cognition depends on our recognizing things as presentational symbols. She speaks of a 'more basic function of symbols' than reference and communication, namely 'to formulate experience as something imaginable in the first place' (*P of A*, p.132). This would make redundant the '*need for symbolization*' (*PNK*, p.41) she invokes elsewhere.

Although this means that Langer's quasi-phenomenological account of presentational symbolism cannot be regarded as explanatory on its own, it might still be explanatory in an oblique sense if having postulated 'presentational thinking' as basic she is then able to derive a theory of the form of thought and knowledge appropriate to discursive symbolism. Her efforts to do this centre on claims about the role of metaphor. Here she is heavily influenced by Cassirer's view, espoused also by many others, that metaphor, being the source of abstraction and generality in thought, is the root of language (*Language and Myth*, Ch.6). In essence the claim here is that once a symbol denotes an individual thing it has the potential to be applied generally because it can be extended metaphorically to other things, the eventual literal meanings that words acquire being faded metaphors.

Langer believes she can use her theory of presentational symbolism to explain this process of metaphorical extension. 'It is in this elementary, presentational mode that our first adventures in conscious abstraction occur' (*PNK*, p.141). Her account of this sometimes uses the idea that *images* of the meanings of symbols, i.e. images of what they denote, can be presentational symbols. 'In a genuine metaphor, an image of the literal meaning is our symbol for the figurative meaning, the thing that has no name of its own' (*PNK*, p.139). However, the simpler, underlying thought is that a symbol can be metaphorically extended to those things that are presentational symbols of the same feeling as the original thing. The law of metaphorical extension is that 'a word designates any quality that can symbolize a certain feeling' (*P of A*, p.171).

Two grounds for dissatisfaction with this account are that it introduces the new idea of symbols having denotation and, more seriously, that it is implicitly circular because the notion of metaphor is needed at the outset in characterizing presentational symbols. The chief characteristic of art, and so presumably of any presentational symbol, is 'that its import is not separable from the form (the picture, poem, dance, etc.) that expresses it' (*F and F*, p.394). Here 'symbol and meaning appear as one reality' (*P of A*, p.26). The sense in which they symbolize the feeling is that they themselves metaphorically contain it: the feeling is metaphorically present in the symbol. Without this notion of metaphorical containment we would have to return to the Crocean notion that the symbols of feeling are feelings which symbolize themselves.

It may appear after this that Langer's theory of presentational symbolism achieves little but to render in a different idiom the same points about the pervasive expressiveness of our experience as we heard from Dufrenne. It cannot be said that she offers a viable positive account of the form of knowledge we derive from art. Nevertheless her work supplies some possible clues as to how an improved theory might go. Two separate points emerge from her discussions about our interest in works of art: we are interested in properties the works themselves possess; and these are properties they possess only metaphorically. A symbolic feature works of art share is that they have a relation to their own properties. But Langer tries to explain this as if it were due to the particular metaphorical properties the works possess. This is certainly a mistake. Things can have a symbolic relation to their own literal properties. Goodman cites the case of a tailor's sample which exemplifies the pattern and various other properties of a cloth. This symbolic relation, which contrasts with denotation, is widespread and by no means confined to works of art. But despite the varied list of semantic and syntactic attributes Langer mentions in characterizing discursive symbols, she attempts no more than a crude dichotomy of kinds of symbolism. A more refined classification of varieties of symbolism is certainly possible. This may pave the way for a genuinely explanatory account of art in terms of the particular symbolic attributes it combines.

5. *Art and the general theory of symbols: Goodman*

Echoing Langer, Goodman writes that 'The difference between art and science is. . . a difference in domination of certain specific characteristics of symbols' (*Languages of Art*, p.264). He aims to lay the foundations of a 'general theory of symbols' (ibid., p.xi) which can throw light on the peculiarities of works of art.

Goodman draws a basic distinction, already alluded to, between two modes of 'reference'. On the one hand, there is the case where a symbol applies to or *denotes* what it refers to. Denotation in Goodman's sense can take a wide range of forms, verbal, pictorial and diagrammatic. On the other hand, there is the more complex case where a symbol *exemplifies* something, as with the tailor's sample of cloth. A symbol *exemplifies* when it refers to some of its own properties. Since Goodman insists on nominalist grounds that strictly 'only labels [not properties] may be exemplified' (ibid., p.57), he concludes that 'exemplification implies the converse of denotation' (ibid., p.58), i.e. an exemplifying symbol refers to a label which denotes the symbol.

Goodman goes on to develop a battery of syntactic and semantic distinctions by which to refine this basic classification. For example, he describes as *linguistic* any system of denotational symbols that satisfies certain purely syntactic requirements, roughly of having a vocabulary of clearly defined elements. Beyond this he classifies as *notations* those linguistic systems that also satisfy certain stringent semantic requirements to the effect that a 'score' written in the notation unambiguously determines what complies with it, so that the score can be recovered from any accurate 'performance'. Ordinary natural languages are obviously not notations – objects do not uniquely determine their correct description in English.

Although Goodman does not discuss exemplification as thoroughly as denotation, he holds that symbols that exemplify can be classified using the same syntactic and semantic distinctions, or appropriate generalizations of them, as apply to denotational systems (ibid., pp.233–4). These distinctions, which relate to much of what Langer had in mind when contrasting discursive with presentational symbols, thus cut across the basic classification.

However impressive all this may be technically, it is, of course, only relevant to the issues concerning us if it helps in explaining notions important to the arts and aesthetics. Goodman does indeed make interesting use of his distinctions, for example in arguing that works of art are *fakable* when and only when they belong to an art form that does not use a notation (ibid., Ch.III, sections 4–5), and in showing that there is no theoretical barrier to creating a notation in his strict sense for dance (ibid., Ch.V, section 8). But these topics are peripheral to the central issue of what we achieve when we use art symbols. Very often paintings depict or *represent* things; and in general works of art interest us because they are *expressive*. Unless Goodman can apply his apparatus to such notions as these he can hardly claim that his approach explains much about art.

Regarding pictorial representatation his provocative thesis is that this consists in being a symbol that belongs to a denotational system which is non-linguistic because it is 'dense', i.e. because it 'provides for infinitely many characters so ordered that between each two there is a third' (ibid., p.136). Goodman particularly relishes the point that here 'resemblance disappears as a criterion of representation' (ibid., p.231). Regarding expressiveness he claims that 'What is expressed is metaphorically exemplified' (ibid., p.85). For example, a picture expresses sadness if it metaphorically exemplifies 'sad'; and 'The picture metaphorically exemplifies "sad" if "sad" is referred to by and metaphorically denotes the picture' (ibid., p.85). Thus representation and expression are, in Goodman's view, special cases respectively of denotation and exemplification.

Although Goodman argues convincingly, as have many others, that resemblance cannot explain pictorial representation, since our capacity to recognize resemblance derives from and does not precede familiarity with the use of symbols, he clearly overstates this point if he denies altogether that representations can resemble what they depict. He himself admits that representation is more than just a variety of denotation; for he agrees that a picture never merely represents *x* but always represents *x as* something or other; and he holds that *representation as* is a matter of exemplification (ibid., p.66). It ought, then, to be possible to understand resemblance between a picture and what it denotes in terms of its representing *x* as a so-and-so when *x* actually is a so-and-so. But in fact Goodman's explanation that 'a picture that represents a man as a man is a man-picture denoting him' (ibid., p.28) implies, since he regards 'man-picture' as an unbreakable predicate, that one could know that a picture represents a man as a man without knowing that it denotes something as it is. Treating 'man-picture' as an unbreakable predicate amounts to a refusal to examine how the denoting and exemplifying roles of depictions are related. But although resemblance cannot explain representation as such, it is still appropriate, once someone has become familiar with some representations, to say he is able to recognize resemblances between other representations and what they denote.

Goodman's discussion of expression leaves one with a similar feeling that he isolates the area where the difficulties lie without resolving them. If expression is metaphorical exemplification then the key to it lies in understanding metaphorical properties. Goodman explains metaphor as use of a term which is influenced by but departs from previous usage (ibid., Ch.II, section 8). Consequently 'the features that distinguish the literal from the metaphorical are transient' (ibid., p.85). This ought to make it difficult for familiar works of art to remain expressive. But it is a travesty to regard metaphor as a species of novelty. The relationship of the metaphorical to the literal is far more complex; and metaphor though it may contribute to is not essentially a phenomenon of linguistic change. Our understanding of words enables us to use them metaphorically as well as literally; and a proper account of metaphor should explain how it is possible for the *same* understanding to be exercised in these two different ways.

A general feature of Goodman's approach illustrated by his treatment of both representation and expression is his reluctance to examine relations between different ways the same symbols (characters) may be functioning. For him, different ways of using the same characters automatically constitute distinct symbol systems. Except in the sense that one symbol system may include another, or use of one system may causally influence use of others, he never considers that to understand one symbolic function it may be necessary to understand its relation to other functions the same characters can perform. Individuating symbol systems as Goodman does divorces them from questions about interrelations between the capacities we exercise in using these systems. Having thus separated them from questions about what we are *doing* in using these systems, his account is naturally incapable of any good explanation of what we *achieve* in using them.

The position is that Goodman's method of classifying symbol systems gives effect to and depends upon belief in the *pluralistic* character of knowledge. He rejects any demand for a comprehensive theory that explains systematically interrelations between our symbolic skills; he believes it suffices to say that in their multifarious ways 'labels of all sorts are tools of organization' (ibid., p.32). Thus his effective answer to questions about what we achieve in art is that this is precisely to use symbol systems having various of the attributes he catalogues. For example, he dismisses the idea that aesthetic experience is distinctively immediate and ineffable with the scornful remark that '"ineffability" upon analysis turns into density rather than mystery, [and] "immediacy" becomes a matter of exemplification rather than of intimacy – a function of direction rather than of distance' (ibid., p.253). Goodman assumes that our use of symbols having these features reflects the possession on our part of a corresponding form of knowledge; and that nothing further is needed to elucidate this form of knowledge than accurately to describe the symbols' properties.

In the end Goodman tells us that 'aesthetic experience is cognitive experience distinguished by the dominance of certain symbolic characteristics and judged by standards of cognitive efficiency' (ibid., p.262). These standards relate, he explains, to 'how well [the symbolization] serves the cognitive purpose', i.e. to 'how it analyses, sorts, orders, and organizes. . . how it participates in the making, manipulation, retention, and transformation of knowledge' (ibid., p.258). He also says that in art 'The primary purpose is cognition in and for itself' (ibid., p.258). However, it is one thing to say that symbolism is to be evaluated by how well it serves the purposes of cognition; it is another to claim that the purpose of some symbolism is purely cognitive. Goodman does not examine the problems which the latter claim poses.

There is, for example, the question whether this claim is meant to be compatible with the pragmatic idea that the meanings of any symbols consist ultimately in how they help us to attain antecedent wants and needs. This idea – which corresponds to a common interpretation of the doctrine that 'meaning is use' – is a semantic counterpart to the philistine idea that aesthetic enjoyment must have an ulterior purpose in the independent benefits it brings. Conceivably this is consistent with the notion that some symbolism has a purely cognitive purpose in the sense that the aim in using it is to develop useful cognitive skills. But if Goodman believes that some symbolism has an internal cognitive purpose in a further sense then this raises questions about the nature of cognition which his classificatory approach to symbolism does not answer.

Goodman fails, then, to give any clear explanation of our interest in art. He appears to vacillate between a view that does not take us significantly beyond Langer's postulated 'need for symbolization', and an implicitly philistine one according to which the criterion of cognitive efficiency reduces to how well the symbols serve our independent practical goals. A further weakness of Goodman's approach is that it is hardly capable of doing justice to the phenomenological points about expressiveness to which Dufrenne and others draw our attention. To find things expressive is to have experiential knowledge of a form central to aesthetic experience; and Dufrenne brings out how pervasive this form of knowledge is within experience as a whole. But the only explanation Goodman can give of this pervasiveness is to point out that anything can be used as an exemplificational symbol and will be found expressive if it possesses metaphorically the properties it exemplifies. This does not explain the significance of our having the capacity to find almost anything expressive, i.e. of our capacity to think metaphorically.

Perhaps the moral of this is that a fuller understanding of the distinction between the literal and metaphorical use of symbols is precisely what is needed to remedy the deficiencies in Goodman's account of symbolic capacities. Certainly it has often been claimed that to understand what is distinctive of art we need to understand metaphor rather than such symbolic properties as exemplification. This appears in fact to have been Langer's considered view. Recall that she confused the point that works of art are exemplifying symbols with the point that the properties they exemplify are metaphorical. Her true preoccupation was not with any special symbolic attributes of works of art but with the contrast between literal and metaphorical meaning. She was right in this. The prospect of elucidating art by examining symbolic properties allegedly peculiar to it has turned out to be a red herring.

Notice that this shift in approach may also bring a change in the sense in which aesthetic knowledge is to be regarded as 'knowledge by acquaintance'. In the theories of Croce, Langer and Goodman aesthetic knowledge is taken to be experiential on account of its *object*, i.e. because it concerns individual intuited or perceived things with which we are acquainted. But if our concern is with the recognition of expressiveness, as manifested in capacities to describe things metaphorically rather than literally, then our primary interest may lie rather in an experiential *mode* of knowledge. This point will be important later in the theory of aesthetic satisfaction to be proposed.

CHAPTER VI

Art and Metaphor

1. The relevance of metaphor

Metaphor in the narrow sense is one among the many tropes or figures of speech recognized by traditional rhetoric. The *Oxford English Dictionary* defines metaphor in this sense as 'Application of name or descriptive term to an object to which it is not literally applicable (e.g. a *glaring error*)'. Other tropes include simile, hyperbole, metonymy and synecdoche. Nowadays, however, it is common to describe almost any non-literal use of words as metaphorical. It is useful to have a general term to contrast with the literal since the problems posed by metaphor in the narrow sense are shared by many other tropes. The principles behind the traditional classification of tropes are anyway not very clear. (Even a general contrast with the literal might be questioned by those who share Quine's doubts about the whole notion of meaning.)

The term metaphor is also frequently used in even broader senses, as when an allegory or a picture is described as a metaphor for something. Of course the term metaphor like any other can itself be used metaphorically; so let us agree that literally speaking metaphor is a linguistic phenomenon which only exists where a contrast can be drawn between the literal and metaphorical use of words. While not wishing necessarily to reject other uses of the term, these should be regarded as metaphorical.

The aesthetic effect of many literary works depends on their use of metaphor. But metaphor is an important topic in aesthetics for wider reasons. We have seen that many writers characterize aesthetic experience in highly metaphorical terms, for example as embodying feeling, or as involving a fusion of our own experiences with something that is apprehended as an organic totality. More generally, the features of works of art we pick out when expressing our aesthetic responses tend to be ones they possess only metaphorically. The depth of a painting and the way a musical theme moves are not literal properties of the painting or of the sounds. Thus Roger Scruton asserts that 'the ways of hearing *sound* that we consider to be ways of hearing *music*, are based in concepts extended by metaphorical transference' (*The Aesthetic Understanding*, p.79); 'if we take these metaphors away [of movement and space], nothing of music remains, but only sound' (ibid., p.85). In so far as philosophical problems about art have to do with what we *say* about works of art, it is reasonable to suppose that the key to them lies in understanding what we are doing when we speak metaphorically.

Of course, philosophical problems in this area do not end here. For example, we want not only to know what we are doing in describing works of art but also some account of artists' abilities to produce them. But if we have to use metaphor in articulating our responses to art, the natural thought is that artists *create metaphor*. In support of this it may be pointed out that metaphor seems to be anomalous in relation to literal usage in much the way that artistic interests appear to be in the context of our other practical concerns. It is usually easy to say what people are doing when pursuing their ordinary practical objectives; but it is difficult to explain what an artist is trying to do. Similarly, when someone is speaking literally we can usually paraphrase what he is saying; but metaphor is often hard to interpret. Words fail us in explaining both our understanding of art and of metaphor.

It is not surprising, then, that many writers equate art with metaphor. For example, Langer describes a work of art as 'a developed metaphor, [because] a non-discursive symbol that articulates is verbally ineffable' (*Problems of Art*, p.26). Arthur Danto tell us that 'metaphors are minor works of art' (*The Transfiguration of the Commonplace*, p.189), and that 'To understand the artwork is to grasp the metaphor that is, I think, always there' (ibid., p.172). Polanyi says that 'Works of art are in a sense metaphors' (*Meaning*, p.151). Adorno goes as far as to say that 'Every art work is in fact an oxymoron' (*Aesthetic Theory*, trans. C. Lenhardt, p.236) – oxymoron being the figure of speech where contradictory elements are pointedly conjoined (e.g. describing the *Tractatus* as having an 'obscure clarity').

If, literally speaking, metaphor is always linguistic then 'Art is metaphor' is metaphorical. What these writers are suggesting is that art is analogous to or perhaps a further manifestation of the same general phenomenon as linguistic metaphor. Either way we can hope that our capacities to speak metaphorically may serve as a model for our creative artistic abilities. If this view is correct a good theory of linguistic metaphor should equip us to turn 'Art is metaphor' into an *explanatory* metaphor.

2. Theories of metaphor

From the literal point of view metaphorical statements are usually false, though we are sometimes speaking metaphorically even when what we say is literally true, e.g. 'Marriage is not a bed of roses'. And a statement does not have to be obviously true or obviously false when taken literally to be meant metaphorically. In 1940 Churchill might have been speaking either literally or metaphorically in saying 'I intend to write the history of the Second World War'.

How is it that in speaking metaphorically we do not lie in cases where what we literally say is knowingly false? Why are we not contradicting ourselves when we say 'The ship ploughs the sea' while admitting that of course this is not literally true? The first task of a theory of metaphor is to answer this question. Once we can answer this it should be easy to understand what we are doing when we speak metaphorically in saying things that are also literally true.

On the face of it there are five possible answers to the above question other than simply dismissing metaphor as an abuse of language. The first is that words take on new *metaphorical meanings* in metaphor distinct from their literal meanings such that when the metaphorical statements are interpreted according to their metaphorical meanings they can be straightforwardly true. This is to regard metaphor as a species of ambiguity.

A second answer is that in addition to literal truth there is also a distinct *metaphorical truth*. On this view, 'The ship ploughs the sea' is indeed incompatible with literal truth; but in saying this I can still succeed in the different aim of saying something that is metaphorically true without the words taking on any fresh meanings. Here metaphor is thought of as a distinct linguistic activity from literal stating.

A third answer appeals neither to changes in the meanings of the terms used nor to different kinds of truth, but to the idea that in speaking metaphorically we *say something obliquely*, rather as we do in being ironical. According to this the apparent incompatability of metaphor with literal truth should disappear once we recognize the existence of indirect as well as direct ways of making statements.

A fourth answer is that apparent incompatability between metaphorical and literal statements reflects a difference in the *viewpoint* from which they are made. I can easily say without contradiction that 'The house is to the left of the tree', and on another occasion that 'The tree is to the left of the house'. This need not imply a change in the meanings of the terms used; nor that I am aiming at a different kind of truth on the two occasions; nor that I was saying something indirectly in making at least one of the statements. The superficial incompatability is easily resolved by supposing that I was standing in a different position on the two occasions. An analogous solution in the metaphor case would hold that the metaphorical is readily compatible with the literal once metaphor is properly relativized to its 'metaphorical viewpoint'.

The fifth response is the radical one of maintaining that there is no need to reconcile metaphors with literal truth because their contradictoriness reflects accurately a real feature of the world. On this approach the real problem posed by metaphor is to explain how we can live with unresolved contradictions.

Since the notions of meaning and truth may themselves be used metaphorically, it is not always obvious where some authors stand regarding the first two answers. A writer may speak freely of 'metaphorical meaning' or of 'metaphorical truth' without committing himself thereby to either of these positions. On the other hand, it is possible to regard 'metaphorical meaning' and 'metaphorical truth' as metaphorical notions while still subscribing to one of these accounts. Thus Donald Davidson, while holding that 'metaphorical truth' is itself metaphor, still offers an account of the second kind. In his view our aim in speaking metaphorically is quite different from that of (literally) stating some truth, since what metaphors achieve is 'not propositional in character' ('What metaphors mean'; in. Platts (ed.), p.252): they make us *see* one thing *as* another.

Goodman gives an account of the first type; and he regards metaphor as typically a transitional phase in the generation of new literal meaning. 'Metaphor', he says, 'is a matter of teaching an old word new tricks – of applying an old label in a new way' (*Languages of Art*, p.69). But 'As time goes on, the history may fade and the two uses tend to achieve equality and independence. . . the residue is a pair of literal uses – mere ambiguity instead of metaphor' (ibid., p.71).

John Searle holds that 'in metaphorical utterances what the speaker means differs from what he says' (*Expression and Meaning*, p.81). Accordingly he believes that the problem of metaphor 'is a special case. . . of the problem of how it is possible to say one thing and mean something else' (ibid., p.76). His theory develops H.P. Grice's idea that figures of speech are varieties of 'conversational implicature' whereby speakers flout certain 'maxims' of conversation (such as 'Be informative') at the level of what they say, so as to imply something without explicitly stating it (cf. Grice, 'Logic and conversation'). Their theories are examples of the third approach.

Like Davidson, Max Black stresses that the aims of metaphor are different in kind from that of literal talk. He writes that we '*organize* our view of man' in saying 'Man is a wolf' (*Models and Metaphors*, p.41). But he also recognizes that 'metaphorical thought and utterance sometimes embody insight expressible in no other fashion', and that 'some metaphors enable us to see aspects of reality that the metaphor's production helps to constitute' ('More about metaphor'; in A. Ortony (ed.), pp.34–9). The world is necessarily seen from some perspective, and 'Some metaphors can create such a perspective' (ibid., p.40). This hints at an account, at least of some metaphors, of the fourth type.

Jacques Derrida's writings, and perhaps Heidegger's, tend to exemplify the fifth, radical view that there is no genuine problem of reconciling the metaphorical with the literal in the sense agreed by the other approaches.

3. *Literalist and tropist prejudices*

Differences in philosophical temperament reveal themselves especially sharply over the issue of metaphor; and before going further it is as well to mention two contrasting prejudices which are apt to colour perception of the problems in this area. One is 'anti-metaphor' and the other 'pro-metaphor'; and I shall label them respectively the prejudices of the *literalist* and of the *tropist*.

The literalist prejudice is broadly to the effect that the notion of literal meaning is in good order, and that if metaphor has a legitimate function it must lie either in the way it contributes to the formation of beliefs that can be stated literally or in something quite separate from the belief-stating function of language. Against this the tropist regards metaphor as fundamental to language, perhaps on the grounds that it displays the very same capacities to forge meaning that underlie language as a whole, and believes that our tendency to express ourselves metaphorically does not stand in need of restraint or discipline. For the tropist, literal meaning, to the extent that there is such a thing, is only a precipitate of spontaneous metaphorical talk. While literalists are disposed to blame the apparent conflict between the metaphorical and the literal upon misconceptions about metaphor (that metaphors can as such be true in the same sense as literal statements), tropists are disposed to blame this upon misconceptions about the literal (that literal meaning can be anything more than regimented metaphor).

Against the literalist prejudice I would stress that conflict between the literal and the metaphorical does not by itself show that there is any defect in metaphor. As every elementary textbook in logic points out, if an argument leads to an unacceptable conclusion the most we are entitled to conclude on this basis alone is that something is wrong with the argument's assumptions. It may be said that so long as we confine ourselves to literal statements we can reason in the confident knowledge that we can only draw true conclusions from true premisses. Since the intrusion of metaphor may disrupt this, is not metaphor to blame? This would only follow, however, if metaphor itself were no respecter of logic. And this may be doubted. Cannot I securely argue that if music is the food of love, and love is not time's fool, then music is the food of something that is not time's fool? If all my premisses are metaphorically true, cannot I be as confident as I would be if they were all literally true, that logic can only lead to true conclusions?

Giving an affirmative answer to this means, of course, adopting a liberal attitude towards mixed metaphor. If we can reason validly with metaphors, then if music is the food of love, and music is mobile architecture, then mobile architecture is the food of love. Again, if Socrates flattened his interlocutors with his questions, and his questions were razor sharp, then he flattened his interlocutors with something that is razor sharp. These conclusions are incongruous; but that is not a good reason to question the inferences. Incongruous conclusions can be drawn from literal premisses. (If the distant star is emitting violet light, and Aunt Augusta's curtains are violet, then the distant star is emitting light the same colour as Aunt Augusta's curtains.) It would also be wide of the mark to object that mixed metaphors are not merely incongruous but contain overtly incompatible elements. Oxymoron, where this occurs, is one of the figures of speech recognized by traditional rhetoric. There is no essential difference between mixed metaphor and oxymoron. For some purposes it may be wise to avoid certain mixed metaphors, perhaps because they are liable to be found amusing. But that does not show that the mixed metaphors are not true. Indeed, when we are amused by a mixed metaphor that is often because we can see how what is being said can be metaphorically true despite the presence of overtly contradictory elements. I conclude that those who believe the phenomenon of mixed metaphor shows that we cannot reason validly with metaphors have allowed their sense of logic to become impaired by a deficiency in their sense of humour.

Against the tropist prejudice the point ought to be made that even if metaphor does not pose the kind of problem literalists believe, that does not show that there is no problem with metaphor at all. Certainly metaphor has an affinity with the spontaneous process by which language comes into being. In both cases meaning can evolve without any explicit intention to create it. But language is not just a meaning-forming process. If metaphor is what creates meaning, and if in this sense all speech is to some degree metaphorical, it still has to be explained what the connection is between engaging in this meaning-forming activity and using language for the diverse purposes to which we put it. Even if there is a sense in which all language is metaphorical, there remains a distinction to be understood between the literal and the metaphorical use of words.

The positive lesson to be learned from tropists is that metaphor permeates language, and so any theory which regards it as peripheral is likely to be wrong. The positive point that literalists make is that it is obscure what someone is doing when speaking metaphorically in a way that it is not when he speaks literally, since in the latter case we can at least explain what he is doing by giving a literal interpretation of his words. My sympathies are with tropism; but it is not really a question of taking sides. It is only in a metaphorical sense, if at all, that all language is metaphorical. Language ability in fact comprises equally the capacity to use words literally and to use them metaphorically without either kind of use being explicable in terms of the other.

4. Dead and faint metaphor

We have good reason to be dissatisfied with the fifth answer listed in section 2 if this is proposed merely out of tropist prejudice; and if it is not this type of answer rapidly becomes a version of the fourth answer. So we need only consider the first four answers. In deciding between them, an important issue is how the different approaches handle the phenomena of dead and faint metaphors.

Dead metaphor abounds. And although 'the mouth of the river' may be as dead as any metaphor can be, the metaphorical potential of such dead metaphors can still be resurrected, as any reader of poetry knows. Faint metaphor is perhaps even more common than dead; so much so that we may hesitate before deciding whether 'The sea is menacing' is only metaphor or whether it is literally true in a secondary or extended sense of 'menacing'. Since the faintness or vividness of a metaphor is a matter of degree it is natural to equate dead metaphor with metaphor that has become so faint that it is imperceptible; and to equate the mortality of a metaphor with its propensity to fade. Metaphors do not fade, however, just by becoming familiar. That there is a familiar, well-established practice of describing some colours as 'hot' and some others as 'cold' does not show that this usage is literal.

Another phenomenon which any theory of metaphor ought to recognize is that our capacity to draw appropriate conclusions from what people say is not usually inhibited by their using words metaphorically. If someone says 'Do not go sailing today if the sea is menacing', it would be perverse to reply that since 'The sea is menacing' is metaphorical it is impossible to comply with the order. And we need not dispute that there is metaphor here to appreciate this. The point has nothing to do with the faintness or vividness of the metaphor. We know perfectly well what it is to comply with the advice, even if this is vividly metaphorical, to 'Remain calm if he tries to obliterate you with criticism'.

This poses an immediate problem for an account such as Davidson's which denies that metaphorical truths are true in the same sense as literal ones. The premisses I use in drawing a conclusion must all be assumed true in the same sense if the inference is to be valid. So on Davidson's view, when we are prepared to draw literal conclusions from apparently metaphorical premisses, as in the above examples, the premisses cannot really be metaphorical after all. Davidson's approach minimizes the extent of metaphor, confining it to isolated utterances.

But Davidson cannot simply ignore the broader phenomenon of metaphor where the metaphorical and the literal rub shoulders. This poses a problem for his approach similar to that posed by malapropisms. To accommodate metaphors we reason with he will have to accept that the literal meaning of a term can fluctuate depending on the intentions of speakers, the usage being metaphorical not in relation to the meaning the term currently has but in relation to a background meaning. But this introduces 'metaphorical meanings' under a new name: metaphorical meanings, like those of malapropisms, are among words' fluctuating meanings – metaphor is like deliberate malapropism. Moreover, this undermines the principle on which Davidson's account of metaphor was originally based, namely that we recognize it because what is said is too obviously false (or occasionally too obviously true) for us to take the speaker to be intending to assert a proposition. Certainly something is likely to be wrong with our interpretation of someone's words if according to it he is uttering obvious falsehoods. But there are now the two possibilities that he is either trying to achieve something 'not propositional in character' by his utterance, or he is using words in a special literal meaning. We need to be able to tell whether or not the utterance is being made with a non-propositional aim before we can decide whether to revise or merely to qualify our interpretation. Davidson's explanation of how we recognize metaphor presupposes, on the contrary, that we already understand sufficiently well the speaker's words.

Davidson's account recalls the theory of Ogden and Richards that language has distinct 'scientific' and 'emotive' functions (*The Meaning of Meaning*, pp.149–50). Ogden and Richards said that the 'best test of whether our use of words is essentially symbolic or emotive' is the relevance or irrelevance of its truth or falsity 'in the ordinary strict scientific sense' (ibid., p.150). But we cannot know the 'ordinary strict senses' of a speaker's words without knowing the kind of use to which he intends to put them. The two supposedly distinct functions of language are interwoven and inseparable. In his discussion of malapropisms Davidson concludes that we have to reject the idea of language as 'a clearly defined shared structure' which speakers use to interpret individual utterances ('A nice derangement of epitaphs'; in Le Pore (ed.), p.446). If the aim of interpretation is to discover *literal* meaning we should also conclude that there is no clearly defined objective for any such shared structure.

Nevertheless Davidson is surely right, as against Searle, to stress that when we speak metaphorically we do not mean something other than what we say. The gist of Searle's account is that when someone says metaphorically 'The ship ploughed the sea' he says indirectly something of the form 'The ship does. . . to the sea', and conveys that the space is to be filled by finding 'a relationship like ploughing' (*Expression and Meaning*, p.102). To the point that we cannot usually fill these spaces with an explicit and accurate literal paraphrase Searle replies unconvincingly that metaphors often serve precisely to 'plug such semantic gaps' (ibid., p.83). But even the most accurate literal paraphrase will be deficient. As Searle himself admits:

> The best we can do in the paraphrase is to reproduce the truth conditions of the metaphorical utterance, but the metaphorical

> utterance does more than just convey its truth conditions. It conveys its truth conditions by way of another semantic content, whose truth conditions are not part of the truth conditions of the utterance.
>
> (ibid., p.114–15)

But if metaphor is only an indirect means of making statements then so far as achieving that end is concerned there is no evident necessity for metaphor. If we have an aim in speaking metaphorically which is unavoidably lost in literal paraphrase, then metaphor is more than just an indirect means of making literal statements; and, if whatever can be said can be said literally, then, as Davidson insists, this distinctive element in metaphor is not something that is *said*.

Since Davidson and Searle both regard metaphor as a different usage of words from direct literal statement, their theories have similar problems in accounting for dead and faint metaphor. For both, the death of a metaphor has to be abrupt and the existence of faint metaphor is hard to acknowledge, because it is supposed that we understand an utterance metaphorically only because it is pointless to take it literally.

Goodman's theory may appear to have the advantage here. In regarding metaphor as an extension of previous linguistic habit he can explain how new literal meaning emerges gradually by claiming that metaphorical usage may only slowly cease to require support from the old habit. But this advantage is only apparent. Goodman, Davidson and Searle all agree that when I speak metaphorically I have a special intention to do so, even if they interpret the content of this intention differently – to convey something non-propositional; to say something indirectly; or to use words in an extended sense. Without such an intention I would, in their view, simply be making a mistake. Goodman needs such considerations anyway if he is to answer the point that metaphor does not fade and die just by becoming established – the influence of previous habit may endure just in the continuing intention to allude to that usage. So even if the intention to depart from and yet to reflect previous usage is one that utterances can realize in varying degrees, its presence or absence divides sharply the metaphorical from the literal.

The truth is that we recognize metaphor because we understand the words used: we do not first have to decide questions about metaphorical intentions but can infer the speaker's intentions from what we understand him to have said. Davidson makes just these points against the notion that there is (literally) a metaphorical meaning alongside literal meaning: we use the same understanding of words in interpreting metaphorical utterances as we do in interpreting literal ones; so the notion of a special metaphorical meaning is not explanatory. But he fails to appreciate that for the same reason it is not explanatory to credit the utterer of metaphor with a metaphorical aim different from that behind literal utterance. Davidson overlooks this because he infers that if there is no such thing as metaphorical meaning distinct from the literal then all meaning is literal meaning. But this does not follow. All that follows is that words have the same meaning when they are used metaphorically as when they are used literally. To conclude that all meaning is literal is to display literalist prejudice. This conclusion creates the bogus problem that in speaking metaphorically we must be speaking with an aim which the meanings of our words do not properly reflect.

5. Viewpoints and exponability

Meaning as such is neither literal nor metaphorical. Sometimes we use words literally and sometimes metaphorically; but the words have the same meaning in the two kinds of use. To get straight about dead and faint metaphor we need, however, to recognize that people often have another distinction in mind when describing utterances as metaphorical. Sometimes individual statements or utterances are described as metaphorical because it is difficult to spell out what follows from them. In this sense metaphor can be a matter of degree: an utterance is more metaphorical the more difficult it is to say fully what it entails, i.e. to paraphrase it.

If an utterance is metaphorical in this sense then it must have been made using some words metaphorically. And if the words used in making an utterance are all used literally then the utterance will not be metaphorical. But it is possible to make a non-metaphorical utterance despite the fact that some of the words are being used metaphorically. An utterance is non-metaphorical, in the sense just explained, even when it uses some words metaphorically, if various things clearly follow from the utterance but these differ from what follows in other contexts where the word is used literally. At one time an example of this might have been the sound engineer's use of the term 'white noise'. (This is not to be confused with the point that someone may be speaking metaphorically though he would still have been saying something true had he been speaking literally, as in 'No man is an island'.)

This double use of the term 'metaphorical' explains much of the confusion about faint metaphor. To avoid this it is wise to use another term when speaking of the distinction of degree that applies to utterances. Let us say that an utterance is *exponable* to the extent that we can spell out what it entails. Being exponable is a weaker notion than being *paraphrasable* if paraphrase has to give the meaning of the original without remainder. By contrast whether or not words are being used literally is not a matter of degree. (I borrow the term 'exponable' from Meredith's translation of Kant's *Critique of Judgement*. Here we read that an 'aesthetic idea may be called an *inexponable* representation of the imagination' (Pt.I, p.212).)

As I have been indicating, 'literal meaning' should not be confused with 'true meaning'. The notion of 'literal meaning' should be explained by reference to the use of words in making exponable utterances. Roughly, the literal meaning of a word depends upon the generalizations we can make about what follows when that word is used in making exponable utterances. More exactly, the literal meaning of a word, i.e. what follows when that word is being used literally, is what follows when the word is used in making those exponable utterances where the role of the context of utterance in determining this does not need specially to be taken into account. A word is being used literally in making an exponable utterance when what follows from this utterance accords with such generalizations. On the other hand, words are being used metaphorically in making an exponable utterance if we have to consider the case individually to tell what follows. (For this reason metaphors are bound to remain hopelessly intractable for anyone who wants a general explanation of the conditions under which they are true.) On this account, whether or not words are being used literally is not decided by any special intentions on the part of the speaker.

These distinctions explain how a metaphorical usage can remain metaphorical however familiar it becomes. A metaphorical usage only fades and dies if it becomes increasingly definite what follows when words are used in that way. Metaphor is mortal when it is liable to elaboration and accretion rather than when it can be literally paraphrased. And the transition from metaphor to new literal meaning can be gradual even though it is not a matter of degree whether or not words are being used literally, because a usage may only gradually develop to the point where it becomes sufficiently exponable to qualify as a case of ambiguity.

An analogy may help to make the distinctions just used more vivid.

If I am known to be speaking of their representations on a map when I say 'The river is to the right of the mountain' then my utterance does not leave their actual relationship undetermined in the way it would have done had it been made on the basis of visual observation from some unknown spot on the ground. Consider the class of utterances about the spatial relationships of geographical features. Let us say that an utterance is *spatially explicit* to the extent that we can infer actual spatial relationships from it without knowing the spatial context in which the utterance was made. And let us say that words are being *used cartographically*, as opposed to *observationally*, if the inferences we can make derive from them having been used with reference to a cartographic representation. We can now see that if an utterance is not spatially explicit then it must have been made using some words observationally; and if all the words in an utterance are used cartographically then the utterance is spatially explicit. But there is the further possibility that an utterance may to some degree be spatially explicit even though it uses some words observationally. For example, if I say, using 'to the right of' observationally, that 'The river is to the right of the mountain, and the mountain is to the right of the lake' it can be inferred that the mountain lies between the river and the lake. Here 'cartographic' corresponds to 'literal'; 'observational' to 'metaphorical'; and 'spatially explicit' to 'exponable'.

All this amounts to a version of the fourth approach to metaphor as outlined in section 2, according to which apparent conflict between literal and metaphorical uses of words is to be removed by relativizing the utterances to their appropriate viewpoint. Not that, in the terms of the analogy, these two ways of using words correspond directly to different positions from which spatial relationships can be described: rather the distinction between metaphorical and literal uses of words corresponds to the distinction between statements of spatial relationship that require relativization to the speaker's point of view and ones that do not because they refer to a map. This furnishes us with a metaphor for the literal: when we use words literally our words refer to our map of the world.

6. Art as metaphor

Since in describing works of art we typically use metaphor, it is not surprising that theories of what we are doing in verbally expressing our aesthetic responses reflect the various approaches to metaphor listed in section 2.

The first idea is that in describing a painting metaphorically as 'sad' or as 'spacious' we are using these terms ambiguously to refer now to special *aesthetic qualities* of the work. This is in keeping with the aims of some of the empiricist philosophers who tried to develop a theory of aesthetic taste. The second idea is that we are not asserting any propositions in uttering these descriptions but engaging in a different kind of activity, such as expressing an imaginative response. Scruton attempts a theory of this type. The third approach is that we are referring obliquely to certain features of the painting by describing it as 'sad' – qualities which hearers can pick out perhaps by recognizing some sort of analogy between the painting and sad people. This is consonant with the idea that the role of critical observations about works of art is not directly to describe them, but to draw attention to certain of their features. The fourth approach implements the proposed view of metaphor, maintaining that 'sad' can have the same meaning as applied to a painting or a person, but that to understand its use in the former case there is a sense in which it is necessary to grasp the particular 'viewpoint' of the speaker. Corresponding to the final approach to metaphor there is the notion that our capacity to describe both people and inanimate objects as 'sad' is simply an irresolvable paradox. This appears to be Adorno's view. He speaks of the 'unintelligibility' of works of art (Aesthetic Theory, p.173), stressing that art is a 'balancing act in which the impossible is realized' (ibid., p.155).

The problem, of course, assuming this final approach is to be rejected, is to explain the connection between the properties of works of art and such qualities as human sadness. Since this is a special case of the relation between the literal and the metaphorical, many writers are led astray by misconceptions about metaphor. Scruton, for example, supposes that if an utterance is not meant literally then it cannot be an assertion. He believes that such descriptions as 'The music is sad' have 'an unasserted character. Indeed, if he is to count as understanding them, the subject must show that he does not mean them literally' (*Art and Imagination*, p.122). He consequently maintains that 'The music is sad' is 'only superficially... of propositional form', and that we should adopt an 'affective' theory which attempts 'to describe aesthetic descriptions not in terms of a property of the object but in terms of an experience that it expresses' (ibid., p.54). The basis of this is Scruton's literalism. (Interpretation of a work of art 'is not primarily cognitive: it does not aim at literal truth' (ibid., p.122). 'A metaphor may be apt, appropriate, vivid or compelling, but it cannot be true' (*The Aesthetic*

Understanding, p.17). It is anyway only plausible to hold that a theory of imagination of the kind that Scruton is interested in can explain the connection between artistic and human sadness in cases where the work *represents* something sad. It can then be maintained that in describing the work as sad we express an act of imagination in which what is imagined, were it real, would be literally sad. But this does not apply to sadness in abstract paintings, or in general to sadness as an expressive quality of works of art. Here the problem of metaphor re-emerges, as Scruton finds when he is reduced to saying that 'the experience of hearing the sadness in the music is in some irreducible way analogous to hearing the expression of sadness – say, in another's voice' (*Art and Imagination*, p.127).

Naturally, the proposed theory of metaphor makes superfluous any special theory of aesthetic qualities or of the artistic imagination. The more interesting question, I think, is whether our understanding of the problems behind linguistic metaphor now helps us to turn 'Art is metaphor' into an explanatory metaphor as regards creative artistic abilities.

A good case can, I believe, be made out for maintaining that the distinction between using words literally and metaphorically has a parallel in that between exercising our productive capacities for utilitarian purposes and using them with aesthetic aims. For this to be so there has to be the potentiality for apparent conflict here analogous to that between the literal and metaphorical use of words. And this can indeed occur. There are, for example, ceramics and pieces of furniture which are not meant to be practical but to be contemplated aesthetically as examples of the potters' or cabinet makers' art. Since, however, some statements are both literally and metaphorically true, the parallel does not demand that the aesthetic evaluation of artefacts should actually conflict with their evaluation by utilitarian criteria. The analogy requires only that the aesthetic estimate of an artefact which also serves a utilitarian purpose cannot be explained merely by how well it serves that purpose. For this reason it is too brisk to try to resolve conflict of the present type by maintaining that a cup that is not meant to be drunk from or a chair that is not meant to be sat upon is only metaphorically a cup or a chair. We want a solution that applies also to cases where an artefact's aesthetic purpose does not exclude its utilitarian one.

To confirm the parallel we can trace aesthetic analogies to faint and dead metaphor. A statement is faintly metaphorical if it is exponable but uses some words metaphorically. Similarly, we can apply some artefacts, as intended, to utilitarian purposes while recognizing that their makers had used their productive skills aesthetically. (For example, there is tableware that is reserved for special occasions.) The fact that skills were so used need not prevent the artefact from having a utilitarian purpose any more than the fact that words were being used metaphorically need prevent us from drawing appropriate conclusions from what was said.

Finding an aesthetic parallel to dead metaphor does not necessarily mean allowing that things' aesthetic qualities wear off through familiarity. However dead a metaphor may be its metaphorical potential can be resurrected. An aesthetic parallel may simply be the sort of case where people become so accustomed to thinking of something in utilitarian terms that they cease to notice its aesthetic merit.

In regarding 'Art is metaphor' as possibly explanatory of artistic abilities we are no longer, when asking about aesthetic counterparts to the various approaches to metaphor, merely enquiring about their application to our descriptions of art. Corresponding to the first approach which equates metaphor with ambiguity, there is now the view that exercising productive skills aesthetically is only a different way of pursuing practical goals of the same type as we pursue in exercising other productive skills. Hedonists might well endorse this. By contrast, to belief in a distinct metaphorical truth there corresponds the belief that we have practical aims of a different character in addition to our ordinary ones. This is perhaps something Kant would have accepted. The third notion that in metaphor we convey something indirectly rather than explicitly has a parallel in the idea that we achieve in art practical aims of familiar sorts but in unobvious or indirect ways. Theories which allege that art has an educational or therapeutic function are in line with this.

To the final approach, according to which contradiction is a genuine feature of reality, there corresponds the view that our practical and aesthetic aims are irreconcilably opposed. This idea can be associated with existentialist styles of thought; for if our practical and aesthetic aims cannot be harmonized rationally, then our decisions as to how to act raise questions of bare commitment. On this view, the problem art poses is not a theoretical one but that of making tolerable to ourselves, through the attitudes we adopt, the fact that our aims are inescapably disparate. I assume that this is a position of last resort.

The question of interest is whether an aesthetic counterpart to the fourth approach to metaphor can give a more satisfactory account than the others of the relation between our aesthetic and practical aims. In developing that approach we distinguished two senses of 'metaphorical': *using words* metaphorically, and making utterances that are *inexponable*. This helped in understanding the position with faint metaphor. We can, I think, draw a corresponding distinction in the aesthetic case that will help us to understand why no clear-cut division is possible between aesthetic and utilitarian aims.

The counterpart to the notion of using words metaphorically as opposed to literally is, as I shall put it, that of using productive skills *aesthetically* as opposed to *practically*. When productive skills are exercised practically there is no special need, as there is when they are exercised aesthetically, to know the context – the 'viewpoint' – in order to understand what the maker is doing. And the notion of degree corresponding to the exponability of an utterance is *how utilitarian* an artefact is, i.e. the extent to which it is associated with a definite practice of use.

The parallel requires, and there is no difficulty about this, that if all the abilities the maker used in producing an artefact were used practically then the artefact is utilitarian; and that if the artefact is not utilitarian then some at least of these abilities were exercised aesthetically. Utterances made using words metaphorically though they are still true when taken literally (like 'No man is an island') can be compared to artefacts that display aesthetic skill, such as an elegant chair, without this interfering with their utilitarian purpose. If the parallel holds there should, however, be the further possibility, corresponding to exponable metaphor which is false taken literally, of producing a utilitarian artefact whose use, because some skills were being used aesthetically, differs from the one it would have had if the abilities used in making it had all been used practically. An example of this might be a folly constructed as a landmark and not for the purposes of habitation.

Adapting what was said about literal meaning, we can now regard the 'practical use' of a given type of artefact as roughly the utilitarian purpose which such artefacts generally have. More exactly, the practical use of an artefact, i.e. the kind of use it has when in producing it the maker exercises his productive skills practically, is the kind of use such artefacts have when they are utilitarian and (as is usually then the case) the manner the maker was exercising his skills does not need specially to be taken into account to tell what their purpose is. This means that the use of an artefact should not be identified with its *practical* use any more than the meanings of words should be identified with their *literal* meaning. In itself the purpose of making artefacts is neither practical nor aesthetic any more than meaning is itself either literal or metaphorical. These are two different and not necessarily incompatible ways of exercising our productive skills. Both types of purpose – aesthetic and practical – can co-exist and intermingle as do the literal and metaphorical elements in what we say.

7. Unanswered questions

The above account avoids a dualistic attitude to our aesthetic and practical aims by articulating the idea that aesthetic concerns permeate our productive activities in the same way that metaphor permeates language. Here it has the advantage over the other accounts; but it leaves many questions unanswered.

For one thing non-utilitarian artefacts would seem to constitute a much broader category than works of art. Objects of religious veneration or ones that have mythic significance within a society may have no utilitarian purpose in the present sense; but they are not on that account contemplated aesthetically in the manner that works of art are. And it is hardly enough in order to separate the former to point out that they are often linked with social practices and customs; for the same is true of works of art – we have, for example, such institutions as art galleries. The sense of 'aesthetic' just used in contrasting the aesthetic with the practical use of our skills is broader than the one we are trying to elucidate.

To put the point another way, the distinction between the metaphorical and the literal does not itself explain what it is to use language with aims that are aesthetic in the sense we want to understand. Although literary works often use metaphor, to compose such a work is not at all the same thing as to use words metaphorically. It would be were linguistic metaphor a particular manifestation of our creative artistic abilities. But the comparison is only metaphorical; and while this metaphor is to some degree explanatory its limitation is that it explains a more general phenomenon concerning our productive activities than the one we are primarily interested in.

A reply to this might be that the sense of metaphor we should be concentrating upon is that of *inexponability*. Certainly it is more plausible to equate the artistic use of language with making inexponable utterances rather than just with using words metaphorically; for it is in the sense of being inexponable that our verbal responses to works of art, including literary ones, are typically metaphorical. Furthermore, what we say here often appears to be *radically* inexponable, i.e. to resist altogether the kind of elaboration and development that would permit it to become an autonomous literal usage. The outlined theory of metaphor says nothing, however, to warrant the notion that some utterances are radically inexponable, nor to explain why we should have any special interest in experiences whose verbal expression would be in such utterances.

To remedy these shortcomings an account is needed of what we are aiming to achieve when we exercise productive skills aesthetically in the narrower sense that interests us. What constitutes success and failure in pursuing these aesthetic aims? So far as our utilitarian aims are concerned the criteria for this are clear enough. But no positive account of our aesthetic aims has been offered.

Although application of the outlined theory of metaphor to our productive skills does not by itself supply such an account, the present ideas may nevertheless contribute to obtaining one. We have seen that a central problem about aesthetic experience is the character of the experiential knowledge that constitutes it. After examining in the previous chapter some unsuccessful theories of this form of knowledge we began to entertain the idea that it may be possible to elucidate it by reference to the role metaphor plays in expressing it. The present discussion of metaphor has not addressed itself to this issue, but rather to the more basic question that any theory of metaphor should answer, namely why we do not contradict ourselves when we speak metaphorically. But the proposed theory of this has features that must encourage the idea that experiential knowledge and the phenomenon of metaphor are linked.

To understand a metaphor it is necessary, I have maintained, to know the particular 'viewpoint' of the speaker in a sense other than the way context enters into interpretation of a literal statement. An obvious and I think correct thought is that in the case of inexponable metaphor at least, knowledge of any such 'viewpoint' is something essentially experiential: we have in some sense ourselves to *experience* the speaker's viewpoint to have true understanding of any such metaphor. (Not, I would want to add, that there is no experiential dimension to understanding literal meaning; only here this is already taken account of in the literal interpretation of the speaker's words.) However, to develop this idea, and in particular to use it to explain how there can be such a thing as aesthetic satisfaction, we will first have to look into some difficult questions about the nature of pleasure and of cognition.

CHAPTER VII

Virtues and Indirect Pleasures

1. A problem about pleasure and 'completeness'

It is well for us to reflect upon the kind of explanation of aesthetic satisfaction we are now envisaging. Assuming that aesthetic enjoyment is pleasure in having some or other form of knowledge, there are serious general difficulties about this. We need some idea of how we propose to resolve them in order to know the right questions for our purposes to ask about cognition.

Were pleasure always like a sensation with which our actions are sometimes associated it ought to be possible to give a teleological explanation of aesthetic pleasure simply by considering its effects. We have seen that this is not possible; but this does not in itself constitute an obstacle since Aristotle's theory of pleasure, which suggests a different pattern of explanation, is so greatly superior to those which treat it like a sensation. Aristotle's idea is that pleasure is a way of experiencing our own actions: we experience true pleasure when the action in question is 'perfect' or 'complete'. This perfection is the *formal* cause of the pleasure. Explaining pleasure by reference to such formal causes connects in its own way with teleological questions because an activity is 'perfect' when it achieves its aims or purposes.

There is, it is true, the problem that we apparently cannot give a direct, explicit account of the formal cause of aesthetic pleasure, since what makes an experience aesthetically enjoyable cannot be put into words. I have suggested that this might be overcome by developing a theory of experiential knowledge. There is, however, a further difficulty. Aesthetically pleasurable activities are ones of perceiving and apprehending things in various ways. Directly to apply here Aristotle's theory it has to be shown that these activities have aims whose fulfilment explains the pleasure. But Aristotle himself described these cognitive activities as 'complete' in themselves in the very sense that is supposed to explain what it is for pleasure to 'complete' an activity. ('The act of seeing is regarded as complete at any moment of its duration. . . . Now pleasure also seems to be of this nature. . . . For this reason pleasure is not a process' (*Nicomachean Ethics*, trans. J.A.K. Thomson, Bk.X, Ch.iv, p.318).) If, as Aristotle claims, pleasure is a 'supervening perfection' experienced when an activity is complete, it ought to follow that cognitive acts are pleasant as such. He admits the difficulty when he suggests shortly after the passage just quoted that fatigue may explain why we do not feel pleasure continuously.

A better conclusion, perhaps, would be that only processes can be experienced pleasurably and that cognition is never pleasant as such. The choice Aristotle faces is either to regard his account of pleasure as not directly applicable to cognitive activities, or to apply it by seeking to maintain that although all such activities are complete some are, so to speak, more complete than others.

However, Aristotle believes in any case that there are many pleasures to which his theory does not apply directly but which require indirect explanation. There are, for example, harmful and restorative pleasures. Aristotle reconciles his theory with the existence of these by appealing to such factors as impairment of our faculties and the entrenchment of bad habits (ibid, Bk.VII). He also acknowledges that some pleasures are incidental; he says, for example, that it is not the sight of a deer or a wild goat that pleases a lion but the prospect of a meal (ibid., III, x). Perhaps aesthetic pleasures can be similarly explained as restorative and incidental pleasures. This appears to be Aristotle's own view when he lists miscellaneous benefits that 'music' can bring – educative, cathartic and for relaxation (Politics, VIII, vii).

At this point Aristotle appears to be adopting the first of the above alternatives, i.e. to be denying that we really enjoy aesthetic experiences for their own sake. Any such theory is, of course, inevitably philistine, though such theories can vary in how gross their philistinism is. On the other hand, in his account of the activities that constitute happiness Aristotle pursues the second alternative. He maintains here that some cognitive activities have special attributes that make possible a direct and peculiarly satisfying pleasure in them. These are not, however, the sorts of cognitive activity associated with the arts, but ones of purely intellectual contemplation. Thus when Aristotle ventures a non-philistine account of cognitive enjoyment he becomes iconoclastic. He accepts that it is possible to enjoy some cognitive experiences for their own sake; but he excludes from this the entire sphere of sense perception. For Aristotle, true beauty is purely intellectual.

I am adopting a broadly Aristotelian view of pleasure in the sense of regarding pleasure as a felt quality of an activity which indicates that the activity's aim is apparently satisfied. The problem we confront, if we are to develop a theory that is neither philistine nor iconoclastic, is to explain how cognition itself can have an aim satisfiable not merely, as Aristotle believed, in intellectual contemplation but in cognitive acts more generally, including perception. The easier course, certainly, is the philistine one of resorting to an indirect explanation of aesthetic pleasures.

A variety of such indirect explanations suggest themselves; but a feature which the most plausible of them share is the idea that aesthetic pleasure has to do with the acquisition of *virtues* in the sense of *desirable habits* whether of character or of thought.

2. *Cognitive virtues*

Aristotle's theory of how we acquire *moral* virtues – virtues of character – gives an elegant indirect explanation of the pleasurableness of some actions.

Aristotle believes that we experience the desirability of things quasi-perceptually in finding them pleasant: ('. . . to experience pleasure and pain is to be active with the perceptive mean in relation to good or bad as such'; *De Anima*, trans. H. Lawson-Tancred, III, viii.) As with sense perception, it is possible for these experiences to be delusive. Indeed, Aristotle believes they often are until we have acquired the moral virtues of finding the right sorts of things pleasant and painful: ('. . . it is the things that seem valuable and pleasant to the good man that are really such' (*Nicomachean Ethics*, X, vi, p.327).)

Now, Aristotle maintains that 'Anything that we have to learn to do we learn by the actual doing of it' (ibid., II, i, p.91); and so, in particular, virtuous habits are only acquired by actually performing relevant virtuous acts. Since the possessor of a virtue derives pleasure from exercising it, the learning process, though it may not be pleasant at first, must become so if it is to succeed. This point can be extended. If a virtue, once acquired, will wither unless it is practised regularly, then some actions may serve the purpose of sustaining the virtuous disposition; and they will be found pleasant if they succeed in doing this. The pleasantness of these actions will thus have an indirect explanation in the desirability of possessing habits of finding the right sorts of things pleasant.

In general, a virtue for Aristotle is simply an excellence that makes something good at its function (ibid., II, vi). It ought therefore to be possible to apply this notion to other habits besides those of moral character, for example to habits of thought. Aristotle does indeed discuss various 'intellectual' virtues, such as prudence and wisdom, as well as the moral ones; but he gives a different and far less coherent account of them. He contrasts intellectual with moral virtues saying that the former owe their inception and growth 'chiefly to instruction' rather than to habit (ibid., II, i, p.91). He seems to overlook the possibility of there being cognitive virtues which resemble the moral ones more closely. It is reasonable to suppose that we understand the world using learned systems of beliefs, and that some of these systems serve this purpose better than others. So there should be scope to apply here the general notion of a virtue, the excellences now in question being those that enable such systems to perform well the function of making the world understandable – properties like coherence, depth and simplicity. It is as plausible as in the moral case to say that it is through practice that we learn these cognitive virtues, i.e. that we learn to prefer systems which have these virtues – and thus which tend to be good at their function – by practice in using systems that actually possess them. There is no evident obstacle to holding that in this respect learning these cognitive virtues is like acquiring the moral virtues.

Clearly this could have an important bearing on aesthetics if aesthetic experience is cognitive experience in which cognitive virtues are exercised. And this is a plausible assumption. Do not we admire in works of art the very same features of coherence and depth, strength and simplicity as we admire in theories? If so, and if cognitive virtues resemble the moral ones in requiring regular exercise, cannot we explain the phenomenon of aesthetic satisfaction by saying that we admire these works because we have learned the cognitive virtues while at the same time this admiration serves to sustain us in these virtues? After our discussion of metaphor it is not a very convincing objection that a painting, a piece of music, and a system of beliefs cannot all be coherent, simple, etc. *in the same sense*. Even if works of art only possess these virtues metaphorically that is not a good reason for denying that in recognizing them here we are exercising the same capacities as we do in recognizing them elsewhere.

Although Goodman does not explicitly endorse an account of this type, he perhaps verges on doing so when he says that aesthetic experience is 'judged by standards of cognitive efficiency' (*Languages of Art*, p.262), especially considering he holds that scientists are primarily concerned in their theories with such quasi-aesthetic merits as simplicity and scope (*Ways of Worldmaking*, p.18; cf. *Languages of Art*, Ch.6, section 7). Some of Collingwood's ideas could also support in a different way the notion that art's role is to instil cognitive virtues. The virtue (he does not so describe it) he is primarily concerned with is a form of truthfulness which is supposed to relate directly to consciousness – a fundamental truthfulness about our emotions, not truthfulness in the sense opposed to deliberate lying (*Principles of Art*, p.288). Collingwood believes that all our actions express emotions, but there is a constant danger of consciousness becoming corrupted. He speaks of art as a 'medicine for the worst disease of mind, the corruption of consciousness' (ibid., p.336). If this means that our general capacity to recognize truthfulness in actions – recognition of which is important to our broader welfare – is reflected in and sustained by our capacity to recognize it in art, then his theory is in keeping with the outlined view that aesthetic pleasure is pleasure in exercising a cognitive virtue.

3. A pragmatic theory of beauty

The earlier theories that tried to link art directly with a practical purpose stumbled over the point that this purpose has somehow to be internal to the experience of art. Enjoying art is enjoying certain cognitive experiences. And there are aesthetic criteria for the appropriateness of this enjoyment. If this enjoyment serves a direct practical purpose this must be attained in experiencing aesthetic enjoyment that is appropriate by aesthetic criteria. Theories which claim that art is valuable for therapy, instruction, recreation and the like all suffer from the weakness that there is no very clear connection between something's being good art and its serving any of these functions. These theories in fact only describe some of art's incidental uses. The inference is that if art brings direct practical benefit then enjoyment that is aesthetically appropriate must be something good in itself. But this conclusion sets us on the route to an aestheticism which subsumes our other practical goals under that of experiencing true beauty.

The idea of a cognitive virtue neatly circumvents this. Thinkers are prompted to ask about the purpose of art because pleasure which is not pleasure in something desirable is at best gratuitous. Unless we abandon altogether use of aesthetic criteria in evaluating art, this means that good art, as judged by these criteria, must be desirable in itself. But we can now see that it does not follow that it has to be desirable in a moral sense. It is desirable to develop cognitive virtues in one's thinking not because this is a morally good thing to do, but because it enhances one's capacity to achieve one's practical goals whatever these might be. Previously it was thought that 'desirable in itself' must mean 'desirable for its own sake alone'; but we can now interpret it as meaning 'desirable irrespective of one's specific practical goals'.

It has become a commonplace that through art we can enlarge and develop our capacities – to notice things, for imaginative insight and the like. What is needed to round this view out, to explain why the capacities in question are of general interest and importance, is to maintain that the capacities whose development is central to good art are the cognitive virtues. This is to concur with Plato's association of art with education, though not with his belief that its role lies specifically in moral education.

A difficulty Plato failed to resolve is how the experience of beauty serves its educative function, namely, as he saw it, to enable us to appreciate beauty in yet higher forms. Hence the need he saw for censorship. Plotinus's aestheticism makes a bold attempt at solving this difficulty. But it is easy, drawing again upon Aristotle's ideas, to give a more straightforward account of how the cognitive virtues develop and the role which art may have in this.

Aristotle believes that 'the pleasure proper to an activity intensifies it' (*Nicomachean Ethics*, X, v, p.322), i.e. roughly, that people become better at activities they enjoy doing. This is really a corollary of his view that we develop virtuous habits by exercising them. In that case good habits must have a tendency to reinforce themselves. We become better at any virtuous activity by actually performing it; and the pleasure we derive from this encourages us to continue performing the activity, and to perform it again, and so to become still better at it. Applying this to the enjoyment of art, there is no difficulty, if this is enjoyment in exercising cognitive virtues, in seeing how exposure to good art will encourage development of artistic appreciation and thereby contribute to art's educative purpose. Nothing corresponding to Plato's censorship is needed here provided that among the art people encounter there is enough that is good.

If beauty is taken to be the general term we use in commending things that exhibit cognitive virtues, then the present theory may appropriately be termed a pragmatic theory of beauty. Pragmatic theories of truth seek to understand it as the feature our beliefs need to possess if they are to serve us well in achieving our practical goals. In the present theory beauty is similarly understood as a feature of our belief systems that enables them to serve well their purposes, including of course helping us in our practical goals. The theory explains why we should have a desire for beauty by relating beauty to our practical goals but without putting it on the same level. Our desire for beauty is a desire for effective means by which to achieve our various goals; and it can be satisfied independently of pursuing any particular such goals.

Interestingly, this type of theory was foreshadowed in Hutcheson's *Inquiry*. Having identified beauty with 'uniformity amidst variety', Hutcheson recognizes that there is beauty where 'one *Theorem* contains a great Multitude of Corollarys', and 'in the knowledge of some great *Principles*, or universal *Forces*, from which innumerable Effects do flow' (*Inquiry*, pp.33–4). This prompts him, when he ponders why the deity should have endowed us with a sense of beauty, to stress the value to us, as creatures of limited understanding and power, of knowledge of universal theorems and causes (ibid., p.98). The sense of beauty would, he says, conflict with reason and interest 'if *irregular Objects, particular Truths* and *Operations* pleased us' (ibid., p.101). It is a short step to explaining our capacity to recognize true beauty as the capacity to recognize general items of knowledge that are useful to us.

Hutcheson saw it as a mark of providence that we possess a sense of beauty that meets our practical needs. Were explanation required of the effectiveness of our sense of beauty most modern writers would prefer one in terms of evolutionary adaptation. But it is not evident that any such explanation is needed. For it is not necessary to think that a beautiful theory is more likely to yield truths than an ugly one. A beautiful theory – one that exhibits the cognitive virtues – may just be one that is well adapted to the thought processes of human beings: it may, in short, simply be one that is easy and convenient for us to use. If beauty and truth are both desirable attributes in a theory, that is not necessarily because truth is beautiful, but may only be because there are two aspects to how well a theory works: whether it gives the right results, and whether it is easy to manipulate. No doubt the sense of beauty has evolved; but there is no evident need over and above this to explain why it should have so evolved that our practical needs are better met by beautiful than ugly theories.

Few, perhaps, would insist on there being a sharp distinction between the uses to which a theory may be put and the features internal to it which make it beautiful or ugly. After all, one of the primary uses of a theory is to explain and to understand events; and features internal to it influence how well we consider that it accomplishes this task. Indeed, according to Goodman, truth is often secondary to explanation as a scientific objective. Most scientific laws, he remarks, are 'sweeping Procrustean simplifications' (*Ways of Worldmaking*, p.121). The scientist 'seeks system, simplicity, scope; and when satisfied on these scores he tailors truth to fit' (ibid., p.18).

Having made these qualifications it has to be admitted that it is no longer clear quite independently what functions the cognitive virtues are supposed to help a theory to accomplish. But this need not undermine the claim that simplicity, etc. are virtues of a theory in the sense explained. For it is no more possible to say independently what purposes a possessor of the *moral* virtues can achieve especially well. It is easy to tell whether or not an artefact, like a knife or a hammer, is good at its function; and there is, perhaps, little difficulty in the concept of a flourishing animal. But for a human being a 'good life' is partially constituted by awareness of the aspects of desirable behaviour that make it desirable. So if we are modelling an account of the cognitive virtues on the moral ones, it is not a convincing objection that we have to refer back to these virtues to explain the functions of a theory which they help it to perform.

Nevertheless the analogy with the moral virtues is, I think, unsound. The analogy exploits an ambiguity in the notion of a virtue – as an acquired habit of performing actions of a kind that serve well some function, or as an attribute of the actions so performed. We describe both people and conduct as virtuous, conduct being virtuous if anyone who is in the habit of performing such actions possesses a virtue. By 'cognitive virtues' it is proper, then, sometimes to mean the habits of so thinking that one's thoughts perform well the functions of thinking, and sometimes the features of our thoughts that enable them to perform well these functions. But the analogy gives no warrant for supposing that we are exercising cognitive virtues in recognizing that, in the latter sense, a system of thought exhibits cognitive virtues. It is not enough in order to acquire a moral virtue that one merely *recognize* that certain actions are virtuous: one must actually *perform* such actions. It is not an objection to the pragmatic theory of beauty that it is only metaphorical that works of art possess the same cognitive virtues as theories, but it is an objection that it does not explain how recognizing these works as possessing these virtues can itself be an exercise of the virtuous habits.

If recognizing that something exhibits cognitive virtues itself exercises these virtues, then, since there is pleasure in exercising a virtue, recognizing this is bound to be pleasurable. But this, of course, is a distinctive feature of beauty: one cannot perceive beauty without delighting in it. We have thus got ourselves into the position of trying to explain our capacity to appreciate beauty by an assumption to the effect that we have recognitional capacities that already possess one of the very features we want to explain. The difficulty has only been postponed.

This does not mean that there are no cognitive virtues or that works of art cannot display them. It shows rather that the order of explanation has been the wrong way around. Simplicity, coherence and the like are virtues in a theory; but these should be understood as *aesthetic* properties. Attempts to characterize them as if they were formal properties of theories can have only limited success. What we are referring to here are experientially known attributes – ones whose presence can only be detected through actual understanding of the theory. This is why recognizing where the cognitive virtues are exhibited itself demands exercise of the virtuous cognitive habits. The result is that it is necessary to understand how aesthetic pleasure is possible *before* we can explain what it is for simplicity and depth, strength and coherence to be virtues in a theory.

4. Art as recreation

We concluded that aesthetic pleasure cannot be explained by reference to any immediate practical benefits because the evaluation of art according to practical criteria would have to square with its evaluation by internal aesthetic ones. If, alternatively, we try to connect aesthetic criteria with cognitive virtues, it is problematic how we can be assumed to be exercising these virtues merely in contemplating works of art.

Perhaps the solution to this is to deny that there are, in the sense assumed hitherto, internal aesthetic criteria for evaluating art. Perhaps we should be more thoroughgoing in thinking of the purpose of art as something external to our experiences in apprehending it. Our error, it may be said, has been a misguided belief in artistic autonomy. Instead we should recognize that art is unintelligible unless placed in its social context – in the same way as is true, for example, of participation in recreational games. Obviously it would be absurd to try to explain why people play games just by reference to the games' rules. The rules of recreational games are to a degree arbitrary because up to a point these do not matter provided the participants agree on them and enter into the right spirit. It is not the rules themselves that matter but what people are doing in following them. To explain the latter it is necessary to refer to the social value of recreational games, specifically to their value in promoting amicable relations among the participants. It can be argued that what people are doing in appreciating art is something analogously external: what we are here enjoying is the activity in the course of which the appreciation of art takes place.

Indeed art is often actually assimilated to the class of recreational activities. Kenny invites this view when, having recognized a class of actions that are simply 'done for pleasure', he cites as 'typical examples' such activities as 'the taking of a holiday, the playing of a game, the pursuit of a hobby, the watching of a spectacle, the production of a work of art' (*Action, Emotion and Will*, p.145). The problem of explaining aesthetic enjoyment and our interest in art would then become part of the more general problem of explaining recreational activities. Clearly this view has some plausibility. To say that something is a good work of art but nobody likes it is absurd. But it is also absurd to say that something is a good game but nobody enjoys playing it. Are not the two cases alike? The phenomenon of humour might be considered an intermediate case. It is nonsense to say that something is a good joke but nobody finds it funny. Obviously humour plays a large part in many recreational activities. However, appreciating a joke also has a cognitive dimension, and so bears an affinity to aesthetic enjoyment. A formula for good jokes is as impossible as one for beautiful paintings.

What, then, is the general pattern of explanation for recreational activities? There is little difficulty in applying to some of these the Aristotelian ideas sketched earlier about the acquisition and preservation of virtuous habits. Let us take it that amiability is a social virtue and that recreational games provide the opportunity to exercise it. The situation here can readily be regarded as one where a virtue reinforces itself. In general, a game succeeds in its social role provided the participants play it in the right spirit, their intention to do so being an initial manifestation of the amiable disposition which the game intends to promote. We were unable satisfactorily to explain beauty as a *cognitive* virtue because it is obscure how we can be exercising this virtue just in contemplating theories or works of art. But it is easy to see that recreational games give opportunities for exercising social virtues.

Kenny believes nevertheless that there is a general difficulty in explaining enjoyment in recreational activities. 'There must', he says, 'be some criterion for success in φing *other than* enjoyment if we are to explain enjoying φing in terms of φing successfully' (ibid., p.146). But if pleasure is itself the criterion for success in recreational activities there cannot, Kenny believes, be an independent basis for the explanation: 'once we give such a criterion, then our account of enjoyment seems plainly false: one can enjoy painting a bad picture and derive pleasure from a game that one loses' (ibid., p.146).

If what we have been saying about virtuous habits is sound then Kenny is mistaken here. The existence of learning activities designed to inculcate the right habits shows that we need not be prevented from explaining why an activity is pleasurable by the point that pleasure is necessary to the activity's success. Nor, because there can be false pleasures, does the possibility of deriving pleasure from an action which is unsuccessful according to the proposed explanation necessarily refute the explanation, provided it appears to the agent that his action is successful. This possibility reflects the quasi-perceptual character of pleasure. And false pleasure may survive the knowledge that it is false rather as an optical illusion may remain effective even when measurement exposes it.

Kenny's difficulty comes from supposing not merely that pleasure is necessary to the success of recreational activities but that it is the sole criterion of their success. This is at odds, certainly, with the generally accepted view that these activities often help to restore and sustain desirable mental dispositions. But perhaps there is a subclass of recreational activities that are engaged in purely for pleasure. Explaining these would indeed pose the problem Kenny describes. Judging from his discussion of what constitutes a good wine, Kenny's proposed solution is essentially the same as Hume's regarding the 'standard of taste', i.e. that a good wine – one that is truly pleasant to drink – is one that those with discriminating palates find pleasant, powers of discrimination being testable independently of enjoyment (ibid., pp.149–59).

It has to be said that even assuming such a criterion is valid it is only in a restricted sense that its existence explains pleasure in wines. It can be used to explain why someone does or does not enjoy a particular wine in terms of his powers of discrimination: it does nothing to explain why we should have the capacity to enjoy wines. But there is no reason to pay attention to expert preferences unless some purpose is achieved when the experts agree. Without this Kenny's view is tantamount to holding that we enjoy some entirely gratuitous forms of pleasure, though of course given that such pleasures exist social purposes might be served by, for example, showing willingness to provide guests with the opportunity to indulge these pleasures.

It is doubtful that there are any such entirely gratuitous forms of pleasure. The wine case cannot be taken as a serious example in view of the physiological functions of drinking. Expert preferences alone cannot decide that a wine is good to drink; it first has to be assumed that the wine is not poisonous. But even if there are gratuitous pleasures, this cannot help much in trying to understand art and aesthetic enjoyment. While it might be explanatory to assimilate art to those recreational activities that instil desirable dispositions, it is hardly explanatory to group art along with a class of supposedly gratuitous pleasures.

What, then, of the possibility of explaining aesthetic pleasure along the lines sketched for explaining enjoyment in recreational games, namely as enjoyment in the exercise of social or moral virtues? If a framework of social practices surrounds art, as it does games, then there should be no obstacle to identifying its purpose with inculcating those social virtues which this framework of practices provides the opportunity to exercise.

The difficulty with this is that although art is often associated with social practices, these do not appear to be as definite as those surrounding games, and so the connection between art and its alleged social role is correspondingly tenuous. Broadly, there are two responses open to a defender of this approach: either to identify a central artistic purpose, regarding other purposes as peripheral to or distortions of this true purpose; or to maintain that the comparison with games does not depend upon identifying a prior purpose that art serves. The first response means assigning to art a more specific function than is immediately obvious; the second means crediting artistic social practices with a capacity to create their own purposes.

5. The 'institutional' theory of art

Many recent writers have emphasized the social and 'institutional' character of art. Wollheim, for instance, asserts that 'Art is, in Wittgenstein's sense, a form of life' (*Art and its Objects*, p.104), meaning by this that works of art and the experiences with which they are associated are inseparable from a complex of habits, skills and practices. This implies, he says, that 'we should not think that there is something which we call the artistic impulse or intention, and which can be identified quite independently of and prior to the institutions of art' (ibid., p.105).

A natural thought, if art is inseparable from a social, institutional framework, is that it has purposes which can only be realized within this framework and so can only be understood by reference to it. This does not follow however. Consider motorized transport. There are elaborate presuppositions behind an intention to take a journey by motor vehicle. But these do not have to be mentioned in stating the purpose of such a journey. The means of transport may only be that – a means to an independently intelligible end. If the institutional framework of art has a deeper significance it must somehow be *constitutive* of art's purpose, not merely a channel through which purposes of the kind we have in art can be attained. For a defender of the game comparison, whether art has a central purpose or can serve multifarious purposes depends largely on whether or not artistic institutions are constitutive of art's purpose. If they are then art can assume different purposes as its institutions evolve. If they are not then it is proper to ask if the institutions are effective in helping us to attain art's antecedent purposes.

The question whether artistic institutions are constitutive of *art* is not, then, the same as the question whether they are constitutive of art's *purpose*. George Dickie fails, I believe, to distinguish these questions in his 'institutional analysis' of art. He is impressed by the Dada phenomenon of ready-mades. Dadaism, he claims, 'reveals the institutional essence of art' (*Art and the Aesthetic*, p.32), because it shows that status as a work of art is something conferred upon artefacts by people acting on behalf of the 'artworld', which is an institution in the sense of 'an established practice' (ibid., p.31).

Dickie appears to believe that since the decisions of the artworld determine which things are works of art, we can explain what art is by analysing its institutional character. The confusion here can be brought out by comparing a similar one Searle makes when contrasting *constitutive* with *regulative* rules (*Speech Acts*, Ch.2, section 5). The latter are supposed to 'regulate a pre-existing activity', in the way, for example, rules of etiquette regulate eating behaviour. But the former 'constitute (and also regulate) an activity the existence of which is logically dependent on the rules' (ibid., p.34). Searle's favourite examples here are the rules of games like chess or football; he also cites voting as an example of behaviour that needs the backing of constitutive rules. But regulating a pre-existing activity is not incompatible with constituting a new one. Whether a rule is regulative or constitutive is generally a matter of how the rule is regarded. Rules of etiquette, for example, may be regulative in relation to eating; but they are constitutive in relation to polite behaviour within the relevant social group. The rules of football are constitutive when it comes to scoring a goal; but they can regulate otherwise uncoordinated play with a ball. Again, the constitutive rules behind voting are regulative in relation to the process of determining political leadership. Once this point is accepted the project of explaining activities just by analysing relevant 'constitutive rules' loses credibility. Unless it can be shown that the function of the rules is *exclusively* constitutive there will be a level at which they are regulative; and to understand the rules it will be necessary to understand the actions they regulate and how they regulate them.

Returning to Dickie, the point is that an institutional framework may well be constitutive so far as the existence of art is concerned, and yet be regulative in relation to the purposes that art serves. Compare the situation with decision-making about the rules of a recreational game. Once formulated such rules can be put to many kinds of use. For example, the aims of professional sportsmen are not the same as those of amateurs. But the original purpose of the rules was to regulate play so as to make it more effective in its recreational function. If art's social dimension is really like that of games, it should be sought in the first instance at the level of the activities artistic institutions regulate, not among activities which their existence helps to constitute. It is for this reason, if I follow him, that Wollheim, while emphasizing that art has '"institutional" characteristics', does not accept the 'institutional theory' of art (Art and its Objects, p. 166).

On this understanding, comparing artistic institutions to those that surround games means identifying an underlying purpose art serves notwithstanding that these institutions may be constitutive in relation to a range of other activities. What can this purpose be? The purpose of ordinary games, I suggested, is to promote social virtues; but the institutions of art as we know them are not in any clear sense concerned to provide opportunities to exercise these virtues. Indeed if we believe that the underlying purpose of art is to promote social virtues, there would seem to be grounds for concluding with Tolstoy that art as we know it has lost its true purpose and become corrupt. This could be explained in terms of the possibilities artistic institutions create for new forms of activity. The present state of the 'artworld' might be compared to one where people have no true interest in games but use them only to bet on the outcome. Again, there is the idea that art is a vehicle by which a cultural elite exerts its authority, so that what the admirers of art are really enjoying, though they may not be aware of this, is their eligibility for membership of a socially superior group (cf. Charles Harrison, *Modern Art and Modernism*, pp.63–4).

The alternative is to take a more favourable view of the potential of artistic institutions to create new forms of activity, maintaining that art has positive purposes of its own in these activities rather as professional sport has its own aims. But what are these purposes? Professional sport exists because many games can provide an enjoyable spectacle. The element of taking sides does of course add zest to this; but the spectacle has first to be able to hold viewers' attention. And the explanation for this lies chiefly in our capacity to derive aesthetic enjoyment from, for example, the way a stroke is played. It would be circular, then, to try to explain how art can give aesthetic satisfaction by comparing its institutional framework to, say, the governing body of a sport. The decisions of such a body presuppose capacities for the form of enjoyment we are trying to explain.

There is, in fact, often an aesthetic aspect not merely to pleasure in the spectacle of a game but to our pleasure in participating in ordinary recreational games. Naturally there is no scope to exercise social virtues in games of solitaire. One of the reasons why games serve their social purpose is that they provide an opportunity for shared aesthetic enjoyment. Hence there is undoubtedly an affinity between art and play. But while this makes it natural to compare the two it prevents the comparison from being explanatory. It could only explain art were it possible to relate art to an independent purpose such as many recreational activities have; but doing that would almost certainly mean regarding artistic institutions as we know them as corrupt.

In view of these points some care is needed over the notion that humour can unite the recreational with the aesthetic. Amusement, like aesthetic enjoyment, is a form of cognitive enjoyment; and we can find things funny without sharing the joke. But this does not mean that amusement, like enjoyment of solitaire, is a species of aesthetic response. (Scruton takes a different view; cf. *The Aesthetic Understanding*, Ch.12.) For humour does, I think, have a definite underlying purpose, namely to encourage the right attitude to mishaps and failures. The proper object of laughter is unimportant mishap: it is proper to laugh if someone slips on a banana skin – but only if they do not hurt themselves. Since humour has a proper object, it is possible to have a warped or cruel sense of humour. Clearly it is of value to have one that is properly developed – we are better able to surmount difficulties if we can see the funny side of things. Creatures like ourselves who can anticipate danger benefit from a sense of humour; and its proper development is related to such virtues as fortitude. Amusement, then, is a form of cognitive enjoyment; but an indirect one. It is enjoyment of cognitive acts in which there is opportunity to exercise desirable dispositions of character.

So indirect forms of cognitive enjoyment are certainly possible: humour is the prime example. If we want to picture aesthetic experience as cognitive experience in the course of which we exercise certain virtues, then perhaps the best such account would be one in which the virtues in question are not identified with the cognitive virtues, as earlier, but rather with the sorts that a properly developed sense of humour exemplifies. But unless we are prepared to take a philistine view with all its consequences, aesthetic enjoyment unlike humour is a direct, non-adventitious form of cognitive enjoyment. This difference is not blurred by the undoubted fact that it is possible, besides being amused by them, to enjoy good jokes aesthetically. We can derive two distinct forms of enjoyment from a joke as easily as we can admire aesthetically an artefact which is also enjoyable to use in its utilitarian purpose.

6. Cognitive pleasure: Aristotle on happiness

This brings us to the question of how it might be possible to take direct pleasure in activities of the kind Aristotle describes as 'complete' in themselves, i.e. various kinds of cognitive apprehension. As mentioned, Aristotle believes this is possible; but only for a narrow range of cognitive acts which are, so to speak, 'complete' to an exceptional degree.

His view is to the effect that cognition (the intellect) has its own *internal* aim which we achieve when we contemplate a good theory. The contingent truth of a thought or perception can never, he believes, explain why cognition is pleasant in itself. If we derive pleasure from awareness of a contingent truth our pleasure is not in the awareness as such but rather in the prospects and opportunities which the truth suggests to us, as with the lion's delight in the sight of a deer. But the situation is different, Aristotle believes, where *necessary* truth is concerned. He maintains that we appreciate for its own sake contemplating demonstrations of 'universal and necessary' truths from intuitively known first principles. Indeed he holds that this is the only activity that can be appreciated entirely for its own sake (*Nicomachean Ethics*, VI, vi-vii; and X, vii), and that for this reason true happiness consists in intellectual contemplation. Here the intellect, which 'is in the fullest sense the man', achieves its highest aim (ibid., X, vii, p.331).

This conception of happiness is so narrow and austere that it is easy to agree that something must be wrong with it: we want a broader notion than Aristotle allows of appreciating things for their own sake – one that can include such things as the love of beauty and the cultivation of friendship. It is less easy to say where exactly Aristotle errs.

One reason why Aristotle limits this notion to intellectual contemplation is that he regards happiness as peculiarly self-sufficient. He takes it that true happiness must consist in activities that have no preconditions beyond the necessities of life (ibid., X, vii), perhaps because if happiness depended upon anything more specific it would not, as Aristotle wants to regard it, be something we have the power to achieve if we are free enough to achieve anything. But activities vary enormously in how demanding their preconditions are. Intellectual contemplation may lie at one extreme, as an activity which can be practised in the widest variety of personal circumstances; but there is a whole spectrum of cases beyond. If Aristotle's point were only that contemplation is the form least vulnerable to circumstances that happiness can take, then we could easily suggest a broader conception of happiness, either by allowing it to take a range of secondary forms or by adopting a less sanguine view of our capacities to attain it.

But Aristotle's point goes further. When he describes a morally virtuous life as 'happy in a secondary degree' this is not merely because moral virtues depend upon the opportunity to exercise them (e.g. a man can only display bravery in the face of danger), but 'because activities in accordance with [moral virtue] are human' (ibid., X, viii, p.331), whereas intellectual activity is the 'divine' element in us (ibid., X, vii). This expresses figuratively the point that even apart from the question of its preconditions intellectual contemplation is pleasurable in itself in a stronger sense than virtuous conduct. The virtues are desirable as necessary means to attaining our true aims. But delight in contemplation, Aristotle believes, is truly intrinsic: this is the only form of pleasure possible for a divine being who lacks altogether the wants and needs characteristic of human beings. Pleasure in a *process*, in Aristotle's sense, such as eating, is related to the outcome of that process; and the activity is pleasant because its outcome makes good some deficiency. So if there are any activities that are pleasing just by themselves, irrespective altogether of wants or needs, then these cannot be processes. They must be of the inherently complete kind, i.e. cognitive activities. Aristotle's belief that we are capable of positive pleasures in this sense expresses his conviction that human beings have a goal of happiness over and above that of animal contentment.

Certainly, in identifying happiness with contemplation, Aristotle may be accused of overlooking that a much wider range of activities can be satisfying for their own sake. But he is not to be challenged merely by questioning his belief that happiness is self-sufficient. This is not a mere assumption. Aristotle holds that the only activity that is intrinsically satisfying in the strong sense is contemplation since this is the only form that pleasure in a complete activity can take. Hence, if happiness consists in intrinsically satisfying activities, happiness is self-sufficient because contemplation is. To challenge Aristotle's conception of happiness it must be shown either that he misunderstands the relation between happiness and activities that are intrinsically satisfying or that pleasure in complete activities can take a wider range of forms than he supposes.

The latter is the course we are interested in pursuing. But, assuming a broadly Aristotelian view of pleasure, cognitive pleasure that is direct, i.e. not adventitious like the virtuous pleasures we have been discussing, ought to be explicable in terms of attaining aims internal to cognition. And the goal of rational explanation – of recognizing relationships between truths – appears to be the only candidate for such an aim. The moral to be learned from the one-sidedness of Aristotle's view of happiness is that if we want a non-iconoclastic aesthetic theory, which allows aesthetic enjoyment to take perceptual as well as abstract forms, it will be necessary to identify an unobvious aim internal to cognition to explain this.

CHAPTER VIII

The Aim Behind Perception

1. Cognition and the essentially metaphorical

Effectively the choice before us is either to think of art as a recreational game whose rules tend to be abused by the 'artworld', or to pursue the question of what an internal, unobvious aim of cognition might be – an aim besides that of rational explanation. The other possibilities are to identify true beauty exclusively with intellectual contemplation as Aristotle does, or to dismiss aesthetic enjoyment as inexplicable and gratuitous. Unless we can understand how the potentiality for aesthetic enjoyment is inherent in our ordinary perceptual capacities we will eventually be driven into one of these other positions.

A number of considerations support the idea that aesthetic enjoyment reflects something general about our cognitive capacities. Although animals enjoy sensory pleasures like the taste of food, we do not think of them as experiencing aesthetic enjoyment as we do. A capacity for this depends on having conceptual or intellectual and not merely sensory cognition of things, i.e. having an *understanding* of what one is experiencing. Some phenomenological writers even detect an *empathic* element in ordinary perceptual experience. For example, Merleau-Ponty says that 'to look at an object is to inhabit it' (*Phenomenology of Perception*, trans. C. Smith, p.68). Lipps himself spoke of 'natural empathy' asserting that 'things as grasped by the understanding are necessarily permeated by my activity' ('Empathy and Aesthetic Pleasure'; in Aschenbrenner and Isenberg (eds), p.409).

This last remark has a bearing on *intentionality*, i.e. the phenomenon whereby when I think about them I have in my mind all manner of things – tables, galaxies, numbers, other people's thoughts, etc. Intentionality can seem an absurd and self-contradictory phenomenon as easily as empathy can. Carritt objects that 'The *Einfühlung* theory attempts to solve the paradoxes of the aesthetic problem by offering us bare contradictions, which it endeavours to render palatable by metaphor' (*The Theory of Beauty*, p.190). But just the same complaint can be brought against the idea that something non-mental and wholly distinct from me, like Mount Everest, is somehow in my mind when I direct my thoughts upon it. The absurdity in the notion that I feel my way empathically into things when I experience aesthetic enjoyment is not very different from the absurdity of holding that things distinct from me are within my mind when I think about them. Maybe, as Lipps appears to be suggesting, the two phenomena are connected. In that case, assuming that empathy is a distinctive element in at least some kinds of aesthetic experience, the nature of this experience ought to be explicable by an adequate theory of cognition.

Against this there is not only the difficulty that there is no obvious candidate for an internal cognitive aim that might explain aesthetic enjoyment: in view of Aristotle's doctrine that cognitive activities are not processes it is hard even to understand what it can mean to say that individual such activities have an aim.

In its negative aspect Aristotle's doctrine is easy enough. It means that thinking and perceiving do not in themselves have any outcome or end result separable from these activities. There are no thoughts and perceptions without thinking and perceiving. But this point becomes difficult when we consider its implications for a positive account of these activities. Abilities are differentiated by what people achieve in exercising them. And we tend to picture what is thereby achieved as making a difference to the pre-existing state of affairs, and thus as some kind of end result or outcome of the activity. But if thinking and perceiving are not processes then apparently this general pattern for explaining abilities does not apply to them. We must, however, be able to do better than just to say that what we are doing in thinking and perceiving is something internal to these activities. If nothing else what we are doing here is related to what we are thinking about or perceiving.

One response would simply be to insist that cognition is a process after all; for example one of 'synthesizing intuitions', as Kant thought. But cognition yields knowledge; and what is known is true. So were cognition literally a process, then known truth would literally be the outcome or end result of our cognitive activities. And how can this be so without truth itself being their outcome? Just this has of course been held by many idealist philosophers. But it does not harmonize well with the identification of aesthetic enjoyment with cognitive enjoyment. Were cognition literally a knowledge-yielding process then cognitive enjoyment ought to be pleasure in gaining knowledge. But, *pace* Hegel, the beautiful is not the same thing as the eminently cognizable. Kant realized this, though he never overcame in his aesthetic theory the problem that his previous account of how our cognitive faculties produce conceptual knowledge leaves no room for a different manner of exercising them which is pleasurable on its own account. If aesthetic enjoyment is cognitive enjoyment, then its existence shows that his idealist account of cognition is defective.

Another response is to concede that cognitive activities are not literally processes, but to grant them as such only a *notional* or *virtual* existence. The idea might be that our descriptions of people as having specific beliefs and perceptions are only part of the framework we use in describing and explaining their behaviour: they are not on the same level as direct descriptions of what they do any more than, say, the dating of events is on the same level as stating what happened. If I understand him, Quine advocates a view of this sort. It gives, perhaps, a fair account of the beliefs and mental states of animals. But we are looking for a theory of cognition which can explain aesthetic enjoyment; and in this respect a Quinean view fares no better than a frankly idealistic one. If the aim behind thoughts and perceptions is really the explanatory aim of those who ascribe them, then we are still without a plausible candidate for a cognitive aim behind aesthetic enjoyment.

We picture abilities as being aimed at producing an outcome, differences in abilities being reflected in differences in the outcome produced. No other way of picturing them is feasible. But anything that literally produces an outcome is a process; and cognition, we have said, is not a process but is complete in itself.

Idealism is the natural consequence of regarding cognition as literally a process. Idealists try to evade the absurdities of their position by saying that it is of course only metaphorical that we 'create' the world we experience. The moral, I think, is that we ought to take seriously from the outset the idea that cognition is only understandable in essentially metaphorical terms, i.e. it has to be understood as if it were a process, but in this respect our account is bound to be metaphorical. This feature does not mean the account is only provisional or in need of supplementation. Rather the account will illustrate, as against literalists, the deep truth of metaphor. Metaphor lies at the basis of cognition not because the first language is metaphorical, but because the use of certain metaphors is necessary in explaining what cognition is. What we say in describing both cognition and aesthetic experience is *essentially* metaphorical in the sense that it could not constitute an autonomous literal usage. If we resist this, conceiving cognition as literally a process, we will still in the end find it necessary to resort to metaphor to escape the absurdities of idealism.

It has, in any case, seemed to many writers that the need Carritt deprecates to use metaphor in characterizing empathy is in fact common to descriptions of many kinds of mental activity. For example, Geach, who equates analogy with metaphor, asserts that many psychological concepts are 'irreducibly analogous' (*Mental Acts*, pp.76–8). Again, Searle denies that a visual experience can be literally yellow (*Intentionality*, p.38). And the point is often made that we rely extensively on manipulative metaphors in characterizing thought and perception. Thus we speak of *grasping* ideas, having a *firm grip* on an argument and *holding* thoughts in one's mind. Polanyi, for one, speaks of a 'kinship between the process of tool-using and that of perceiving as a whole' (*Meaning*, p.37). He claims that 'the way we know in perception' is like the way my '*subsidiary* awareness of my feelings in my hand [when I use a hammer] is merged with my *focal awareness* of my driving the nail' (ibid., p.33).

These comparisons of Polanyi's are, I think, apt. There is, I believe, important truth in the idea that perception contains something metaphorically like one's kinaesthetic experiences in performing ordinary physical actions. The theory to be sketched will attempt to show the respect in which our understanding of cognition needs to be metaphorical by explaining the essential role of kinaesthetic metaphors in describing cognitive processes.

2. The intellect and the senses: Aristotle

Animals have senses. A dog can see that the rabbit is in the field. But we can also *perceive* this. We *understand* what we are seeing: unlike animals, we *conceptualize* what we sense. Since we sometimes derive aesthetic enjoyment from perceiving things but animals do not, we take it, from sensing them, it is natural to suppose that the capacity for this enjoyment derives from the role of the intellect, i.e. from the faculty by which we understand sense experiences.

Descartes took it that the peculiarities of perception (along with other mental activities) show that perceptions as such are special objects which reveal themselves completely to the knowing mind. The sceptical difficulties he consequently found himself in suggest that this account neglects the ordinary sense in which perceptions generally result from interactions with things perceived. Even if perceiving is unlike ordinary activities in being complete in itself, perception is still in some sense an outcome of the way things affect us through our sense organs.

Aristotle does not deny this. He distinguishes two kinds of 'affection' (*De Anima*, II, v). Perception is not a process because it is not the kind of affection where a thing changes from one actual state to another: it is the kind of affection where something potential becomes actual. This reflects the positive meaning Aristotle gives to his notion of 'completeness' or 'perfection'. A thing is more complete the more fully it is actually what it can be potentially. Perceptions are complete in themselves because having them consists not in change from one actual state to another but rather in our perceptual faculties becoming actually something they were previously only potentially.

This account suits the principle basic to Aristotle's metaphysics that *form* is what actualizes things, i.e. makes them what they are. Form actualizes matter making it whatever it actually is, matter on its own being a mere potentiality to receive form. If perceiving actualizes our perceptual faculties then perceptions also consist in the reception of form. This gives Aristotle a ready account of how a perception relates to what is perceived: the connection lies in the identity of the form which actualizes both the matter of the perceived object and our perceptual faculties. The latter 'becomes like and is such as what acts on it' (ibid., 418a, trans. Lawson-Tancred); 'the sense is the recipient of the perceived forms without their matter' (ibid., 424a).

A limitation of this account is that it fails to make clear how our perceptions differ from the sensory knowledge of things that animals have. This is a key question in view of the suggestion that we could explain the capacity for aesthetic enjoyment if we understood more fully how these differ. But Aristotle's answer is unsatisfactory. Sometimes he suggests that the senses and the intellect differ in what is knowable through each – the particular or the universal. At other times he suggests that the intellect and the senses know the same objects – the forms of things – but know them in a different way (e.g. ibid., III, iv, 429b). Apparently he believes that intellectual and sensory modes of knowing forms correspond respectively to knowledge of universals and knowledge of particulars (i.e. to knowledge of the major and minor premisses of a syllogism). What we want to understand, however, to explain how perceiving differs from sensing, are different modes of knowing the same *particulars*.

Aristotle fails to give an account of this. When he distinguishes intellectual from sensory knowledge of forms, e.g. distinguishing knowing 'what it is to be straight' from knowing merely 'the straight' (ibid., 429b), this bears upon the difference between *thinking* and perceiving rather than between perceiving and sensing. For intellectual knowledge of forms is knowledge of them wholly apart from matter. ('In the way. . . that things are separable from matter in general, in that way are the things connected with the intellect' (ibid., 429b).) In thinking this knowledge we have 'images', which are 'like sense-data but without matter' (ibid., III, viii, 432a), this form of knowledge not being concerned with particular things at all (ibid., 417b). No doubt Aristotle was prompted into this view by the thought that having a form in the senses, unlike having it in the intellect, is equivalent to believing that some particular thing has it. Unless having a form in a sense faculty amounted to believing that some particular thing is white, sweet, etc., an animal's senses would be no use to it.

According to Aristotle, then, we receive through our senses the forms of particular things, and through the intellect we know these forms in a further way which yields knowledge of 'universals'. But this only explains how in sensing things we have the opportunity also to exercise intellectual capacities: it does not explain how these two capacities co-operate in perception. To understand how our perceptions differ from the sensory experiences of animals we need to understand our capacity to think about the particulars we sense. Having separated the objects of intellectual and sensory knowledge there is now a problem in explaining how they are related when we think about what we are sensing.

From Aristotle's point of view, if a thought relates to specific particulars that apparently can only be because it is juxtaposed with sensory elements. It will be the relation of the thought to these that gives it reference to individual particulars. This doctrine has, of course, been held by many philosophers down to the present day. For example, Geach writes that 'The content of the judgment is always intelligible and conceptual. . . but an act of judgment performed in a particular sensory context may therefore be referred to particular sensible things' (*Mental Acts*, p.64). There is, it is true, assumed to be no difficulty in understanding how intellectual thought can relate to certain individual *images* – the images we have in thinking the thoughts. But these are not the particulars we are interested in when asking about the relation in perception of thought to individuals: we are interested in thought's relationship to the particulars we know through our senses, not to sense-data themselves. A question thus arises about how the 'particular sensory context' confers on a thought a relationship to the particulars we sense.

Russell's theory of descriptions claimed to answer this question. But the problem is really symptomatic of a broader failure to explain the fusion of the intellectual and the sensory in perception. There is a problem for Aristotle in how we can even think that our thoughts relate to particulars. My seeing something is supposed to consist in the actualization of my visual faculty by the same form as actualizes the seen object. Similarly, the forms of things known through the intellect are supposed to be present in the intellectual faculty. But a form must actualize our cognitive faculties in a different manner from the way it actualizes the things known, or my visual faculty would literally become white when I see something white, and my intellect would literally become a rabbit when I think of rabbits. Prompted by this consideration, Aquinas distinguished two different ways forms can be actualized: with *esse naturale* or with *esse intentionale*. As Geach explains this, 'what makes [something] to be a *sensation or thought* of an X rather than an actual X or an actual X-ness is that X here occurs in the special way called *esse intentionale* and not in the "ordinary" way called *esse naturale*' (*Three Philosophers*, p.95). But clearly what it is that makes the actualization of a form something 'natural' cannot itself be actualized in our minds without the natural not merely intentional thing existing within our minds. But I have to be able to think that a form is actualized naturally and not merely intentionally in order to think that what I am seeing is real and not merely imaginary. Dark thoughts about the unintelligibility of matter hardly constitute an adequate response to this point. The true implication is that the difference between thought and reality is unintelligible, so that I can never *think* about real things at all – except, perhaps, my own thoughts.

3. Further problems in understanding particulars

Russell's theory of descriptions may make the above conclusion palatable; but the problem has roots further back. Aristotle assumes, quite properly, that faculties are differentiated according to what they enable their possessors to do. Evidently there are such differences as between the senses and the intellect since we recognize that many creatures have the former but not the latter. Aristotle takes it, however, that cognitive faculties differ fundamentally in the *objects* known through them.

This is questionable. When discussing knowledge by acquaintance (Chapter 5, section 1) we saw that forms of knowledge can vary in their *objects*; in the *mode* of knowledge; and in their *source*. It is not in dispute that the intellect and senses are distinct sources of knowledge. But it should not be taken for granted that further explanation as to how they differ has to uncover differences in the objects known as opposed to differences in the mode of knowledge.

This should be fairly evident as regards the distinctions between *perceiving* something and merely *sensing* it as an animal might, and between *perceiving* something and *thinking* it. With each pair there are differences even when the objects of the knowledge are the same. Both truths and particulars can be either sensed or perceived; and both can be objects of thought. I perceive a rabbit; a dog sees it. I perceive that it is running; the dog sees that it is. And I can both think of the rabbit, and think that it is running. Yet sensing, perceiving and thinking are all different; for animals sense without perceiving, and we can think something without perceiving it.

The commonly accepted picture is of two basic cognitive capacities – the senses and the intellect – the former being exercised in perception and the latter both in perception and thought. Since, however, some thoughts are entirely general, the intellect appears to differ from the senses not only in making possible a different mode of knowledge of particulars but also in yielding knowledge whose objects are different from the particulars known through the senses.

One objection, certainly, to the idea that the senses and the intellect differ fundamentally in their objects – the one the theory of descriptions tries to circumvent – is that it is beyond the competence of either faculty to apprehend the relation between what is known through them. If, however, the intellectual is regarded as a non-sensory mode of knowing the particular, there is the problem why the intellect is not simply a further kind of sense. Among the senses there are obviously different modes of knowing the same object. One can both see and hear the same thing; and there are properties knowable through more than one sense, for example motion and shape can be both seen and felt. But were the intellect like an additional sense it would not be necessary to have ordinary sensory experience before the intellect can operate.

Aristotle explains why this is necessary by regarding the intellect as a capacity to know in another way whatever is already known through the senses: we know through our senses what things are; but through the intellect we know what it is for them to be what they are. But notice that this account not only fails to explain how it is possible to know particulars in both sensory and intellectual modes but also implicitly undermines the original conception of the senses as giving knowledge of particulars. If we can know intellectually whatever is knowable through the senses, and the intellect yields knowledge of forms not particulars, it follows that we do not know particulars through the senses either, but only forms. We said earlier that when a form is in the senses this is equivalent to knowing that some particular has this form. But it now appears that the sensory knowledge can only be that something or other has the form. Not merely, then, are particulars unintelligible, i.e. not the objects of intellectual knowledge, nor are they as such possible objects of sensory knowledge. *This* problem cannot be evaded along the lines of the theory of descriptions by regarding sensory experiences themselves as the ultimate particulars we know.

To escape these difficulties we need to understand how in perception a non-sensory mode of knowledge of particulars is fused with sensory knowledge and does not merely exist alongside it. In one way there is no difficulty in seeing how sensory and non-sensory knowledge can sometimes be so fused; for this is characteristic of knowledge of one's own actions. In performing an action I can both see what I am doing and experience my action inwardly. It is hard, however, to understand how this can be relevant to perception in general since only physical actions can literally be known simultaneously in both these ways.

Aristotle was, of course, well aware that we have a special inner knowledge of our own actions – and in particular that this gives craftsmen a special knowledge of the artefacts they make. When a carpenter makes a table he knows what makes it a table in a sense that an observer unskilled in carpentry cannot. Indeed, the meaning of *form* for Aristotle is largely governed by this analogy: the craftman's inner knowledge of artefacts would appear to be his model for intellectual knowledge of forms, i.e. for knowing what it is to be a table as opposed simply to being able to recognize tables. His notoriously obscure doctrine of the 'active' intellect which is supposed to have the capacity to bring all things about (*De Anima*, III, v), is probably intended as a reply to the objection that one can only literally know in this way things one has made or at least has the ability to make. Aristotle appears to believe that in some deeper sense, for which artefacts serve as an analogy, everything is related to our minds as something we could make. Not surprisingly many commentators have maintained, since only the divine creator could literally have this inner knowledge of everything, that this model requires that in our intellectual capacities we participate in the powers of the divine mind.

Be that as it may, the account does not overcome the objection that knowing what makes something in one's senses whatever it is, is, for Aristotle, knowledge of a form and not of a particular. If we can know anything we sense as if it were something we had made, and in making something we have interior knowledge of its form, then the forms of things, rather than the things themselves, must be what we know in our senses. (Aristotle admits that things themselves are not in our sense faculties when we cognize them, 'since, clearly, stone, for instance, is not in the soul' (ibid., III, viii, 431b).)

Nevertheless, the maker's knowledge of an artefact is an appropriate analogy for our intellectual knowledge of particular things. Aristotle's error, like that of idealist accounts of cognition, is to recognize too late, if indeed he does so at all, that the analogy is metaphorical. (This error comes out in his theory of the active intellect.) The analogy is appropriate because our inner knowledge of our actions – the knowledge that comes from so-called kinaesthetic sensations – does not exist alongside sensory knowledge but blends with it as inner and outer knowledge of the same thing. When Merleau-Ponty speaks of us as 'inhabiting' things we perceive, or Lipps of us as 'permeating' them with our activity, they make the point that this feature of knowledge of our actions is metaphorically present in perception. The problem is to reach an understanding of perception that can explain why such metaphors are appropriate. This will give the understanding of it we need for aesthetics.

4. The imagination as a pseudo-capacity

Through the right sort of theory of the imagination it is possible, I think, to secure the desired explanation of the appropriateness of describing cognitive processes using kinaesthetic metaphors.

The term 'imagination' has been applied to a very diverse range of capacities. At one extreme it means only the capacity to retain and perhaps to recall images. At the other it designates a capacity for inventive and creative insight. In between there is a sense of 'imagining' something more or less equivalent to supposing it to be true. There is also a sense where to imagine something is to engage in make-believe.

Further uses of the term include adverbial ones, as when we describe actions as having been performed imaginatively.

Thinkers have held very different attitudes to the imagination. Some, like Descartes, have regarded it as dangerously deceptive and consequently in need of control by our higher rational faculties. The Romantics, by contrast, saw it as a source of insight into nature more profound than reason. Again, the imagination has been thought of, for example by Hume and Kant, as one among our cognitive faculties, of little intrinsic interest perhaps, but as essential to cognition as a whole.

In a way all these attitudes are correct. The imagination in its basic sense, as an activity of spontaneously forming images, would not be a positive capacity at all. It would be like a propensity to hallucinate. A creature that had imagination in this sense but did not recognize its products for what they are would be liable to serious error. But in other senses imagination is positive. The verbal transmission of knowledge would be impossible unless we had imagination in the sense of a faculty of envisaging possibilities besides those taken to be actual. And if there is an imaginative element in the experience of beauty, then in this role it is evidently something positive.

It is not, I think, accidental that we group together these diverse mental activities; for they are related. In its basic sense the imagination would indeed be deceptive. By itself it would only be a pseudo-faculty, not a positive one. To become a genuine, positive capacity it needs to be understood and controlled by the intellect – though not in the manner Descartes envisaged. In being so understood the original imaginative faculty is transformed into, among other things, an element in perception. My view is that the imagination in its positive senses is a collection of capacities that result in various ways from the transforming effect of the intellect upon the original deceptive faculty.

The importance of this is the light it can throw reciprocally on the intellect, i.e. the capacity which differentiates perceptual from merely sensory experience. I suggest we can understand the intellect itself in terms of its basic role being that of transforming the original imaginative pseudo-faculty into a genuine one. This has consequences contrary to the tradition which tries to understand the intellect by referring to objects of knowledge peculiar to it – universals, concepts and the like. Instead I shall be interpreting intellectual knowledge, in the first instance, as having the same objects as that of the senses, but as knowing them in a different experiential mode.

This approach identifies an aim underlying intellectual cognition: that of so understanding the workings of the original false imaginative capacity that it is transformed into capacities that are no longer inherently deceptive. I hope to show that understanding of this aim will enable us to explain aesthetic satisfaction as cognitive enjoyment.

Such an explanation is feasible because there is more than one way this aim behind intellectual cognition can be achieved. What is before my mind when I now imagine things, whether in make-believe, recollection, or as an element in perception, is not inherently deceptive because I have intellectual capacities. Through these I know what these imagined things are in a way an animal does not know the things it senses. My knowledge of this may well be expressible in literal (exponable) statements about the things. This knowledge as to what something is corresponds to intellectual knowledge of the thing's *form*, as Aristotle understood this. But over and above this I may have an understanding of what is before my mind that is only expressible metaphorically (inexponably). In the next chapter I shall be advancing the thesis that occasionally when this occurs the aim behind cognition is achieved in such a way that one's experience has peculiarities of the sorts associated with aesthetic satisfaction. This theory connects the intellect at root with the kind of experiential knowledge involved in understanding metaphor.

The question to begin with is what a creature needs to be able to do to turn an imaginative capacity of the original deceptive kind into something positive or at any rate harmless. By chance it could happen that what the creature imagines is true. (A dog might dream that a rabbit is nearby when one actually is.) But this would not remove the problem with the false capacity, namely that the imaginer knows neither when it is exercising it, nor what it is doing when it does so. Without knowing either of these things the imaginer's experience would tend to be chaotic in proportion to how frequently it exercises the false capacity. The pseudo-capacity would disrupt its normal sensory capacities.

We can hardly say that the imaginer might render this pseudo-capacity harmless simply by learning to exercise it at will. For by hypothesis the capacity is spontaneous: it cannot be brought under voluntary control, at least not directly. Nor can we suppose that the imaginer might escape error simply by learning to detect when he is exercising the pseudo-capacity. By hypothesis there is nothing manifest when it is exercised to reveal this; hence there is no immediate basis for detecting when it is being exercised. But if the capacity cannot be brought under control in either of these ways how can it be made harmless?

An answer lies, I think, in there being senses in which one can know what one is doing that differ from *knowing that* one is doing something in particular. For example, there is a sense in which I can know what I am doing when I am tying a shoelace even if for some reason I do not do so successfully (e.g. the shoelace breaks). Our imaginations are no longer inherently deceptive because we know what we are doing when we perceive things or appear to be – not in the sense that we know straight away whether or not we are really perceiving them, but in the sense that we know what it is to be perceiving these things. This enables us, if the perceptual belief is mistaken and given suitable opportunity, to detect our error later even if there was nothing originally to reveal this.

5. Perception and kinaesthetic experience

As regards any ordinary physical action, I know what I am doing through kinaesthetic experiences. These experiences encompass *how* I experience what I am doing. Their presence differentiates actions from mere physical movements.

It is sometimes said that the difference between doing something deliberately or accidentally lies in whether or not the agent *intended* to do it. This has some plausibility for actions like dropping something. But if an intention to perform a given action is always something that could have been formulated before actually performing it, this criterion applies only to a limited range of actions. Many things we do involve skilful performance of learned abilities; and in such cases it is frequently impossible to specify one's actions in detail in advance of performing them. A pianist may be unable to say how a given passage should be fingered before actually playing it. This does not make the fingering he then uses merely accidental. In response to such considerations, Searle distinguishes 'prior intentions' from what he calls 'intentions in action', which he identifies with the 'experience of acting' (*Intentionality*, p. 91). But having allowed 'intentions in action' – which correspond to what I mean by 'kinaesthetic experiences' – the presence of these and not of prior intentions is what counts in separating genuine actions from accidental ones and from things that merely happen to us.

In our kinaesthetic experiences we experience certain things we do as actions of ours – as things we are able to do. This is why 'kinaesthetic sensations' are often rather elusive: for they are not sensations properly speaking at all. We do not know our actions through an inner sense since what we know here is not like a sense quality. Knowing what I am doing as something I am able to do involves knowing my capacities in respect of the specific action being performed. This is not knowledge of a general truth about the sorts of things I can do; it is experiential knowledge of the particular action. In this sense even animals that lack conceptual knowledge know what they are doing. And knowing this includes knowing potentialities along with knowing the actual. I know what I am doing as something I am able to do only if I know what doing this entails and what else I could go on to do.

My suggestion is that we can understand how the imagination loses its inherently deceptive character by considering imagining and sensing as if they were actions of ours like ordinary physical actions. Since ordinary actions are often quite spontaneous, not something we could have deliberated about, it is not a good objection that we cannot think out in advance how we are going to exercise this form of imagination. The point of the comparison is to regard perception (real or illusory) as if we had kinaesthetic experiences by which we know here what we are doing. With this the imagination ceases to be deceptive because knowing what one is doing in apparently perceiving something equips one to tell whether or not the perception is genuine for the same reason as knowing what one is doing in performing any ordinary action equips one to tell whether or not one succeeds. A lion hunting a deer knows what it is doing; and if it fails to capture it, it knows this because it knows what hunting a deer entails. Similarly, in apparently perceiving something we know what we are doing; and we can tell whether or not the perception is genuine because we know what is entailed in genuinely perceiving that thing.

The central difference between ordinary actions and perceptions is that in the former case a description of what someone has done can be perfectly accurate even if it turns out that he has no ability to do this. In practice we would only ask if, for instance, dropping something was a genuine action if we thought the agent could either have done this or, had he chosen, refrained from so doing. (The question would be pointless were he known to have inadvertently picked up something very hot.) But whether or not he has the ability we can still describe what he did as his dropping the thing. In the case of the imagination, however, a person who has developed a genuine ability to exercise it is not thereby able to do something which he may previously have done but only accidentally. In its original guise imagining is not merely something the person does involuntarily, so that a positive imaginative capacity is the ability to do that very thing but in a more controlled way. The imagination is originally a false capacity not just in the sense of not being a capacity, but in the sense that what is done through it is not something one could have a true ability to do. Unless the imagination were transformed by knowing what one is doing in exercising it, the only thing would be to hope it could somehow be eliminated. As I have said, when it is transformed it becomes, among other things, an aspect of our perceptual capacities.

This difference between ordinary activities and the imaginative/perceptual ones makes it metaphorical to speak of kinaesthetic experience in connection with the latter. It is thereby responsible for the peculiarities of intellectual cognition. In general an action has two components: what the agent does; and the fact that in doing this the agent knows what he is doing. Thus in knowing what he is doing an agent knows a necessary part of what makes his action the action it is. In general this is only a necessary part since, as we have said, a person can know what he is doing and yet for various reasons fail in fact to do it. But in the case of the imaginative activity there is not the same contrast between a person knowing what he is doing and what he actually does. The latter cannot be detached from the former. There is not in perception the further component, as there is in ordinary physical activities, of doing something that could be specified independently of one's having the ability to do it. This is why perception is not a 'process' but is 'complete' in itself. Our intellectual faculties are 'creative' in the sense that exercising them are types of activity different in kind from any that precede them. In this case if one knows what one is doing then one knows what one's action is.

The other side to this is that the notions of success and failure apply differently to cognitive activities as compared to ordinary ones. With the latter, performing them successfully, or unsuccessfully, simply means accomplishing, or failing to accomplish, what they entail, where any attempt to perform the action will produce one or other outcome. For example, a lion hunting a deer will either succeed or not succeed in capturing it. The lion may not know what its action is just by knowing what it is doing; but provided its senses are functioning properly it will be able to tell whether or not it succeeds in what it is trying to do. With a perception, by contrast, I know what my perception is just in having it; but the perceptual act does not itself accomplish, or fail to accomplish, what it entails – knowing what a perception is does not by itself answer the question whether it is real or illusory.

Nevertheless, the same distinction between success and failure as applied to other actions still applies to perceptions. Without this distinction we would succumb to the Cartesian illusion that we can perform infallible inner mental acts. But in the perceptual context the distinction gains a new significance. Here we know our action without remainder in knowing what we are doing; but this is offset by the point that success (or failure) in perception, in the sense of achieving (or failing to achieve) what the activity entails, is not, as with ordinary activities, something one knows merely in the course of engaging in it. In perception there is no gap between knowing what one is doing and knowing what one's action is: instead there is a gap between one's action and what one's action entails. Thus the concept of truth applies to perceptions.

The gap is bridged by the point that in knowing perceptions one knows what they entail despite not knowing thereby whether or not what they entail is actual. But how are we to conceive of this knowledge of what a perception entails? How, if it can exist independently of one's having the opportunity to exercise it, does it equip one, as I suggested, to tell whether or not the perception is genuine?

6. Productive skills and conceptual empathy

I said that we can tell whether perceptions are genuine on the same basis as we can tell whether an ordinary action has been successful, namely because we know what we are doing, which involves knowing what our action entails. This needs qualification in view of the differences just noted. The appropriate comparison is not with actions in general, but specifically with those in which we exercise productive skills. Because we know what our perceptions are merely in having them, we know the things we perceive as if metaphorically speaking they were things we had made.

Another way to see this is to note that the general form of error to which an imaginer is liable before his pseudo-capacity for imagination is transformed, though of course he could not put it like this himself, is to suppose that he can bring things about just by imagining them. It is false that he has any such capacity; and this is still literally false even when the transformation has been effected. What is then true is that by imagining things he can make them in his mind.

This last statement is *literally* true because of the meaning of 'mind'. But to understand this we need to see why the metaphors that give the notion of mind its meaning are appropriate. As I said, the appropriate metaphor in describing perception is comparison with the processes by which we make things. Metaphorically speaking we know things we perceive as things we can make in the way a potter knows pots. In looking at a pot, a potter understands what he sees – he can make it in his mind. This is confirmed by his practical abilities to make pots. Similarly, the perceiver's capacity to make what he perceives in his mind is manifested in his capacities explicitly to make these things: not to make them literally, of course, but to make them in words. The metaphor of language as a tool has, since Wittgenstein, become a commonplace. He, however, thought of it as a tool whose uses are irreducibly diverse; but I would maintain that it has an essential use in our capacity for actively making things in our minds. Essentially language is the means used by the imagination understood as an active capacity for envisaging and contemplating possibilities. Thus our intellectual faculties as manifested through language are 'creative' abilities not only in the sense noted earlier, namely that what is accomplished through them differs in kind from any preceding type of activity, but in the sense that metaphorically speaking they are abilities for making things.

Our capacity to tell whether or not a perception is genuine is like the ability of a competent potter to tell, if he can examine it closely enough, whether or not a pot is well made. The capacities one knows in perceiving something might alternatively be exercised in making that thing verbally – in saying what it is. This makes explicit what the perception entails. This verbalizable knowledge can be pictured as equipping us to tell, as experience unfolds, if the perception is genuine. But the capacities to tell if the perception is genuine and to say what it entails are really two different ways of exercising the same capacities in respect of the perception. And they are not the only ways. In verbally expounding what a perception entails we are using words literally; and this makes explicit what follows if the pèrception is genuine. So to be able to tell if perceptions are genuine we have to be able to use words literally. But this by no means exhausts our capacities to make explicit our knowledge of what perceptions are; for there is also knowledge that is expressed using metaphor. If we explain the notion of *form* as what one knows in knowing what makes a perceived thing what it is, then this ought now to be recognized as a more general notion than Aristotle's.

His notion of form can be identified with what one knows in knowing what makes something what it is where this knowledge is expressible using words literally. The more general notion is what is needed for the purposes of aesthetics.

What I have been saying endorses, with significant modifications, the ancient idea that intellectual knowledge of things is knowledge of what makes them what they are. It also vindicates, again with major qualifications, the idea of Lipps and others that there is an empathic element in ordinary conceptual experience. In a broad sense we are using empathic metaphors whenever we speak of ourselves as having kinaesthetic experiences of things other than our own physical actions. And, as Polanyi maintains, this is how we need to understand ordinary perceptual experiences even when the knowledge this experience yields is itself expressed literally. But it is a mistake to suppose, as many of those who are sympathetically disposed to this point imagine, that this demands an idealistic explanation. We should explain why cognition has to be understood as a process of making things not by appeal to idealistic conceptions but in terms of its only metaphorically being a process. Because of this one knows what makes a perception what it is merely in knowing what one is doing in having it: in knowing what one is here doing one therefore knows what one is perceiving as if it were something one had made. However, it remains true, as Lipps believed, that empathy in the sense that figures in aesthetic experience is not a peripheral addition to cognitive experience but a manifestation of a more general phenomenon intrinsic to intellectual cognition as a whole.

CHAPTER IX

Aesthetic Satisfaction

1. Peculiarities of aesthetic enjoyment

Tradition associates experience, the particular and the concrete with the senses, while associating our conceptual, intellectual faculties with generality, the abstract and with their own non-perceptual objects of knowledge – concepts, propositions and the like. A variant of this, trying to bring these faculties together, is to think of the intellect as arranging or synthesizing the material received through the senses.

It is impossible to understand aesthetic enjoyment, considered as enjoyment of experiential cognition, without modifying these conceptions. Without a broader notion of experience than the sensory no credible account can be given of our capacity to derive aesthetic enjoyment from theorems, explanations and many kinds of literature. Any type of thing, whether perceptible through the senses or graspable only in the mind, e.g. a mathematical proof, can be found beautiful. Even aesthetically enjoyable perceptual experiences are forms of experiential knowledge that depend upon the intellect. In all these cases the experiences are satisfying because of the way they meet the aim behind intellectual knowledge. But if the intellect deals with the abstract and the general, or the arrangement of sensory material for the purpose of intellectual knowledge, there is no reason why any knowledge of particulars should ever be satisfying. In that case, cognitive enjoyment ought, as Aristotle held, to be confined to knowing intellectually satisfying truths. This was clearly a problem as soon as Baumgarten introduced the term 'aesthetics' in the modern sense. He gave no good reason for believing that aesthetic (experiential) as opposed to logical (conceptual) knowledge has its own autonomous 'perfection'. His view that the senses are 'inferior' cognitive faculties that serve the 'superior' faculty of the intellect should mean that excellence at the sensory level consists only in contributing to excellence at the level of thought.

In the previous chapter, while accepting the distinction between sensory and intellectual faculties, I rejected the idea that knowledge of the particular is confined to the former. I maintained that we have experiential knowledge of particulars which is intellectual, this being comparable metaphorically to kinaesthetic experience of our own actions, specifically of actions of making things. The task before us is to use this account to explain the special character of the experiential knowledge we have in aesthetically enjoyable experiences. We shall find that this involves not only breaking the exclusive association of experience with the senses but also, conversely, accepting that our understanding of what makes things what they are is sometimes made explicit experientially rather than verbally. The functions traditionally divided between experience and thought in fact cut across them.

My general thesis is that aesthetic pleasure is direct, non-adventitious cognitive enjoyment. In the previous chapter I argued that the aim behind perception (intellectual cognition) is to transform an imaginative pseudo-capacity into a genuine one. This, I claim, makes it possible for a wide variety of cognitive activities to be enjoyable in themselves consistently with the Aristotelian idea that pleasure is to be explained by reference to the aims of the pleasurable activity. There is nothing, certainly, especially pleasurable about the routine way this aim is attained, namely in having the sort of knowledge about what one is perceiving that would be expressed verbally in a literal statement. Delight in this would only be adventitious delight in what is perceived. But the aim can exceptionally be attained in other ways, if for example one has an understanding of what one is perceiving that is verbally expressible only in metaphor. This can yield knowledge to which the distinction between the real and the imaginary does not apply. To defend my thesis I need to explain the forms that non-adventitious cognitive enjoyment can accordingly take, and to show that these exhibit the peculiarities we associate with aesthetic enjoyment.

These peculiarities can be classified as (a) *logical*; (b) *epistemological*; and (c) *phenomenological*.

(a) When someone enjoys doing something we can usually distinguish the activity he enjoys from his experiences in enjoying it – he could have engaged in the activity without finding it enjoyable. But since the enjoyed activity in aesthetic enjoyment is precisely one of having certain experiences, there is not in this case the same contrast as usual between enjoyed activity and enjoyable experience. At the same time, however, the experiences we find aesthetically enjoyable are intentional cognitive acts having their own intentional objects – things seen or heard, etc. So far as these are concerned, aesthetic enjoyment can have any type of object whatever. In one sense, then, the object of aesthetic enjoyment is always something of the same type – a cognitive experience of something; in another it can be any type of thing, namely what the experience is an experience of. Aesthetic enjoyment belongs to a logically special category of enjoyment in the sense that there is a different relationship here from elsewhere between the enjoyment and its object.

(b) Aesthetic enjoyment has the epistemological peculiarity of being *self-intimating*. With other activities one may only realize that they were enjoyable after the event. But if I derive aesthetic enjoyment from listening to a symphony I must be aware of this at the time. Thus we conceive of beauty as 'necessarily pleasurable' in the sense that one cannot experience beauty without being aware of one's delight. Aesthetically enjoyable experiences are always accompanied by a *feeling* of pleasure.

(c) Different forms of aesthetic enjoyment exhibit a variety of remarkable phenomenological features. Empathy is perhaps the most striking of these. Not that this feature is always conspicuously present when we enjoy things aesthetically. There may be little empathy in, for example, enjoying the abstract beauty of mathematics. But aesthetic enjoyment of perception is usually empathic. Here we sense the things perceived as exhibiting a quasi-organic unity and as somehow embodying the feelings we experience in perceiving this unity. A noteworthy point is that this embodiment of feeling is often perceived as giving a clarified insight into the feelings embodied. However, even when aesthetic enjoyment is abstract rather than empathic, it still tends to have phenomenological peculiarities. There is, for example, a distinctive sense of *rightness* about an elegant proof.

The idea that the experience of beauty is *intrinsically* pleasant can combine the logical and epistemological points just mentioned. To mean by so describing it that what is enjoyed is internal to the experience is to allude to the logical points. On the other hand, to mean by this that one is bound to delight in the experience of beauty is to make the point that aesthetic pleasure is self-intimating.

The logical point about the inseparability from aesthetic enjoyment of the enjoyed activity is responsible for the difficulties in explaining aesthetic pleasure, and as such is more fundamental than the epistemological point; but many writers have been more preoccupied with the latter. For example, Plato's idea that in experiencing true beauty we apprehend the good is an attempt to explain why beauty is intrinsically delightful in the epistemological sense. The same explanatory objective can also motivate the idea that in experiencing aesthetic pleasure we enjoy exercising a virtue in the sense of a desirable habit of thought or character.

Note, as this last kind of view shows, that there are forms of pleasure that are intrinsically satisfying in the epistemological but not the logical sense. If the experience of beauty is identified with aesthetic enjoyment, and this has the peculiarities just listed, then a philistine is anyone who denies that there are any forms of enjoyment with all these peculiarities. So it is possible to be a philistine while in one sense agreeing that there are intrinsically satisfying forms of experience. Because of the ambiguity in the notion of intrinsic pleasure, philistines may not always show themselves in their true colours.

Assuming we want a non-philistine theory, it is necessary, then, in defending the thesis that aesthetic pleasure is cognitive enjoyment, to show that this enjoyment does indeed possess these peculiarities. Up to a point we are already in a position to do this. For example, it can be said that the sense in which the object of this enjoyment is not detachable from the experience of the enjoyment is the same as that in which thoughts and perceptions are not detachable from activities of thinking and perceiving. Aesthetic enjoyment is not a means to an end but is complete in itself in the same sense as intellectual cognitive activities are not means to an end, i.e. are not processes, but are complete in themselves.

But this does not explain why cognitive enjoyment should be self-intimating. This is so only if one is bound to be aware of how any enjoyable cognitive activity is experienced; and it is not obvious that this must be the case.

Again, identifying aesthetic with cognitive enjoyment does not by itself explain its phenomenological peculiarities. This should be evident from the point that aesthetic experiences are diverse phenomenologically. To explain this an account is needed of the different forms cognitive enjoyment can take. I shall be maintaining that it can take two basic forms – empathic and abstract – though these can be combined in various ways.

2. Perceptual knowledge

Actions that are truly pleasant are so because the aim of the activity is achieved. Pleasures thus vary according to the activities found pleasant. Cognition produces knowledge. Hence cognitive pleasures should yield a form of knowledge – 'aesthetic knowledge' – which can be elucidated by reference to the manner in which cognitive abilities are here being exercised. Aesthetic knowledge is not, as Baumgarten believed, knowledge obtained through a specific aesthetic cognitive faculty.

Nor, of course, is aesthetic knowledge merely the verbal knowledge that something is beautiful or knowledge of the accuracy of any description of the beautiful object. One could know these on the word of a reliable informant without experiencing any aesthetic enjoyment. Aesthetic knowledge is experiential rather than verbal. But the distinction between experiential and verbal knowledge is hard to explain.

We have seen that at least three things can be meant by describing knowledge as 'experiential': that it has an experiential *source*, e.g. it is known through the senses; that what is known is known in an experiential *mode*, e.g. it is known perceptually as opposed to merely verbally; or that the knowledge has an experience as its *object*, i.e. it is actually about an experience. Obviously, aesthetic knowledge is not just knowledge that has experiences as its object – we often have knowledge about experiences without deriving any aesthetic pleasure from this. Nor is it knowledge that merely has a special source – the mode in which the knowledge is possessed is crucial. This is not however like another mode of perception; for perceptual knowledge has its own objects but any type of thing can be apprehended with aesthetic pleasure. The position would seem to be that in aesthetically enjoyable experiences we have knowledge that is experiential in a further sense beyond the above three. Here we have knowledge of our own experiences in a distinctive experiential mode. But what sense can we make of the idea of having experiential knowledge of our own experiences beyond merely having them?

We will not be able to answer this without first having an answer to the more basic question of how perceptual and verbal modes of knowledge differ. There is little difficulty, to be sure, in distinguishing our perceptual knowledge from the sensory knowledge that animals have. Our perceptual knowledge involves intellectual capacities that animals lack. When we perceive things we do not merely recognize them as animals do but have an understanding of them: we know what makes them what they are. This knowledge can be made explicit through our verbal capacities. But this does not help in distinguishing perceptual from verbal modes of knowledge. What is the difference and what is the connection between perceiving that something is the case and knowing it only because one has been told? It is hardly disputable that often the same item of knowledge could have had either a perceptual or verbal *source*. But why should this make any difference after the knowledge has been acquired to the mode in which it is possessed? If verbalizing the knowledge makes explicit what is known implicitly in having the perception, how can there be a positive respect in which knowing it perceptually differs from knowing it verbally?

This question tends to prompt two sorts of answer. One is that perceptual experience of a truth brings us directly into contact with it in a sense that a verbal report cannot, so that this experience, unlike that of understanding a report, by itself warrants the claim to know the truth. The other is that perception of a truth has a richness of content lost in any verbal description – a verbal report unavoidably abstracts from the perceptual experience.

These conceptions both raise many problems. They do not suffice to explain the difference between perceptual and verbal modes of knowledge. The first suggests that perceptual knowledge is knowledge where what is known does not extend beyond the boundaries of our experience of its truth. It is hard to make this requirement precise; but in any case when we say that we have seen something for ourselves rather than merely heard it reported we certainly do not usually mean that it has fallen within experience in this sense. (We would accept that the knowledge claim rests on further assumptions.)

It is also hard to formulate satisfactorily the idea that perception of a truth has a richer content than a description. Were this only a question of perception being finer textured than language then the discrepancy could be overcome or at least reduced by developing a more refined vocabulary. If, on the other hand, perception contains elements that no language, however refined, can communicate, then the difference between perceptual and verbal modes of knowledge lies in the former comprising, in addition to verbalizable knowledge, some knowledge whose *object* is not verbalizable. But how can a difference in *mode* of knowledge be explained by differences in *objects* of knowledge?

Conceivably a non-verbalizable knowledge of experiences – a kind involved in actually having them – might be a source of verbalizable knowledge. But even supposing that while actually perceiving the book on the table I have non-verbalizable knowledge of my perceptual experience, afterwards I know simply that the book was on the table. I may associate this statement with imagery, of course; but so might someone who had not perceived its truth. It cannot plausibly be claimed that perceptual and verbal modes of knowledge differ in that the former is associated with more vivid or definite imagery. Some people are good at visualizing things described to them; but that does not make their knowledge perceptual; and all imagery is indeterminate to some degree. There is of course the difference that what is known perceptually originally had its source in perception, and subsequent imagery may recall the perceptual experience. But this only means that present knowledge and imagery share a common source. This does not explain what persisting difference the origin of the imagery can make to the manner in which the perceptually acquired knowledge is known.

If there is a persisting difference between perceptually and verbally acquired knowledge consisting in having in the former case non-verbalizable knowledge of perceptual experiences, then although this knowledge may not be verbalizable it must still be detachable somehow from the experiences so that it can be possessed in a more enduring form. Otherwise it would simply cease to be relevant. The suggestion that this form relates to our power of imagery is effective only if we can distinguish perceptual imagery from the imagery with which a verbal report may be associated by someone who has not perceived its truth. But there does not appear to be any inherent difference. The suggestion presupposes but does not explain a difference in capacities for imagery.

Were the difference to lie in the mode in which images are known then the original question about how modes of knowledge differ would simply have been replaced by another. If there is some other difference between the images it must apparently consist in qualities that are altogether ineffable. It has indeed been widely held that perceptual experiences have qualities that cannot be fully expressed in words. But if this means it is quite impossible to say what these qualities are, then knowing something perceptually as opposed to verbally reduces to knowing it along with certain ineffable associations. This view encourages the conclusion that how we experience things is 'subjective' in the sense that it is not relevant to matters that can be rationally discussed. However, a theory of modes of knowledge ought to explain how the same thing can be known in different modes and the connection between knowing something in a given mode and what is known. A theory which equates perceptual knowledge of a truth with knowing it along with ineffable associations fails to do this.

The difference between knowing something perceptually or verbally is not essentially a difference in *what* is known but in *how* it is known. The notion of ineffable knowledge is not relevant to understanding this: we want to understand how knowing something perceptually differs from knowing it verbally even when the knowledge can be put into words. The distinction to be understood is between the concrete nature of perceptual experience of a truth and the merely verbal experience of it we might have in understanding a report. The former is not confined to current perception of the truth but can survive in memory; and it does not differ from the latter in containing objects of knowledge which cannot be verbalized.

One difference, evidently, is that someone who actually perceived that something is the case, as opposed to someone who has merely been told, is generally in a position to supply further information. If I actually see that there is a rabbit in the field I can be expected to be able to say more about its whereabouts, how it is moving, etc. But this point does not identify a form of knowledge peculiar to perception.

What, however, of the point that first-hand experience is needed to recognize metaphorical (inexponable) truth? Concrete experience is needed to recognize that a theme moves erratically, that two shapes in a painting balance one another, or that the tension in one line in a drawing is greater than in another. Can we say, then, that the difference between knowing something perceptually and knowing it merely verbally is that in the former case one is in a position to recognize such metaphorical truths? A problem with this is that it is not clear that I myself need concrete experience to know such truths. It is not denied that they can be formulated verbally. So I can know that the composition in a painting is balanced even though I have not seen it myself if I have a reliable first-hand informant.

There is naturally a big difference between knowing such a metaphorical truth experientially and knowing it merely verbally. However, this point is no help for present purposes unless we can explain this difference without presupposing that between perceptual and verbal knowledge. But if we can give an independent account of how these two kinds of knowledge of metaphorical truth differ, it should be possible to use this to explain the difference between perceptual experience of a truth and the verbal experience of it we have in understanding a report.

Such an independent account is possible, I think, by applying again but in a new way the distinction between knowing something and understanding it – the distinction we used to differentiate knowing something in the way an animal might from knowing the same thing perceptually, as we can.

The tendency is to assume that knowing something perceptually differs from knowing it verbally in that verbal statement of a truth formulates explicitly the understanding of it implicit in knowing it perceptually. Were this always so it would be impossible for there to be anything positive in knowing something perceptually rather than verbally. But perceptual knowledge differs from verbal knowledge not because the former contains elements that cannot be verbalized, but because verbalizing it does not always make our perceptual understanding explicit. It does so when what we know perceptually can be stated literally; but not where perceptual knowledge can only be stated using metaphor. I can know that the painting is sad because I have been told; but I do not know thereby what makes it sad. Only someone who has seen that it is sad knows this. In knowing this he has an understanding of what he is perceiving which someone who only knows the verbal truth lacks. The latter knowledge is comparable to that which animals have of literal truths. A dog can see that there is a rabbit in the field, but does so without understanding. Similarly, someone who knows that the painting is sad only because he has been told does not understand its sadness – he does not know what makes it sad.

Understanding as opposed to knowledge of a metaphorical (inexponable) truth demands, then, concrete experience of its truth. It is insufficient for this merely to know the meaning of a verbal report. Reversing this we can explain the difference between knowing something perceptually as opposed to verbally by saying that only in the former case has one understanding and not just knowledge of metaphorical truths about the object of knowledge. This explains without postulating ineffable knowledge the sense in which perceptual experience has a richer content than a verbal description. It can also explain what is meant by saying that an experience brings one directly into contact with a truth – though rather than thinking that a perceptual experience warrants a knowledge claim because it does this we should understand what it is for an experience to give direct contact with a truth in terms of the types of knowledge claim the experience warrants.

This account entails, clearly, that metaphor is not an accidental feature of language. The notion that we have a direct, perceptual grasp of reality depends on our having the ability to use words metaphorically.

3. Aesthetic understanding (1): empathic enjoyment

We have two distinctions to bear in mind: that between knowing something and understanding it; and that between implicit and explicit understanding. Metaphorical truth differs from the literal in that understanding of the latter but not of the former can be made explicit by verbally expounding it. Understanding of a metaphorical truth, by contrast, has to be experiential rather than verbal.

The question arises how in that case experiential understanding of a metaphorical truth might be made explicit. In ordinary perception this understanding is only implicit. But by general principles it ought to be possible to make it explicit, at least sometimes. In perceiving something I know what I am doing, this being knowledge of my capacities in respect of the specific perceptual act in question. My implicit understanding of what I am perceiving is my knowledge of these capacities – capacities which can be described as enabling me actively to make what I am perceiving in my mind. In exercising these capacities I make explicit my previously implicit understanding of my perception. In particular, then, I ought to be able to make explicit my implicit perceptual understanding of metaphorical truths, even if this cannot be done simply by formulating them verbally, by exercising those capacities which I know in having this implicit understanding.

In doing this I will have an experience of the metaphorical truth in which my understanding of it is explicit. Understanding of metaphorical truth must always be experiential; but experiential understanding of it need not always only be implicit. There is, then, I claim, such a thing as *explicit experiential understanding* of a metaphorical truth: the kind of understanding we have when we understand metaphorical truth explicitly. My thesis about the *empathic* variety of aesthetic enjoyment is that we experience it when we have such explicit understanding of metaphorical truths. But how can this occur?

We have followed Aristotle in holding that cognitive activities such as thinking and perceiving are not processes but are complete in themselves. This is also an essential feature of any actions that make our understanding of our experiences explicit. It is thus a commonplace that complete sentences are the unit of verbal communication, not isolated words and phrases. In the same sense as is true of perceptions, a meaningful utterance is not the outcome of a process but is complete in itself. There are no statements over and above the activity of stating any more than there are perceptions over and above the activity of perceiving. The meaning of a sentence is not a construct out of the antecedent meanings of its parts; rather its parts have meaning only as a reflection of their role in sentences. Recognizing that an utterance is something complete in this sense is part of the experience of knowing what it means.

Verbal utterances made using an established vocabulary possess (or if defective fail to possess) this property of completeness in a literal sense, i.e. we can spell out – by referring to syntactic and semantic properties of the words used – why an utterance constitutes (or, if defective, fails to constitute) a meaningful statement. However, the case that now interests us – the one relevant to explicit understanding of metaphorical truth and to empathic aesthetic experience – is where things have this sort of completeness *metaphorically*.

As a general principle, in knowing perceptually as opposed to verbally a thing's metaphorical (inexponable) properties we know what makes it the case that it has these properties. In particular, then, in recognizing that something has metaphorically this property of completeness we know what makes it complete, this being something that cannot be spelled out but can only be understood experientially. Since this completeness is a matter of relationships between a thing's parts or properties, having an essentially experiential understanding of it means recognizing relationships between a thing's perceived metaphorical properties. Metaphorical completeness is not just one metaphorical property alongside others but rather a relationship among them.

Now, by the above principle, knowing this relationship among a thing's metaphorical properties is knowing what makes it the case that these properties are related in the ways they are. However, the relationships between individual metaphorical properties are part of what it is for the thing to have these particular properties – the individual properties are not the same apart from their relationships to others. Ordinary experiential understanding of metaphorical properties and the exceptional kind we have in recognizing metaphorical completeness thus have the same type of object, namely what makes it the case that the relevant thing has its metaphorical properties. But in a definite sense to know metaphorical completeness is to have a further understanding of metaphorical properties beyond the ordinary implicit understanding we have just in perceiving such properties individually. If the ordinary understanding of this is *implicit* understanding, the understanding one has in recognizing something's metaphorical completeness can be regarded as *explicit* understanding of its metaphorical properties – a form of explicit understanding that is experiential.

Having an understanding of some metaphorical truths is the element in an experience of a perceivable truth that makes it concrete rather than verbal. Hence the explicit understanding we have in recognizing something's metaphorical completeness is explicit understanding of the element in this recognition that makes it a concrete experience.

The other side to this, drawing upon what we have said about metaphor, is that such explicit understanding is understanding of *how* one is experiencing something, i.e. of one's subjective view of it. To know the meaning of a metaphorical statement one has to know the speaker's viewpoint – how things seem from his point of view. In the case of inexponable metaphor only actual experience of this viewpoint can constitute understanding of what is said. Understanding such metaphors demands active imagination. But we have already said that in recognizing something's metaphorical completeness we have explicit understanding of that element in what we are experiencing that cannot be understood without actually experiencing it. And this is the same as having an understanding of the subjective viewpoint in this experience. Therefore in understanding explicitly a thing's metaphorical properties I simultaneously understand how my experience is *felt*.

Recognition of metaphorical completeness is thus at the same time both an experiential understanding of what one is experiencing and of how subjectively one is experiencing it. To have this twofold understanding is to experience the thing perceived as empathically embodying one's feelings in experiencing it. A mark of this is willingness to apply organic and personal metaphors to the thing perceived – to describe it as alive, having character and so on – as if it mirrored one's experience.

These points explain what it is to have empathic experience. There is no difficulty in seeing that this experience achieves in an exceptional way the aim behind intellectual cognition, namely to escape the original deceptiveness of the imagination, and is thus a form of cognitive experience that is satisfying in itself. In this case our intellectual aim is not achieved by being able to tell whether what we are perceiving is real or illusory (though this may also be true), but rather by having a form of knowledge to which this distinction between real and illusory does not apply: an understanding of one's own experiences. It is not possible to have this form of knowledge without being aware of those features of the enjoyable act that make it enjoyable; so this cognitive satisfaction has the required attribute of being self-intimating. It is also easy to see that it is impossible here to separate what is being enjoyed from one's experiences in enjoying it. Hence this form of enjoyment also has the logical peculiarities associated with aesthetic experience.

Given that pleasure is always a quality of an activity and perceptual experiences are sometimes pleasurable in themselves, it is not altogether surprising that the qualities of these enjoyable perceptions that make them pleasant will appear to be qualities of the objects perceived. I have tried to explain this by saying that we are here recognizing that something has the property of metaphorical completeness, i.e. we have here an experiential understanding of the metaphorical possession by something of that property which distinguishes intellectual cognitive activities from processes.

This account could, perhaps, serve as a gloss on some of Dewey's ideas. Dewey stresses that the conditions out of which aesthetic admiration arises 'are the conditions and factors that make any ordinary experience complete' (*Art as Experience*, p.12). As such the aesthetic 'is no intruder in experience from without' but 'is the clarified and intensified development of traits that belong to every normally complete experience' (ibid., p.46). To explain this Dewey tries to develop a notion of '*an* experience' which is 'a whole and carries with it its own individuating quality and self-sufficiency' (ibid., p.35). This quality 'pervades the entire experience in spite of the variation of its constituent parts' (ibid., p.37). I would concur with Dewey's sentiments here. However, the account of empathic aesthetic enjoyment just given concerns perceptual experience; and not all cognitive enjoyment is perceptual. When it is the enjoyment is typically empathic; but there are also abstract, non-empathic forms of aesthetic enjoyment. These require separate treatment.

4. Aesthetic understanding (2): beauty and necessity

We can derive aesthetic satisfaction from purely abstract sources. Theorems and the solutions to problems can be beautiful as well as flowers and paintings. This prompted Worringer to contrast the aesthetics which proceeds from 'man's urge to empathy' from that which proceeds from 'his urge to abstraction'. He writes that:

> Just as the urge to empathy as a pre-assumption of aesthetic experience finds its gratification in the beauty of the organic, so the

urge to abstraction finds its beauty in the life-denying inorganic, in the crystalline or, in general terms, in all abstract law and necessity.

(*Abstraction and Empathy*, trans. M. Bullock, p.4)

I have maintained that empathy, in the sense usually meant by writers on aesthetics, is a manifestation of a more general phenomenon basic to intellectual cognition as a whole. So it should not be surprising that cognitive (aesthetic) enjoyment can take forms not characterized by empathy in the narrow sense. As Worringer suggests, aesthetic enjoyment takes two main forms – empathic and abstract; though it should not be overlooked that these are often combined in the same experience. To explain abstract aesthetic enjoyment we need a generalization of the account of cognitive enjoyment already given.

In the empathic case one has explicit understanding of metaphorical truths. My thesis about the *abstract* variety of aesthetic enjoyment is that we experience it when we have explicit understanding of the grounds of a necessary truth, e.g. in recognizing the cogency of a proof. The two cases are united by the point that in both we have explicit understanding of a kind of truth that cannot be understood, i.e. one cannot know what makes it true, without concretely experiencing it. The generalization needed to assimilate both cases is thus in the notion of concrete as opposed to merely verbal experience. The general thesis is that we experience aesthetic enjoyment when we have explicit understanding of concrete experience. Such understanding, in contrast to explicit understanding of perceivable literal truths, is always experiential.

Perceptual experience is one variety of concrete experience; and we have perceptual experience of something when we understand metaphorical truths about it. But metaphorical truths are not alone in not being understandable merely through knowing the meaning of a verbal report. The same can apply to necessary truths. To know what makes a painting sad one has to see it. Similarly, to know what makes something necessarily true one has to see why it is true. Understanding of a metaphorical truth is made explicit when one recognizes that something is metaphorically complete. Understanding of the grounds of a necessary truth is explicit in, for example, seeing that the truth follows from certain premisses.

That there should be something satisfying about seeing this is explained by the notion that intellectual capacities aim to escape the original deceptiveness of the imagination. For clearly there is not in the recognition of necessary truth the same distinction between the real and the imaginary. (This is not to deny, of course, that there can be other sorts of errors in proofs.) Thus we can agree with Aristotle that intellectual contemplation of necessary knowledge can be a source of satisfaction while rejecting his own explanation of this. Aristotle did not tackle the special problems posed by cognitive enjoyment, but rather argued that since true happiness must lie in activities that are intrinsically satisfying, in the sense that they do not make good any deficiency, it must consist in intellectual contemplation, because this is the only activity that fully meets this requirement. One of the unfortunate consequences of this was to encourage neglect of the possibility of deriving aesthetic satisfaction from perceptual experiences.

In speaking of the satisfaction that can be derived from appreciating a proof we are not speaking of mere verbal acceptance or acknowledgement of a necessary truth but an understanding of what makes it true in which (unless we are mistaken) we know its truth. To have explicit understanding of a valid proof is simultaneously to experience the truth of its conclusion: in recognizing the validity of a proof we experience the truth of its conclusion in a sense that we do not experience perceived literal truths. Understanding of the latter is separable from concrete perceptual experience. (One can understand these literal truths, for example as verbally reported, without having concrete experience of them.) But in the recognition of necessary truth explicit understanding and concrete experience of the truth coincide.

Necessary truths are the only literal (exponable) truths that fall within experience in this sense. But they share this feature with truths about feelings known empathically when we have explicit understanding of something's metaphorical properties. To have this explicit understanding of metaphorical properties is not only to experience the truth that the thing has these properties (in a sense over and above merely knowing, as one might from a report, that it has them), but to experience them as giving an understanding of the feelings which the thing embodies. Explicit understanding of metaphor bears the same relation to understanding of empathic feeling as explicit understanding of a proof does to understanding of the necessary truth proved. Hence there is a genuine parallel between the point that one must see the beauty in a beautiful painting if one understands it correctly and the point that if one grasps properly a valid proof then one must see that the conclusion follows.

Referring to the peculiarities of aesthetic satisfaction listed earlier, we can now see that the satisfaction from appreciating a proof counts as aesthetic even though it is not perceptual. Given that explicit understanding of a proof is a matter of how one experiences it and that recognition of a proof's validity is satisfying, it follows both that the delight entailed in grasping a valid proof is self-intimating and that the enjoyed activity has the logical characteristic of being inseparable from our experiences in engaging in it. Also this satisfaction, though not empathic in the ordinary sense, has related phenomenological features. In both cases the barrier which separates perception of literal truth from reality is broken down. In empathy things partake of our feelings. In apprehending necessity literal truths are absorbed into the mind. The latter can be thought of as a kind of 'reverse empathy'.

This point is sometimes expressed by saying that our rational powers mirror the essential form of reality. This way of speaking is, of course, no more explanatory in itself than are the metaphors that surround the ordinary notion of empathy. But this is not a good reason for rejecting it. If it is rejected, necessary truths will tend to seem no more than a record of verbal conventions and habits. Once that way of regarding them takes root, bogus problems arise about the possibility of people diverging in what they accept as necessarily true and about what it is for necessary truths to be true to the things we experience.

Ordinary empathy and the reverse kind are, then, two species of the same genus. It ought to be evident in any case that there is an affinity between our capacity to recognize necessary truths – considered as something internal to what we say – and to experience aesthetic enjoyment – considered as something internal to certain cognitive activities. We can explain neither necessary truth nor aesthetic enjoyment by reference to something external – a necessary fact or an independent purpose. There is hence a severer beauty than that we know when we experience things as echoing our feelings: a beauty we know when we experience necessity.

5. Beauty and experiential knowledge

These two sorts of beauty do not exclude one another. We admire works of art not only because they embody feelings with which we can empathize but for abstract qualities like balance and proportion. Works of art, along with theories, are praised for exhibiting rightness, depth and coherence.

Conversely, thought even about the most abstract matters is often supported by imagery. Understanding of a truth proved, in so far as it demands capacities for imagery, can have an empathic aspect – one appropriate to the feelings we experience in abstract thinking. The two forms of aesthetic satisfaction far from being mutually exclusive are often two elements within the same experience.

Not surprisingly, therefore, many writers link art and aesthetic enjoyment with necessity. For example, Fiedler tells us that artists develop their 'visual conceptions' to a degree where they 'take on the character of necessity' ('On Judging Works of Visual Art'; in Aschenbrenner and Isenberg (eds), p.368). Dufrenne speaks of the 'self-sufficient necessity' within a work of art (*Phenomenology of Aesthetic Experience*, p.396) and Clive Bell compares the appreciation of art with that of pure mathematics (*Art*, p.25).

Sometimes when we say there is a necessity or rightness about the arrangement of shapes in a painting we are only applying our understanding of literal necessities, for example if we say this because we see the painting as exemplifying a regular geometric pattern, or because we regard certain features of it as essential to what it represents. This has made possible a debate among some artists and critics about the relative importance of 'form' and expressive 'content' in art. But it is a confusion to think there can ever be any real conflict between abstract (formal) and empathic (expressive) aesthetic enjoyment. If something is apprehended as metaphorically complete, a necessity in the relation between its parts being one of its perceived metaphorical properties, then this necessity must be perceived as integrated with its other metaphorical properties. Necessity has to be something understood experientially in order to be a cause of aesthetic enjoyment. There can be nothing aesthetically satisfying about merely applying understanding of a literal necessity.

It is clear that the present thesis that aesthetic enjoyment consists in having an experiential form of knowledge is quite different from Baumgarten's thesis that aesthetic enjoyment is enjoyment of 'aesthetic' (sensory) experience. We agree that aesthetic enjoyment is cognitive; but the theory that we experience it when we have explicit understanding of concrete experience severs its specific association with the senses. The thesis, as Baumgarten understood it, that aesthetic enjoyment (the experience of beauty) is the enjoyment of aesthetic experience is false.

Baumgarten's error was not just wrongly to identify the objects of aesthetically enjoyable cognition but to believe that the form of experiential knowledge relevant here is to be differentiated according to its objects. When cognitive experience is enjoyable this is not because of its object but rather because of its mode.

This error fuels what would otherwise be a rather obviously sterile debate about the ontological status of 'aesthetic objects'. In so far as any type of thing can be apprehended with aesthetic enjoyment, questioning their ontological status only poses the general philosophical question 'What sort of things can we apprehend?' However, a uniform account will be demanded by those who suppose that aesthetic enjoyment involves a form of knowledge with its own kind of object.

The only feasible such account is that the knowledge in question is a special knowledge of our experiences themselves. One of the ways this error is perpetuated is in the notion of the 'aesthetic attitude', i.e. the notion that we enjoy aesthetic experience only when we adopt a specially detached attitude in which we attend to what we are seeing, hearing, etc. for its own sake. But we would then face the choice either of holding that it is not really the apprehension of ordinary things that we enjoy aesthetically but only this special knowledge of our own experiences, or of interpreting ordinary things along idealistic lines as having no existence over and above what we know when we know our experiences aesthetically.

This error tends to encourage the doctrine which Croce held for other reasons, that the true work of art lies in the experiences of those who apprehend the physical object the artist produces. Dewey, for example, tells us that:

> The *product* of art – temple, painting, statue, poem – is not the *work* of art. The work takes place when a human being cooperates with the product so that the outcome is an experience that is enjoyed because of its liberating and ordered properties.
>
> (*Art as Experience*, p.214)

This doctrine is made possible by the logical peculiarities of aesthetic enjoyment. Against this it is insufficient to argue, as Wollheim does, that physical objects can themselves have expressive properties and so nothing prevents physical objects from being works of art (*Art and its Objects*, sections 15–19). Even if physical objects can have expressive properties, on this misguided approach it will be our experience of apprehending them that is the object of the aesthetic experience. What is needed to refute this doctrine is explanation of how a form of enjoyment is possible that has the logical and other peculiarities noted.

This will explain without literally identifying them how experience and what is experienced are united in aesthetic enjoyment.

The point that aesthetic knowledge is a distinct mode of knowledge rather than a form of knowledge with its own objects is important not only in allowing us to acknowledge the full diversity in aesthetic experience but also in connection with the dilemma which, as I said (Ch.3, section 2), confronts attempts to explain aesthetic experience in words. The problem is that we can only know what makes an aesthetically enjoyable experience enjoyable by actually experiencing it; so is not it beyond the power of words to give any true explanation of this enjoyment? If aesthetic enjoyment is cognitive then it seems that either what is known here cannot be put into words; or if it can then knowing it does not alone suffice to explain the enjoyment. Either way efforts at explanation appear to have been frustrated.

This dilemma remains intractable so long as it is supposed that experiences are the objects of knowledge of aesthetically enjoyable cognition. But the reason why one must have the experience to know what makes the cognition enjoyable is not that this is knowledge about experiences but that experience is needed to understand what is known. The knowledge can be stated verbally; and one can know the meaning of this statement without having such experiential understanding. To explain the enjoyment a theory is needed which allows understanding sometimes to take an experiential form, and which can connect this with satisfaction of an underlying cognitive aim. Otherwise there is no escape from the accusation that it is absurd, because what it concerns is essentially experiential, to try to explain aesthetic enjoyment using words.

CHAPTER X

Art and Artistic Abilities

1. Questions about art

Philosophical questions about art can be grouped under three main heads: (a) Questions about the relation between the satisfaction we derive from art and from natural beauty. In what ways do these differ and in what ways are they the same? (b) Questions about the nature of creative artistic abilities. What sort of account of these is possible? And (c) questions about the value and importance of art. What is the role of art in human life? What is the difference between great and minor art? Is some art positively bad?

The account of aesthetic satisfaction in the previous chapter hardly broached these issues. To accept that account is to accept, as against philistinism, that there really is such a thing as the experience of beauty, i.e. experience that has the peculiarities we associate with aesthetic enjoyment. But this does not deal with iconoclastic reservations about the capacity of human beings to create things of beauty. It has often been held that our appreciation of art and of natural beauty are fundamentally different, the satisfaction we derive from the former having nothing essentially to do with aesthetic satisfaction. For example, Danto writes that 'aesthetics . . . hardly touches the heart of art and certainly not of great art, which is certainly not the art that happens to be most beautiful' (*The Transfiguration of the Commonplace*, p.173). There are positive and negative grounds for holding this.

The positive grounds are that the qualities we value in art are quite different from those we admire in natural beauty. There is often a dimension of imagination in appreciating works of art absent from delight in natural beauty. Works of art provide spectators with the opportunity to enter into them imaginatively in the sense of engaging in make-believe; and they are often valued for the imaginative experiences they thus afford – for their richness, depth and universality. By comparison, beauty may appear a subordinate merit, and perhaps even a superficial one. Sometimes we admire works we recognize to be flawed over others that are more perfect.

Certainly our attitude to works of art is very different from that to natural objects. Knowing that something is a work of sculpture and not a piece of driftwood affects our response even if it is impossible to tell which it is just by looking. It is put into a new perspective once it is known to be a product of human artistic activity; for the artist can be presumed to have intended that spectators should notice certain specific features of the work. The question thus arises whether or not spectators do in fact notice those features the artist intended them to. An element of communication, in the sense of grasping the artist's intentions, enters into the appreciation of art which has no parallel – unless one postulates a divine communicator – in delight in natural beauty.

As well as the positive thought that art achieves things that natural beauty cannot, there is the negative idea that it is beyond human capacities to create beauty as such. As Plato saw, a capacity to do this would seem to be very different from other productive skills. There are specific things a carpenter knows how to do; and we can explain how he is able to make a bed or a table in terms of his applying these specific items of practical knowledge to a preconceived end. But no specific practical skills could analogously explain a capacity to make beautiful things if only because there is no class of beautiful things as such.

On Plato's theory, beauty is the appearance of what is good; and a good table, for example, is one that serves well its purposes. Plato allowed that when a carpenter who knows what it is for something to be a good table applies his knowledge practically he makes a beautiful table. However, the problem with art is that it claims a closer relationship with beauty: works of art profess no purpose, save incidentally, but to be apprehended as beautiful. Plato believed this is absurd. If works of art had a valid function they would be capable of beauty on the same principle that beds or tables are, namely in so far as they well exemplify what it is to be good of their kind. But nothing, he believed, can have the kind of relation to beauty that art professes.

We do not have to accept all of Plato's theory to agree that there is a difficulty here. To say artists are concerned with creating things of beauty is not on its own an intelligible characterization of their creative capacities. The first challenge Plato poses is to give an intelligible account of these capacities. A second challenge is to find a way of defending the idea that there is a special sense in which art as opposed to craft activities is aimed at beauty.

Many thinkers in taking up the first challenge have conceded Plato's points as they relate to the second. This is often true of theories that explain art as being concerned with the expression or communication of knowledge. For instance Goodman at one point rejects the term 'beauty', insisting instead that cognitive merit is what matters in art (*Languages of Art*, Ch.6, section 6).

But it is a mistake to think that in taking up Plato's first challenge we must abandon belief in a special connection between art and beauty. That is unavoidable on Plato's own theory of beauty; and many cognitive theories of art make no attempt to maintain to the contrary. But on the theory proposed, to experience beauty and to have a certain experiential form of knowledge (explicit experiential understanding) are one and the same thing. So there is no inevitable incompatibility in holding that art aims both at the expression of knowledge and at beauty. It aims at both simultaneously if the experience of beauty (aesthetic satisfaction) is identical to cognitive enjoyment and artists intend spectators to enjoy for its own sake (non-adventitiously) the cognitive experience of looking at their work.

Given the proposed account of aesthetic satisfaction, and assuming we are not willing to be iconoclastic, questions (b) call for a theory of artistic abilities that explains why successfully exercising them results in the expression of knowledge of the aesthetically satisfying form. The answer to (a) will then depend on what is special about knowledge of this form when it is expressed artistically. The answer to (c) will reflect the answer to (a) and the relation between artistic and other abilities implicit in the answer to (b).

2. *Two theories of artistic abilities*

There has been the problem in understanding artistic abilities that on most conceptions of experiential knowledge it is just as unintelligible how anyone could have an ability to express specific items of such knowledge as it is on Plato's theory of beauty how any skill could be aimed specifically at creating beautiful things. Clearly, if having the knowledge a work of art expresses demands actual experience of it then in this respect the work cannot be preconceived. If Plato is right in believing that artistic abilities are intelligible only if they accomplish preconceived ends, then the theory that artists aim to express experiential knowledge encounters the same difficulty as the claim, on Plato's understanding, that they aim to create beauty.

Cognitive theories of art are thus liable to the same argument that since artistic ends are not verbally explicable, artistic abilities themselves are inexplicable. The notion of genius as a magical faculty deeper than rationality is a tribute to the persuasiveness of this line of thought. Of course, postulating such a faculty is no more a genuine explanation of artistic abilities than is the doctrine of inspiration by the muses or some other outside source that sometimes tempted Plato himself.

The argument might, however, be taken only to establish that artistic abilities cannot be explained in any more basic terms. In that case there are two remaining forms an explanation of them might take. One is a theory which assigns them a basic role among human cognitive capacities. Here they do not receive explanation by reference to their component skills but through an account of their relation to our other, less fundamental capacities. Croce attempted a theory of this sort. He believed that we have creative artistic abilities, but that since they cannot be analysed further they must yield a basic form of knowledge of our own individual expressive acts. This would mean that the individual things each of us knows are all products of his own artistic ('aesthetic') activity – a conclusion which creates insuperable difficulties in understanding how artistic communication is possible.

The alternative is to deny in the interests of communication that our artistic abilities are truly creative. On this view these abilities are not essentially abilities to make anything, but rather abilities to recognize in things qualities of which for some reason it is valuable to have experiential knowledge. Croce held that artistic ends are verbally inexplicable because creative aesthetic knowledge is more basic than conceptual knowledge. The alternative approach concludes that since artists set out with no preconceived ends, they have no specific ends, and are thus in essence no different from searchers for *objets trouvés*. This is in keeping with the 'institutional' theory of art, and with some of Goodman's remarks. The thought behind it has had considerable impact on the actual practice of art.

A feature these two responses share is their tendency to regard art as omnipresent or ubiquitous. In Croce's theory all 'intuition' is expressive aesthetic activity. As Collingwood puts it in expounding his very similar theory, 'Every utterance and every gesture that each of us makes is a work of art' (*Principles of Art*, p.285). So we are all artists. Moreover, at any moment 'The world [the artist] has come to know is a world consisting of language; a world where everything has the property of expressing emotion' (ibid., p.291). So everything is art. In the institutional theory, on the other hand, not everything is actually a work of art; but whether something is depends solely on decisions of the 'artworld', i.e. on whether the artworld confers the status of work of art upon it. On this theory anything is potentially art since no constraints, such as ones to do with the intentions of the object's maker (if indeed it is an artefact), limit which objects can be awarded this status. This is a point where Goodman's theory that works of art are things characterized by certain symbolic attributes makes contact with the institutional theory. As Goodman puts it, we ought to ask 'When is art?' rather than 'What is art?' (*Ways of Worldmaking*, Ch.4). For to be a work of art is to be functioning as a certain type of symbol.

The Crocean and institutional approaches also share, in consequence of regarding art as omnipresent or ubiquitous, difficulty in explaining why we should be interested in art. If art is omnipresent why should we single out some things as works of art in a narrower sense? Or if art can be found anywhere we have the inclination to confer artistic status upon things, what purposes are we pursuing in actually conferring this status? Croce simply postulates that we aim to achieve more difficult and more complex expressions; and Goodman takes it for granted that it is possible to use symbols to pursue cognitive purposes for their own sake.

These shared weaknesses are symptomatic of a common error, namely the belief that since art has to do with experiential knowledge, the ability to produce works of art, if there be such a thing, cannot be understood as an ability to realize by making things any specific artistic intentions. This is to misunderstand the nature of the experiential knowledge with which art is concerned. The underlying mistake is the assumption that this knowledge must be differentiated by its object. This mistake shows up in the inability of either approach to give a satisfactory account, on its own conception of this knowledge, of why we should value art.

3. Creative imagination

Conventional wisdom has it that artists have vivid imaginations, and that this is the source of their inspiration. Technique is needed, of course, to realize what is imagined. But technique and imagination are usually contrasted. It is said that technique, unlike imagination, can be taught; and that while imagination without technique lacks only means for its expression, technique without imagination is simply empty.

Croce was right to reject this dichotomy of imagination and technique. He saw that if artists have the ability to express a form of experiential knowledge, then a technical capacity for expressing this knowledge distinct from the knowledge itself cannot be part of true artistic ability. It is impossible to form the intention to express a specific item of experiential knowledge without already having the *capacity* to express it. But he wrongly held that it is impossible to have knowledge of this form without *actually* expressing it. He reasoned that if artistic ability is the ability to express knowledge of a kind which demands contact with an expression of that knowledge, then having the knowledge at all is an exercise of artistic ability. Croce's error was to assume that having the knowledge to be expressed demands such contact – a natural enough error on conceptions of experiential knowledge which take sensory contact with things as their paradigm.

But not all experiential knowledge is sensory knowledge. Through kinaesthetic experience we have experiential but non-sensory knowledge of our own actions. And in perception, as well as sensory knowledge, we have experiential knowledge that is intellectual: we know what makes the things we sense what they are. Moreover it is possible in imagining oneself exercising one's productive skills to have experiential knowledge of the thing one imagines oneself making which is not merely imaginary sensory knowledge. For just as we can know metaphorically, in perception, how to make things we take to be actual, we can know literally how to make things we know only to be imaginary. Sometimes, of course, I form an image of something, and then imagine myself making it. Here the question arises whether or not I am in fact able to make it. But in the case I am considering the focus is on exercise in imagination of one's productive skills where this does not presuppose a separate image of the thing to be made.

This is creative or productive imagination in the sense of imagining oneself making something. Knowing what one is doing in exercising this creative imagination means knowing one's capacities in respect of an activity of imagining oneself making something, i.e. knowing capacities whose exercise would result in actually making the thing. I understand what I am doing when I exercise creative imagination because I know what makes the thing imagined what it is. And I make this understanding explicit if I actually make the thing.

Creative imagination in this sense is exercised in imagining oneself making any sort of thing whatever that one is genuinely able to make. By regarding artistic inspiration as a special case of creative imagination in this sense we can preserve the inner connection between inspiration and the ability to make the work without identifying the work with the inspiration. This also enables us to see how the work can illuminate the inspiration: it does so by making explicit the understanding of the work which is already present implicitly.

My thesis about artistic inspiration – the kind of creative imagination that leads to the production of works of art – is that it is an exercise of creative imagination that is enjoyable for its own sake, not adventitiously because of its associations or the prospect of benefits that making the thing might bring. In other words, inspiration is an exercise of creative imagination that is aesthetically enjoyable in its own right. This, I think, is the basic point to make in answering questions (b) above. We can use this thesis to define art rather than seek a definition of art and then attempt to understand how an intention to produce works of art can be connected with a capacity actually to do so. To defend the thesis a different connection has to be explained – that between having an inspiration and, if the inspiration is realized, producing something apprehension of which gives aesthetic satisfaction.

4. Inspiration and works of art

The first thing to say about the above thesis is that it widens the scope of aesthetically enjoyable experiences beyond the cases already explicitly discussed.

As explained in the previous chapter, we experience aesthetic satisfaction when we have explicit understanding of concrete experience; and experience of something is concrete rather than merely verbal when it involves experiential understanding of it not just knowledge, i.e. when we do not merely know it but know experientially what makes it what it is. We discussed perception and the recognition of necessary truth as examples respectively of concrete experience of things and of truths. But other experiences are also concrete in this sense. For example, our experience of what we are doing is concrete when we know what we are doing, i.e. when what is being done is a genuine action. For, naturally, in knowing what we are doing we know experientially what makes what we are doing the action it is. (This indeed is the most basic form of experiential understanding.) In particular, we have concrete experience whenever we exercise creative imagination or imagination in the sense of make-believe – as opposed to exercise of imagination in its original deceptive form where we do not know what we are doing.

These concrete imaginative experiences can themselves be aesthetically enjoyable. This does not mean introducing any new forms of aesthetic satisfaction beyond the empathic and abstract varieties already described. Such enjoyment in imagining is typically empathic, though the perceptual experiences with which we empathize here are imaginary rather than actual. Clearly this possibility is important in understanding how literature can be aesthetically satisfying.

It is also important in understanding how artistic inspiration, i.e. aesthetically enjoyable creative imagination, is connected with producing things that themselves yield aesthetic satisfaction. If the inspiration is empathically enjoyable then the experience is the same thing as experiential understanding of the feelings embodied in what is imagined. But this experience is also implicit understanding of what makes the thing imagined what it is, this understanding being the practical capacity to make it. In making this understanding explicit by actually making the thing one would therefore simultaneously make explicit one's understanding of the empathic feelings. Originally, then, the experiential understanding of these feelings in the imaginative experience was only implicit: the artist makes this understanding explicit when he makes what he has imagined. On the theory that aesthetic satisfaction is explicit experiential understanding, it follows that anyone who understands what the artist has made will experience aesthetic satisfaction.

We can use this notion of artistic inspiration, as aesthetically enjoyable creative imagination, to define a notion of *work of art*. In a broad sense, a *work of art*, in contrast to other artefacts, is something produced in exercising the productive skills one knows oneself to have in experiencing such an artistic inspiration. This means there is no need to postulate a class of artistic abilities as such. Our productive skills should not themselves be thought of as either artistic or non-artistic: whether or not something is a work of art depènds rather on the manner in which productive skills were being exercised in making it. (Here I concur with William Morris's conviction that 'the chief source of art is man's pleasure in his daily necessary work, which expresses itself and is embodied in that work itself' (*News From Nowhere and Selected Writings and Designs*, ed. Asa Briggs, p.140). Dewey expresses essentially the same view when he writes that 'any practical activity will, provided that it is integrated and moves by its own urge to fulfillment, have esthetic quality' (*Art as Experience*, p.39).)

These points bring the present discussion into line with the attempt in Chapter 6 to formulate an account of productive skills modelled on that of metaphor. We saw that it is possible to apply to these skills a distinction analogous to that between using words literally and using them metaphorically – a distinction between, as I termed it, using these skills 'practically' or 'aesthetically'. The notion of a 'non-utilitarian' artefact, i.e. one not associated with any definite practice of use, was the counterpart to that of inexponable metaphor. As I said, exercising our skills 'aesthetically' is a broader notion than that of exercising them with aesthetic aims in the sense we are interested in; and the notion of a non-utilitarian artefact is broader than that of a work of art. But we can now supplement the earlier definitions as follows. Productive skills are being exercised *artistically* when in exercising them the agent realizes an aesthetically enjoyable experience of creative imagination. (This is a special case of exercising them 'aesthetically' in the earlier sense.) A *work of art* is an artefact produced in exercising productive skills artistically. Being a work of art in this sense is compatible with being a utilitarian artefact; for example, elegant furniture and functional but aesthetically pleasing pottery might be both. We can easily define, however, a narrower notion of *fine art*: an artefact is a work of *fine art* if it is a non-utilitarian artefact which is also a work of art.

5. Inspiration and artistic success

In a much-discussed passage in his *Philosophical Investigations* Wittgenstein denies that one could invent a symbolism for recording one's sensations just by mentally associating the symbols with the sensations. His objection is that one has no 'criterion of correctness' as to whether or not usage of such symbols preserves a regular pattern of association with the sensations. 'One would like to say: whatever is going to seem right to me is right. And that only means that here we can't talk about "right"' (*Philosophical Investigations*, I, section 258, trans. G.E.M. Anscombe).

The same objection would seem to apply even more forcefully to the idea that artists have a capacity to fulfil specific artistic intentions. There may come a time when an artist stands back from his painting and says 'That is what I meant'. But what criterion does he have for whether or not his impression that the painting is as he intended it to be is correct?

In attempting to apply symbols directly to one's sensations it is at least possible to say that one is attempting to use a symbol in the same way as before. But an artist may be unable to say anything definite about what he takes to constitute success in attempting to produce a given work.

Whereas the case Wittgenstein describes is a hypothetical one designed to expose philosophical misconceptions about the sense in which we have immediate and certain knowledge of our sensations, the problem in the artistic case is actual and of practical importance to artists. Yet, unless we are philistines or iconoclasts, we will accept that we are genuinely able to produce works of art. How is this possible? How can we distinguish success from failure in exercising artistic abilities?

One difference between Wittgenstein's hypothetical case and the artistic one is that I need a criterion of success in recording my sensations to know that I really have an ability to record them, but given that there are no artistic abilities as such, there is no need for a criterion of artistic success to confirm that I have whatever abilities I exercise in trying to produce a work of art. Nevertheless, given that there is a new distinction between success and failure when these skills are being exercised artistically, it is still proper to ask how we can tell here whether we have been successful. It is not uncommon for artists later to reject work which at the time appeared to be going successfully. And critical evaluations are notoriously liable to fluctuate. The distinction between artistic success and failure is often difficult to draw in practice. Might the distinction be illusory?

From the artist's point of view, the main source of difficulty is that artistic inspiration can easily be confused, in practice as well as in theory, with other kinds of experience. Inspiration consists in an enjoyable imaginative experience of making something. This is as opposed, say, to imagining something one would like to make. But the distinction between these is not always easy to observe. Instead of trying to realize a genuine inspiration an artist may simply try to make something he imagines to be enjoyable to look at, hear, etc. This is what lies behind art that is only derivative. In practice the important distinction is not so much between success and failure in realizing a genuine inspiration as between work that is inspired and that which merely appears to be.

Another reason why artists may find this distinction difficult to draw is that making a work of art does not usually realize a single inspiration but rather a succession of increasingly more definite inspirations. This is connected with the role of artistic media and, more broadly, of 'technique'. A genuine inspiration, being an imaginary exercise of productive abilities, is an imaginary exercise of making something using appropriate media (wood, stone, paint, etc.) where the imaginer is genuinely able to use the media to make what he imagines. But works of art usually have a complexity which prevents one imagining every detail in advance. Actually making a work is apt to be a tentative, exploratory process which refines the original inspiration. There is interaction between imaginative activity and use of the medium to realize it. The initial inspiration is genuine only if the artist is able to resolve the problems which realizing it poses with further, more refined inspirations; but it may not be clear to him in advance whether he is able to do this.

This brings out that inspiration should only exceptionally and with qualification be thought of as a separate experience that wholly precedes making a work. That is only possible in the sense that an artist who has an assured technique may sometimes be able effortlessly to resolve the problems that arise in making a work. Inspiration is rather to be thought of as a quality that pervades successful creative activity. This is in keeping with the general point that what makes something I do an action of mine is how I experience it, this being part of what makes the action the action it is. Producing a work of art involves realizing an enjoyable imaginative experience, and this imaginative element is part of the activity of making the work in the sense that it is a necessary element in how the activity is experienced. Croce was wrong to identify 'intuition' with 'expression'; but inspiration is usually interwoven with the activity of realizing it in the same way that any experience of acting is with the action experienced.

This puts the question of whether or not an artist succeeds in realizing an inspiration in its proper perspective as an instance of the question of whether or not someone succeeds in performing the action he intended to perform. As a rule, we cannot first decide what an agent intended to do and then look to see if he succeeded. Provided what someone does makes sense in relation to the other things he does, that is usually enough to indicate that it was something he intended to do. It is a mistake to suppose the question could be resolved more decisively if only we had greater insight into the other's mind. Consider linguistic utterances and the question of whether in making them one achieves what one intends, i.e. says what one meant to say. Saying what one meant to say is only exceptionally a matter of realizing a prior intention of saying something in particular. (It might be when, for example, struggling with an unfamiliar foreign language.) Ordinarily we recognize what we say as something we meant to say not by reference to prior intentions in speaking but by recognizing that what we say makes sense. In this respect a speaker's own position is not different from that of his audience. Similarly, we recognize, as does the artist himself, that he has achieved what he intended, i.e. has successfully realized an inspiration, by understanding what he has made.

Against this it may be pointed out that on the question of whether a speaker has said what he meant hearers can base their opinion on whether his other actions are consistent with his intending to say what his words are taken to mean. But although we speak of interpreting paintings, we are not able so to interpret them that by comparing them with the painter's other actions we can conclude that a given painting was, or was not, one he intended to produce. We can compare what someone says with his actions because his utterances are means by which he pursues the ends behind those actions. But we cannot similarly compare an artist's paintings with his other actions because paintings are not, except incidentally, means for pursuing other ends. This raises questions about what it is to understand a work of art.

6. Understanding art

In reply to the last point it might be argued that symbol systems of all kinds interact and influence one another, and so the apparent independence from language of the systems artists use is illusory. These diverse systems, it may be said, contribute to knowledge jointly rather than separately. (For example, Goodman sometimes suggests that usage of symbolic characters in linguistic systems depends in part on their simultaneous role in various exemplificational systems.) Saying that a painting is as the artist intended might, then, be like recognizing that a speaker has said what he meant to the extent that both rest on the same overall interpretation of the agent's symbolic capacities.

This approach would, however, entail a philistine estimate of art if the joint interpretation of symbol systems were purely a matter of explaining how their use helps agents to secure independently recognizable goals. It is doubtless true that exemplificational symbols such as samples of things are often useful in attaining such goals, and that interpreting what people are doing in using them goes hand in hand with understanding things they say. But if this is how 'artistic symbols' are supposed to contribute to our goals then we abandon the idea that the aims responsible for the satisfaction we derive from works of art are ones achieved within our experiences of apprehending them.

This philistine approach equates understanding symbols of any sort with being able to explain how they serve the user's antecedent goals. But the sense of understanding we want in speaking of understanding art is different. We want a sense more like perceptual understanding. To perceive a tree is not just to know that some particular thing is a tree but to have some experiential understanding of what makes the tree what it is. Similarly, in the first instance at least, to understand a work of art is to have experiential understanding of what makes it what it is.

Now what makes the work what it is, namely the artist's productive activity, makes explicit understanding of the feelings that inspired it – the feelings the artist understood implicitly in imagining the work. So experiential understanding of the work – being the same thing, metaphorically speaking, as the maker's experiential knowledge in making it – makes explicit experientially understanding of these feelings. And this experience is enjoyable in itself. Anyone who understands the work will consequently have an understanding of the maker's aim in producing it which renders superfluous any outside explanation in terms of ulterior goals. This form of understanding does not rest on any further capacity to explain why the maker should have wished to produce the artefact.

Since this understanding is the same, metaphorically, as the maker's experiential knowledge, it is proper to say, metaphorically speaking, that spectators must themselves become artists to understand an artist's work, and that a true artist is someone who enables others to become artists. Of course, spectators do not themselves need technical knowledge of how a work was made in order to have this understanding of it. It should be emphasized, however, that the artist himself also needs this understanding, i.e. notwithstanding that he literally has the experience of making the work, he also needs experience that is metaphorically so described. (It can easily be both literally and metaphorically true that he has the experience of making it. Cf. 'No man is an island'.) Without this he does not understand what he has made and so is not in a position to claim that he has realized his inspiration. Whether or not he has this understanding is his criterion for whether or not his impression that things went well in making the work was correct.

To have this understanding is to have an experience in which a feeling is understood explicitly. On its own neither the empathic enjoyment of natural beauty nor the abstract enjoyment of intellectual beauty has this feature. In the former there is only implicit experiential understanding of the empathic feeling. The difference can be explained from the phenomenological point of view on the supposition that the artistic experience combines abstract with empathic aesthetic enjoyment. Then the work will not only be experienced as embodying the feeling one has in apprehending it, but the arrangement and organization of its parts will be experienced as necessary. Hence the work will be apprehended as embodying with necessity the feeling experienced. The feeling so to speak follows necessarily from apprehending the rightness of the work, while reciprocally it is impossible to have this feeling without apprehending this rightness. In this sense the work makes explicit this particular feeling. The feeling both gives form to and is given form by the production of the work of art. The artist awaits the moment when what he has made 'clicks' and assumes a necessary character; for this is the sign that his inspiration has been realized. In saying this I agree with many of the things Langer said about what art accomplishes, though not with her theory of presentational symbolism. On the question how art is able to accomplish these things, Fiedler was nearer the mark when he spoke of artists developing their conceptions until they assume the character of necessity.

The point that understanding of feeling is made explicit in art differentiates art from natural beauty, and this supplies the basic answer to question (a) above. It is possible, it is true, as some *objets trouvés* show, to see nature as art. But it is better to regard this as a limiting case of artistic ability rather than as undermining or blurring the distinction between art and nature. The institutional theory is right that status as a work of art can be conferred on something just through a capacity to see it as a work of art. But this is because seeing something in this way, i.e. having the sort of experience that constitutes understanding a work of art, is what terminates the activity of making such works, not because an artistic status can be conferred on things at will. The true significance of this for artistic abilities is to bring out how accidents can have a legitimate role in art. Any artist has to be able to recognize that some features in his work though unplanned are worth preserving. Sometimes this can mean turning accidents to advantage. *Objets trouvés* are the extreme case.

In making explicit the feelings of the artist, works of art make possible, as the experience of natural beauty alone cannot, communication of the subjective element in experience. It may be impossible to share one and the same feeling, considered as an individual experiential event; but our feelings are not for that reason unknowable by others. In art we can know that we share the same experiential understanding of them. In particular, when a work has a representational content, e.g. depicts something or tells a story, it can communicate a subjective view of what it represents, because it makes experiential understanding of certain feelings about it explicit. When this occurs in, for example, appreciating a story, the sense in which we enter into the writer's mind and share his subjective experience is that we share explicit understanding of the same imaginary empathic feelings: we empathize with the same imaginary rather than actual perceptual experiences.

This does not necessarily mean sharing any actual feeling. To understand a sad poem – one that makes explicit a feeling of sadness – is not to feel sad about anything but to understand what it is to feel sadness in the things or events the poem describes: it is to know what makes an experience of these a feeling of sadness. If the poem is successful, enjoyment of it will combine empathic with abstract elements. Without the latter – the sense of rightness about how it uses words – it would fail to make any definite feeling explicit. The presence jointly of both forms of aesthetic satisfaction is the criterion for our understanding of the poem being what the writer intended, and thus for our having the same imaginary perceptions as others who agree in finding it satisfying both empathically and abstractly.

The accounts of empathic and abstract aesthetic satisfaction, as applied to imaginary (make-believe) experiences, can thus explain aesthetic enjoyment of literature: this does not demand a fundamentally different account. Note that the possibility of empathizing with imaginary experiences created by words depends on this being concrete, albeit make-believe, experience of what is described. I have maintained that we have concrete experience of something when we have understanding, not just knowledge, of metaphorical truths about it. It is often said that poetry relies on metaphor; but it would not, just by using words metaphorically, convey the understanding necessary for the imaginary experience to be concrete. Poetry relies on metaphor in the sense of depending on metaphorical truths about what the poem says. That poetry can yield concrete experience of what it describes shows that these metaphorical truths have the same basis in the meanings of the words used as do truths about what the poem says literally. This confirms that in itself meaning is neither literal nor metaphorical. What are sometimes referred to as the elements of 'tone' and 'colour' in meaning are not extraneous additions to literal meaning. No literalist can give an account of poetry credible to anyone who is not a philistine.

7. The value of art; aesthetic experience as a source of meaning

In one sense, the problem of why we should have a capacity for aesthetic enjoyment – a capacity that serves no obvious practical goal – is resolved by identifying this enjoyment with cognitive enjoyment. For our cognitive skills are evidently of practical value to us. From the viewpoint of evolutionary biology, this identification would appear to make our capacity for aesthetic satisfaction an agreeable side-effect of skills whose primary purpose lies elsewhere.

But there is also the point that the experience of beauty is intrinsically satisfying in a sense that no other experiences are. Only this experience can qualify as a truly final goal of action. 'Because it is aesthetically satisfying' is the only answer that can on its own terminate positively questions about the point of engaging in an activity.

In apparent contradiction to this it is sometimes said that aesthetic considerations should give way to the demands of morality. In the context of a hedonistic–puritanical debate this sounds like saying that one should sometimes forgo pleasure in order to do one's duty; and that is hard to disagree with. But the antithesis is superficial, as is tacitly conceded by moralists who believe that a promise of heavenly reward awaits those who respect the moral law; for heavenly pleasures can only be aesthetic. It may not be a sufficient condition, all things considered, for a course of action to be desirable that it yield aesthetic satisfaction. This is the aesthete's error. But if there is an ultimate end to be pursued it must be intrinsically satisfying in the aesthetic sense.

How can this be compatible with the idea that our capacity to experience beauty is only a side-effect of our cognitive skills? Unless, by placing the evolutionary process in a broader context, we can harmonize intrinsic satisfaction with survival value, it may well seem, from the viewpoint of our practical welfare, that our capacity to appreciate beauty is something of a deceptive luxury which might get out of hand. Idealistic or religiously inclined philosophers tend to the former alternative. Polanyi, for instance, speaks of a 'gradient of meaning in operation in evolution in addition to purely accidental mutation and plain natural selection' (*Meaning*, p.173). There is, he says, 'a general movement towards the attainment of meaning in the universe' (ibid., p.182). Again, on an idealistic theory like Croce's, according to which art is omnipresent, it is hardly possible to question a concern with art: his theory permits no contrast between such a concern and any independent practical or evolutionary demands. The latter alternative that in ordinary practical terms art is a luxury would be held by those who have no faith that human life is meaningful but who believe that through art we catch a glimpse of what it would be if it were. This is essentially a tragic view – that the pursuit of meaning puts us at odds with uncaring nature.

There is, however, a third view. Because they are intrinsically satisfying, aesthetic experiences can be *final* causes, i.e. ends to be pursued. But they also have something of the character of *formal* causes, i.e. the understanding of all manner of things attained through aesthetically satisfying experiences is a factor in making other diverse actions of ours what they are. Aesthetic satisfaction can thus make actions meaningful not through being sought as a goal but in the sense that previous experience of such satisfaction shapes how we experience what we subsequently do.

This is illustrated by the understanding of other people that art makes possible. There is a sense in which we understand others only if we know what they are feeling. Without some shared aesthetic experience, specifically a shared experience of art, this is unattainable. Hence we have a sense of alienation from cultures that have left no art behind them. This need not necessarily be fine art, of course. But there are types of feeling that can only be expressed in fine art; and works of fine art are especially effective as a source of understanding of feeling since, being non-utilitarian artefacts, they oblige spectators who wish to understand them to do so aesthetically. One can perceive that a beautiful table is a table without perceiving its beauty. But one cannot perceive that a work of fine art is a work of fine art without taking oneself to have the experiential understanding it makes explicit.

How we act towards others is shaped by the understanding of people we gain from art. More generally, we see things through the eyes of art – and in a deeper sense than that we see them *as* works of art, either as *objets trouvés* or as consciously evoking particular works or styles. Aesthetic knowledge does not have direct practical application; but its influence is widely felt on how we experience our actions. Indeed the full sense in which aesthetic experience gives meaning to our actions is, I think, comparable to that in which traditional empiricism held that sense experience gives meaning to our words.

The difficulties with that traditional doctrine spring from differentiating the meaning-conferring knowledge according to its objects. It then becomes a problematic basic knowledge of the 'immediate content' of experience. For the 'immediate content' of consciousness is by itself formless and elusive. Merleau-Ponty makes this point when he writes that 'consciousness, which is taken to be the very seat of clear thinking, is on the contrary the very abode of ambiguity' (*Phenomenology of Perception*, p.332). He stresses, as have others, the affinity between phenomenological writings and the works of novelists and poets. The true moral of this is not, however, that phenomenology can throw light on the nature of art but that the problem of how one can have explicit understanding of the immediate content of experience is the same as the problem of artistic creativity. Only through art is it possible to gain the understanding of immediate experience that phenomenologists seek. The traditional doctrine that understanding of this experience is a source of meaning is correct – it contributes to making our actions what they are. Where the traditional doctrine fails is in not analysing the circumstances in which the required understanding is attainable.

Various aesthetically satisfying experiences are the source of meaning in particular in our linguistic actions. For example, certain such experiences underpin literal meaning, since the literal meanings of phrases depend on what follows when they are not being used metaphorically, and seeing why this follows, in so far as this is an instance of the recognition of necessary truth, brings aesthetic satisfaction. But because it is possible to derive other forms of aesthetic enjoyment from how we use words not all linguistic meaning is literal meaning.

Briefly, the difference between great and minor art is that the former has deeper influence in shaping our experience. Depth of influence is not, of course, the same as prominence or popularity. In saying that great art has deep influence we allude to the point that some types of experience can already be recognized as especially important to human beings. Typically these are ones about which it is difficult to know what to feel. It is in its capacity to give shape to these experiences that the greatness of great art lies.

Since aesthetic knowledge is not restricted to any specific range of objects we are free to recognize that the value of many activities besides the arts themselves is primarily aesthetic. These include the study of history and indeed of philosophy itself. Questions about the point of these activities tend to elicit the same range of philistine and puritanical answers as the same question about the arts. They have been said, for example, to have value as mental exercise, or in educating us about the good for man, or as a kind of intellectual therapy. But no one who really understands these activities could be satisfied with any of these answers. Their true aim is to make our understanding of experience explicit and thereby to contribute to making our actions meaningful.

The opposite of this is a state of confusion and ignorance. Some artefacts promote this by masquerading as art while in fact encouraging us to enjoy apprehending them for incidental reasons. In this sense false art – art that is positively bad – is a genuine possibility and a real danger. Since it is possible to confuse this incidental enjoyment with true aesthetic satisfaction, false art may be hard to detect.

This, I imagine, is what Collingwood had chiefly in mind when he spoke of the 'corruption of consciousness' against which true art has to struggle (*Principles of Art*, p.284). The notion of false art is not, however, one his own theory consistently allows. He is in the same predicament here as Croce is regarding ugliness. As Bosanquet noted, 'For Croce the ugly is the purely inexpressive . . . [But] The inexpressive except by self-contradiction, would be nothing' ('Three lectures on aesthetic'; in Aschenbrenner and Isenberg (eds), p.420). A corresponding point applies in any theory that makes art omnipresent or ubiquitous, or indeed in any theory which interprets the experiential knowledge with which art is concerned on the model of sensory contact with something. For, naturally, this sort of contact has no opposite. But true art gives meaning to our experience; and false art is false not because it somehow gives experience a wrong meaning – that is impossible – but because it appears to give meaning while failing to do so.

This is a positive deficiency. To be taken in by false art, or for that matter by pseudo-philosophy or corrupt history, is to have the illusion of understanding where there is none. When this occurs, in a real sense people do not know what they are doing. Thus the understanding we gain from true art and from all of those activities whose aim is truly aesthetic is certainly no mere luxury. The dangers when false art usurps its place are too great for such a view. Even apart from its sometimes being a goal of action, aesthetic experience in all its forms is what gives meaning to our lives.

Bibliography

Adorno, T.W., *Aesthetic Theory*, ed. Gretel Adorno and Ralph Tiedemann, trans. C. Lenhardt, London, Routledge & Kegan Paul, 1984.

Aquinas, St Thomas, *Summa Theologiae*, London, Blackfriars/Eyre & Spottiswoode, 1964–81.

Aristotle, *De Anima*, trans. Hugh Lawson-Tancred, Harmondsworth, Penguin, 1986.

Aristotle, *The Nicomachean Ethics*, trans. J.A.K. Thomson, Harmondsworth, Penguin, 1953.

Aristotle, 'On the Art of Poetry' (*Poetics*), in *Classical Literary Criticism*, trans. T.S. Dorsch, Harmondsworth, Penguin, 1965.

Aristotle, *The Politics*, trans. H. Rackham, Cambridge MA, Harvard University Press, (Loeb Classical Library, *Aristotle*, Vol.XXI), 1932.

Aschenbrenner, K. and Isenberg, A. (eds), *Aesthetic Theories: Studies in the Philosophy of Art*, Englewood Cliffs, NJ, Prentice Hall, 1965.

Baumgarten, A.G., *Reflections on Poetry* (*Meditationes Philosophicae de nonnullis ad poema pertinentibus*, 1735), trans. K. Aschenbrenner and W.B. Holthner, Berkeley, University of California Press, 1954.

Beardsley, M.C., *Aesthetics from Classical Greece to the Present*, New York, Macmillan, 1966; AL, University of Alabama Press, 1975.

Bell, C., *Art*, London, Chatto & Windus, 1914, new edition 1949.

Berlin, I., *Vico and Herder*, London, Chatto & Windus, 1976.

Black, M., *Models and Metaphors*, Ithaca, NY, Cornell University Press, 1962.

Black, M., 'More about Metaphor', in A. Ortony (ed.), *Metaphor and Thought*, Cambridge, Cambridge University Press, 1979.

Bosanquet, B., 'Three Lectures on Aesthetic' (1915), excerpt of Lecture III reprinted in Aschenbrenner and Isenberg (eds).

Burke, E., *A Philosophical Enquiry into the Origin of our Ideas of the Sublime and Beautiful*, (1757; 2nd edition 1759), London, Routledge & Kegan Paul, 1958.

Carritt, E.F., *The Theory of Beauty*, London, Methuen, 1914, 6th edition 1962.

Carritt, E.F. (ed.), *Philosophies of Beauty*, Oxford, Oxford University Press, 1931.

Cassirer, E., *Language and Myth*, trans. S. Langer, NY, Dover, 1953.

Collingwood, R.G., *The Principles of Art*, Oxford, Oxford University Press, 1938.

Croce, B., *Aesthetic* (*Estetica come scienze dell'espressione e linguistica generale* 1902), trans. D. Ainslie, London, Peter Owen, 1953.

Croce, B., *Guide to Aesthetics* (*Breviario di Estetica* (1913)), trans. P. Romanell, South Bend, IN, Regnery/Gateway, 1979.

Danto, A., *The Transfiguration of the Commonplace*, Cambridge, MA, Harvard University Press, 1981.

Davidson, D., 'What metaphors mean', in M. Platts (ed.), *Reference, Truth, Reality*, London, Routledge & Kegan Paul, 1980.

Davidson, D., 'A Nice Derangement of Epitaphs', in E. Le Pore (ed.), *Truth and Interpretation: Perspectives on the Philosophy of Donald Davidson*, Oxford, Blackwell, 1986.

Dewey, J., *Art as Experience*, NY, Capricorn Books, 1934.

Dickie, G., *Art and the Aesthetic: An Institutional Analysis*, Ithaca, NY, Cornell University Press, 1974.

Dufrenne, M., *The Phenomenology of Aesthetic Experience* (*La Phénoménologie de l'expérience Esthétique*, 1953), trans. E.S. Casey *et al.*, Evanston, IL, Northwestern University Press, 1973.

Dummett, M., 'Truth', *Proceedings of the Aristotelian Society*, 59, 1959; reprinted with a Postscript (1972) in *Truth and Other Enigmas*, London, Duckworth, 1978.

Fiedler, C., 'On Judging Works of Visual Art' (1876), trans. H. Schaefer-Simmern and F. Mood, reprinted in Aschenbrenner and Isenberg (eds).

Fischer, E., *The Necessity of Art: a Marxist Approach* (*Von der Notwentigkeit der Kunst* (1959)), trans. A. Bostock, Harmondsworth, Penguin, 1963.

Freud, S., *Civilization and its Discontents* (*Das Unbehagen in der Kultur*, 1930), trans. J. Riviere, London, Hogarth Press, 1963.

Geach, P.T., *Mental Acts*, London, Routledge & Kegan Paul, 1957.

Geach, P.T., 'Aquinas', in G.E.M. Anscombe and P.T. Geach, *Three Philosophers*, Oxford, Blackwell, 1961.

Goodman, N., *Languages of Art*, IN, Hackett, 1976.

Goodman, N., *Ways of Worldmaking*, IN, Hackett, 1978.

Grice, H.P., 'Logic and Conversation', in D. Davidson and G. Harman (eds) *The Logic of Grammar*, Encino, CA, Dickenson, 1975.

Guyer, P., *Kant and the Claims of Taste*, Cambridge, MA, Harvard University Press, 1979.

Harrison, C., Introduction to *Modern Art and Modernism*, Milton Keynes, Open University Press, 1984.

Hegel, G.W.F., *Introduction to Aesthetics*: The Introduction to the Berlin Aesthetics Lectures of the 1820s, trans. T.M. Knox, Oxford, Oxford University Press, 1979.

Hume, D., 'Of the Standard of Taste' and 'The Sceptic', in *Essays and Treatises*, Edinburgh, 1825.

Hutcheson, F., *An Inquiry into the Original of our Ideas of Beauty and Virtue*, Brookfield, VT, Gregg International Publishers, 1969; facsimile of 4th edition, London, 1738; first published 1725.

Jeffrey, F., 'Essay on Beauty', reprinted in Aschenbrenner and Isenberg (eds); first published 1816.

Kant, I., *Critique of Judgement*, trans. J.C. Meredith, Oxford, Oxford University Press, 1928.

Kant, I., *Critique of Pure Reason* (*Kritik der Reinen Vernunft*, 1781), trans. Norman Kemp Smith, London, Macmillan, 1929.

Kenny, A.J.P., *Action, Emotion and Will*, London, Routledge & Kegan Paul, 1963.

Langer, S.K., *Philosophy in a New Key*, Cambridge, MA, Harvard University Press, 1942.

Langer, S.K., *Feeling and Form*, London, Routledge & Kegan Paul, 1953.

Langer, S.K., *Problems of Art*, London, Routledge & Kegan Paul, 1957.

Leibniz, G.W., *Philosophical Writings*, ed. G.H.R. Parkinson, trans. M. Morris and G.H.R. Parkinson, London, Dent, 1973.

Lipps, T., 'Empathy and Aesthetic Pleasure', reprinted in Aschenbrenner and Isenberg (eds), trans. K. Aschenbrenner, 1965; first published 1905.

Locke, J., *An Essay Concerning Human Understanding*, London, 1690.

Merleau-Ponty, M., *Phenomenology of Perception*, trans. C. Smith, London, Routledge & Kegan Paul, 1962.

Morris, William, *News From Nowhere and Selected Writings and Designs*, ed. Asa Briggs, Harmondsworth, Penguin, 1962.

Ogden, C.K. and Richards, I.A., *The Meaning of Meaning*, London, Routledge & Kegan Paul, 5th edition 1938, first published 1923.

Plato, *Ion*, trans. W.R.M. Lamb, Cambridge, MA, Harvard University Press (Loeb Classical Library, *Plato*, Vol.VIII).

Plato, *Phaedrus*, trans. H.N. Fowler, Cambridge, MA, Harvard University Press (Loeb Classical Library, *Plato*, Vol.I).

Plato, *The Republic*, trans. H.D.P. Lee, Harmondsworth, Penguin, 1955.

Plato, *The Symposium*, trans. W.R.M. Lamb, Cambridge, MA, Harvard University Press (Loeb Classical Library, *Plato*, Vol.I), 1925.

Plotinus, *Enneads*, trans. A.H. Armstrong, Cambridge, MA, Harvard University Press, Vol.I, 1966; Vol.V, 1984.

Polanyi, M. and Prosch, H., *Meaning*, Chicago, IL, University of Chicago Press, 1975.

Reid, T., *Essays on the Intellectual Powers of Man*, Edinburgh, 1785.

Rist, J.M., *Plotinus: the Road to Reality*, Cambridge, Cambridge University Press, 1967.

Russell, B., *The Problems of Philosophy*, Oxford, Oxford University Press, 1967, first published 1912.

Santayana, G., *The Sense of Beauty*, New York, Dover, 1955, first published 1896.

Schelling, F.W.J., *System of Transcendental Idealism*, trans. P. Heath, Charlottesville, University Press of Virginia, 1978, first published 1800.

Schiller, F., *On the Aesthetic Education of Man* (*Briefe über die ästhetische Erziehung des Menschen* 1793–5), trans. E.M. Wilkinson and L.A. Willoughby, Oxford, Oxford University Press, 1967.

Schopenhauer, A., *The World as Will and Representation* (*Die Welt als Wille und Verstellung* (1819, 2nd edition with a supplement of 50 chapters 1844)), trans. E.F.J. Payne, New York, Dover, 1966.

Scruton, R., *The Aesthetic Understanding*, Manchester, Carcanet Press, 1983.

Scruton, R., *Art and Imagination*, London, Methuen, 1974.

Searle, J.R., *Expression and Meaning*, Cambridge, Cambridge University Press, 1979.

Searle, J.R., *Intentionality*, Cambridge, Cambridge University Press, 1983.

Searle, J.R., *Speech Acts*, Cambridge, Cambridge University Press, 1969.

Tolstoy, L., *What is Art?* and *Essays on Art*, trans. A. Maude, Oxford, Oxford University Press, 1930; trans. of *What is Art?* first published 1898.

Wittgenstein, L., *Philosophical Investigations*, trans. G.E.M. Anscombe, Oxford, Blackwell, 2nd edition 1958.

Wittgenstein, L. *Tractatus Logico-Philosophicus*, trans. D.F. Pears and B.F. McGuinness, London, Routledge & Kegan Paul, 1961.

Wollheim, R., *Art and its Objects*, 2nd edition with Six Supplementary Essays, Cambridge, Cambridge University Press, 1980.

Worringer, W., *Abstraction and Empathy* (*Abstraktion und Einfühlung* 1908), trans. M. Bullock, London, Routledge & Kegan Paul, 1953.

Index